KT-483-157

From the Margins of Empire

CHRISTINA STEAD, DORIS LESSING, NADINE GORDIMER

Louise Yelin

Cornell University Press

ITHACA AND LONDON

Copyright © 1998 by Cornell University

All rights reserved. Except for brief quotations in a review, this book, or parts thereof, must not be reproduced in any form without permission in writing from the publisher. For information, address Cornell University Press, Sage House, 512 East State Street, Ithaca, New York 14850.

First published 1998 by Cornell University Press
First printing, Cornell Paperbacks, 1998

International Standard Book Number (cloth) 0-8014-3503-X
International Standard Book Number (paper) 0-8014-8505-3

Printed in the United States of America

Cornell University Press strives to use environmentally responsible suppliers and materials to the fullest extent possible in the publishing of its books. Such materials include vegetable-based, low-VOC inks and acid-free papers that are recycled, totally chlorine-free, or partly composed of nonwood fibers.

Cloth printing   10 9 8 7 6 5 4 3 2 1

Paperback printing   10 9 8 7 6 5 4 3 2 1

Excerpts from *Burger's Daughter* by Nadine Gordimer. Copyright © 1979 by Nadine Gordimer. Used by permission of Viking Penguin, a division of Penguin Books USA Inc., and A. P. Watt Ltd.
Excerpts from *My Son's Story* by Nadine Gordimer. Copyright © 1990 by Felix Licensing, B.V. Reprinted by permission of Farrar, Straus & Giroux, Inc., Penguin Books Canada Limited, and Bloomsbury Publishing Plc.
Excerpts from *A Sport of Nature* by Nadine Gordimer. Copyright © 1987 by Nadine Gordimer. Reprinted by permission of Alfred A. Knopf Inc., Penguin Books Canada Limited, and A. P. Watt Ltd.
Excerpts from *The Golden Notebook* by Doris Lessing. Copyright © 1962 by Doris Lessing. Copyright renewed 1990 by Doris Lessing. Reprinted by kind permission of Jonathan Clowes Ltd., London, on behalf of Doris Lessing, and with the permission of Simon and Schuster.
Excerpts from the 1971 Preface to *The Golden Notebook* by Doris Lessing. Copyright © 1971 by Doris Lessing. Reprinted by kind permission of Jonathan Clowes Ltd., London, on behalf of Doris Lessing.
Excerpts from *In Pursuit of the English* by Doris Lessing. Copyright © 1960 by Doris Lessing. Reprinted by kind permission of Jonathan Clowes Ltd., London, on behalf of Doris Lessing, and by permission of HarperCollins Publishers Ltd.
Excerpts from "The Small Personal Voice" by Doris Lessing. Copyright © 1957 by Doris Lessing. Reprinted by kind permission of Jonathan Clowes Ltd., London, on behalf of Doris Lessing.
Excerpts from *For Love Alone* by Christina Stead reprinted by permission of Margaret Harris, literary executor of Christina Stead.
Excerpts from *The Man Who Loved Children* by Christina Stead, Copyright 1940, © 1968 by Christina Stead. Reprinted by permission of Henry Holt and Company, Inc., and Margaret Harris.

Librarians: Library of Congress Cataloging information appears on the last page of the book.

Contents

Acknowledgments

Working on this book for many years, I have benefited from the advice, assistance, and support of many people and institutions. I am happy to acknowledge their help.

My research was supported by the Purchase College President's Award for Junior Faculty Development in 1989, by a sabbatical leave in 1992, by grants from the Purchase College Faculty Support Fund and the Jim Greenwood Humanities Development Fund, and by United University Professions Continuing Faculty Development Grants in 1993 and 1995. I am grateful for a Ball Brothers Fellowship that supported my work in the Gordimer Collection at the Lilly Library, Indiana University, Bloomington. I thank the staff at the Lilly Library, especially Sondra Taylor, curator of manuscripts, and Rebecca Crane, head of public services, for their efficiency and warm welcome. My stay in Bloomington was made particularly pleasant by the staff of the Center for Advanced Studies in the Humanities, where I was a visiting scholar. Professor H. H. Remak, director of the center, and Ivona Hedin, associate director, anticipated my every need. I also thank the librarians at the Bancroft Library, University of California, Berkeley, where I worked in the papers of the League of American Writers, and the staff of the Harry Ransom Humanities Center, University of Texas, Austin, where I worked in the Stanley Burnshaw Collection.

Portions of this book have been presented at conferences and at colleges and universities; the reception of work in progress helped me refine my ideas over the years. I thank colleagues who commented on versions of chapters presented at the Rutgers University Center for Historical Analysis; the University of Texas, Austin; the Graduate Center, City University of New York; Sarah Lawrence College; the Berkshire Conference of Women Historians; the Columbia University

Seminar on Women and Society; State University of New York at Stony Brook; Bryn Mawr College; and City College of New York. I especially acknowledge the Society for the Study of Narrative Literature, for annual conferences that stimulated my work as it developed.

Many people have helped me complete this book. First, I thank Jennifer Nail, Elizabeth Larsen, Wendy Capron, Annie Fisher, and Marcia Lane for providing stellar child care. I am grateful to Desley Deacon, Hester Eisenstein, and Susan Pennybacker for sharing with me their knowledge of fields I was just entering. Mary Lynn Broe, Angela Ingram, Dale Bauer, and Karen Lawrence helped me to refine early versions of several chapters. Helen Cooper kept me going by e-mail. Hazel Rowley shared with me her work in progress on Stead and made sure I didn't miss anything important. Rosalie Reutershan provided support with unfailing energy and good cheer. I thank Edward W. Said for showing me how to think in ways that led, by a very circuitous route, to this book. I am particularly grateful to Celeste Schenck for encouragement that saw me through the early stages and to Jane Marcus for fostering this project from beginning to end. Geoffrey Field has been an exemplary colleague and mentor; I thank him for the pleasures of our interdisciplinary collaboration. I express appreciation to the University Seminars at Columbia University for assistance in the preparation of the manuscript for publication. Material drawn from this work was presented to the University Seminar on Women and Society. At Cornell University Press, I thank Bernhard Kendler for his encouragement over the years, Shari Benstock for her enthusiasm and support, Nancy J. Malone and Carol Betsch for splendid copyediting, and Margaret R. Higonnet, whose rigor and generosity were a mirror that showed me the book I wanted to write. Mary McGlynn's assistance was invaluable. Very special thanks go to Carla Kaplan for being the reader I addressed as I was writing, and to Bella Brodzki, Françoise Lionnet, and Ronnie Scharfman for friendship and commitment that made a home for my work. Finally, I thank my husband, Robert Friedman, and my son, Willy Friedman, for giving me a reason to stop working at the end of the day.

Portions of this book have been previously published; permission to reprint is gratefully acknowledged. An early version of Chapter 2 appears as "Buffoon Odyssey?: Christina Stead's *For Love Alone* and the Writing of Exile," in *Post/colonial Conditions: Exiles, Migrations, and Nomadisms, Yale French Studies* 82 (1993): 183–203. Parts of Chapter 6 appear in "Problems of Gordimer's Poetics: Dialogue in *Burger's Daughter*," in *Feminism, Bakhtin, and the Dialogic*, ed. Dale M. Bauer and Susan Jaret McKinstry (Albany: State University of New York Press,

©1991), 219–38, and "Exiled in and Exiled from: The Politics and Poetics of *Burger's Daughter*," in *Women's Writing in Exile*, ed. Mary Lynn Broe and Angela Ingram (Chapel Hill: University of North Carolina Press, ©1989), 395–411. An early version of Chapter 7 appears as "Decolonizing the Novel: Nadine Gordimer's *A Sport of Nature* and British Literary Traditions," in *Decolonizing Tradition: New Views of Twentieth-Century "British" Literary Canons*, ed. Karen R. Lawrence (Urbana: University of Illinois Press, 1991), 191–211.

L. Y.

From the Margins of Empire

Introduction: From the Margins of Empire

This is a book about women writers and national identity. It examines the construction of national identity in the novels of Christina Stead, Doris Lessing, and Nadine Gordimer, three white women who were born or grew up in British colonies or former colonies. These writers, whose lives span the 20th century, are situated at the intersection of the colonial and the postcolonial, the modern and the postmodern. As white women, they occupy positions at odd angles to these binaries. Their lives and work encompass a range of national identifications. They exemplify three strategies for negotiating between colonial or formerly colonial "peripheries" and metropolitan "centers": Stead, who lived most of her life away from Australia, where she was born and died, has an unsettled national identity; Lessing is or becomes English; Gordimer identifies as a South African. These identifications are played out in their novels, which raise questions about the role of whites, especially white women, in the contemporary—postcolonial, postimperial—global political and cultural order.

The years between 1940, when Stead published *The Man Who Loved Children*, and 1990, when Gordimer published *My Son's Story*, saw the threat of fascism, a world war, anticolonial struggles and decolonization in Africa, Asia, and the Caribbean, and, finally, the end of apartheid in South Africa. During these years, many new nations emerged, and radical changes occurred in some of the older ones: in the aftermath of European empires, the map of the world was profoundly rearranged. All three writers bear witness to this global transformation; their novels inscribe their own changing national identifications and changing conceptions of national identity itself.

The national identity of Stead, Lessing, and Gordimer is in question in a way that it would not be for writers—white writers, at least—born in the metropole. It differs, too, from the national identity of Frantz Fanon's "native intellectuals," members of colonized groups in colonial, decolonizing, or formerly (post- or neo-) colonial countries who "take their stand in the field of history" and "defend the existence of their national culture."[1] More recent studies of nations and nationalism by Benedict Anderson, E. J. Hobsbawm, Etienne Balibar and Immanuel Wallerstein, and Homi Bhabha treat nationality in the modern world as an artifact, an invented, fabricated, heterogeneous product of what Balibar calls a "fictive ethnicity."[2] The unstable, invented, hybrid character of nationality is especially marked in writers such as Stead, Lessing, and Gordimer, for whom no single set of identity categories can take priority. We cannot, for example, assign them a nationality, nor do they define their own national identities on the basis of race, ethnicity, language, or citizenship. The national identity of each, moreover, is not only a function of the nations in which they find themselves—or which they leave—but is also inflected by gender constraints that may be nationally specific or extend beyond national boundaries. This is not to suggest that the meaning of "woman" or "women," or of the phrase "woman writer," is invariable across different times and places or that gender always influences a subject's nationality in the same ways, but rather, as Joan W. Scott and Denise Riley remind us, that "gender" and "woman" (or "women") are historically constructed and hence variable categories, terms whose meanings fluctuate. These fluctuations in turn affect national identities that are themselves in flux.[3]

Stead (1902–1983) was born in Australia. She left in 1928 and lived and wrote in England, Europe, and the United States, returning to Australia in 1974 after she had effectively ceased writing. Stead's novels re-

[1] Fanon, "On National Culture," 209.

[2] Balibar and Wallerstein, *Race, Nation, Class*, 49. Anderson asserts that "nationality or . . . nation-ness, as well as nationalism, are cultural artefacts of a particular kind" (*Imagined Communities*, 13). Hobsbawm suggests that race, ethnicity, religion, language, and statehood, traditionally identified with nationality, have no intrinsic connection with it (*Nations and Nationalism*, 33, and cf. Hobsbawm and Ranger, *Invention of Tradition*). Ernest Gellner also treats the nation as a fabricated entity, a "contingency, not a necessity," but he stresses the homogeneity of nations and nationalisms as they have been constructed in the modern world (*Nations and Nationalism*, 6, 107, and passim).

[3] As Riley puts it, " 'women' is historically, discursively constructed, and always relatively to other categories which themselves change; 'women' is a volatile collectivity in which female persons can be very differently positioned, . . . while for the individual, 'being a woman' is also inconstant and can't provide an ontological foundation" ("*Am I That Name?*" 1–2). Cf. J. Scott: "Gender is a primary way of signifying relationships of power . . . a primary field within which or by means of which power is articulated. . . . Gender . . . provides a way to decode meanings and to understand the complex connections among various forms of human interaction" ("Gender," 44–46).

flect her wanderings. Often published in England or the United States before they were published in Australia, they are set in Sydney, Paris, London, Washington, New York, and Switzerland, among other places. Stead's nomadic life makes her, at different points in her career, an Australian writer in exile, an Australian American writer, and an English writer. She never quite belongs to any of the nations she lives in. As Lorna Sage puts it, Stead was "un-Australian, un-English, un-American," a displaced person who "explored the meanings of displacement."[4]

Throughout her life, Stead attempted to repudiate, even to deny, limitations of gender that nevertheless followed her around the world. She expressed little or no solidarity with other women and eschewed identification as a feminist or with feminism. Yet, in part because she was a woman, she occupied a marginal position in all the cultures she traversed.[5] Her conflicts about gender complicate, indeed intensify her already unstable national identifications. These conflicts are registered in her novels, which describe the situation of women across several different national locations but, for a variety of reasons, are not easily accommodated by the category of "women's writing" as it has been defined in Anglo-American feminist criticism. Rather, Stead's work exemplifies a posture of exile as Edward W. Said outlines it. Said observes that the intellectual exile exists "in a median state, neither completely at one with the new setting nor fully disencumbered of the old, beset with half-involvements and half-detachments, nostalgic and sentimental on one level, an adept mimic or a secret outcast on another," yet he also notes that exile makes possible a certain "originality of vision."[6] In characterizing the exile this way, he might be describing Stead, who chose to leave the land where she was born and whose life and work ask us to consider what it means to write from the margins.

Lessing (1919–) was born in Persia, grew up in Southern Rhodesia (now Zimbabwe), and in the late 1940s emigrated to England, where she has lived ever since. Lessing began writing in southern Africa but did not publish her first novel, *The Grass Is Singing*, until after she arrived in England.[7] Her early novels focus on the experiences of young white women and men in colonial southern Africa, but since the 1960s,

---

[4] Sage, *Women in the House of Fiction*, 37, 46.

[5] The account of Stead that I give here is close to that of Susan Sheridan, who notes the tension between Stead's "fascination with women's lives" and her "rejection of feminism" and who sees her as "marginal . . . relative to all three Anglophone literatures with which she is associated" (*Christina Stead*, xiv, xii).

[6] Said, *Representations of the Intellectual*, 49, and "Reflections on Exile," 172.

[7] See Lessing, *Under My Skin*, 325, 361, 370, 404–5.

most of her novels—with the exception of the Canopus in Argos series, which imagine their own universe—have been set in England.

The Golden Notebook (1962), Lessing's best-known novel, was hailed in the 1960s by a nascent feminist movement for its exposure of sexism across the political spectrum.[8] Lessing acknowledges in her preface to the tenth anniversary edition of the novel that it describes "what many women were thinking, feeling, and experiencing," but she emphasizes that it was not a polemic for women's liberation (25). Rather, she presents the novel as a cosmopolitan corrective to the provinciality of English literature and represents herself as an English, or British, writer. Lessing's invention of Englishness, as enacted in her novels and other writings, is enabled in part by her status as a white colonial woman in an era when immigration by blacks from Britain's colonies and former colonies was being restricted and the claims of these immigrants to British citizenship, increasingly limited. The "English" texts I discuss in Chapters 3, 4, and 5 raise questions both about the place of white, former colonial women in an English culture hostile to women's aspirations and about the implications of membership in a national culture defined or constituted by racial exclusion.

Gordimer (1923–) was born in South Africa and remains there. Her career virtually coincides with the era of apartheid: she published her first book, a collection of stories, in 1949, the year after the National Party took power (her first novel was published in 1953) and her most recent novel, in 1994, the year when the first democratically held elections took place and Nelson Mandela became president of South Africa. Unlike Stead and Lessing, who left the places where they were born or grew up, and even as white opponents of apartheid like herself were leaving South Africa, Gordimer chose to stay in South Africa and be (or become) a South African writer.

Gordimer initially identified as a colonial; subsequently, she saw herself as a dissident, part of a minority within and opposed to the dominant white minority. Now that the country is no longer ruled by a white minority, she identifies herself as a South African who belongs to a nonracial nation. Her novels, set mainly in South Africa, explore the implications of this belonging. They also constitute, as she puts it, an "offering of what I was learning about the life within me and around me," a "gesture" by means of which "I entered the commonality of my country."[9] The most recent novels especially speculate about the place

---

[8] On feminist reception of the novel, see Chapter 4, notes 53 and 54, below; and especially "Opening *The Golden Notebook:* Remembering the Source," a report on the 1991 PEN symposium on the novel.

[9] Gordimer, *Writing and Being,* 132. Gordimer describes her trajectory in this text, especially in chapter 6, which ends: "That other world that was the world is no longer the

of whites—women and men alike—in a postcolonial future to which they look forward.

The lives and, more important, the novels of these women invite us to explore what it means to *choose* a national identity, to "affiliate," in the sense that Said gives the word, with a particular national (or transnational) culture.[10] The novels of Stead, Lessing, and Gordimer ask us to think about how, or under what conditions, such choices and affiliations are possible. In addressing issues of national affiliation, I examine the ways that novels represent their writers' relationship to dominant and oppositional (residual and emergent) national cultures and transnational political entities.[11] In the process, I consider whether, how, or to what effect whites might translate or refashion colonial origins into new forms of nationness or national identity.

In a recent book on Gordimer, the critic Kathrin Wagner treats Gordimer's self-identification with the nonracial South African nation as a doomed endeavor or, worse, a matter of bad faith. Wagner characterizes Gordimer as a writer "trapped in the historical situation her work seeks to transcend." [12] But a historical situation, even as it defines a set of limits in and against which writers struggle, is not necessarily a trap. In this book, I treat novels as a record of that struggle and as instances of it, acts that resist and rewrite as well as reproduce historical conditions that they cannot imagine away—that is, that perform the cultural work of inventing or constituting identity. Like all acts of invention, the enterprise of these writers does not, cannot proceed free of hindrance. It is implicated in, even when opposed to, the political and cultural formations in which it is written and read. Yet the actuality of struggle, of practice, should not be discounted just because the results might be equivocal.[13]

---

world. My country is the world, whole, a synthesis. I am no longer a colonial. I may now speak of 'my people' " (134).

[10] Said explains that affiliation is a "compensatory order that . . . provides men and women with a new form of relationship" involving choice, will, agency ("Introduction: Secular Criticism," 19).

[11] Raymond Williams explains that "a cultural process is seized as a cultural system, with determinate dominant features" and oppositional elements that he terms "residual" and "emergent." "The residual . . . has been effectively formed in the past, but it is still active in the cultural process, not only and often not at all as an element of the past, but as an effective element of the present." The "emergent" designates "new meanings and values, new practices, new relationships and kinds of relationship [that] are continually being created" (*Marxism and Literature,* 121–23).

[12] Wagner, *Rereading Nadine Gordimer,* 3.

[13] Cf. Said: "To study affiliation is to study and to recreate the bonds between texts and the world, bonds that specialization and the institutions of literature have all but completely effaced. Every text is an act of will to some extent, but what has not been very much studied is the degree to which texts are made permissible" ("Reflections on American 'Left' Literary Criticism," 175).

The novels of Stead, Lessing, and Gordimer, narratives about nationality by writers whose own nationality is in question, urge an eclectic critical perspective. In approaching them both as products of the multiple positioning and complex and shifting national affiliations of their authors and as explorations of the question of national identity, I situate them in (and against) the national cultures in which they are produced and which, in some cases, they attempt to refashion. In the process, I put a feminist critique of gender in conversation with theories of nationalism and national identity.

In *Three Guineas* (1938), Virginia Woolf characterizes women—the class of women she identifies as the "daughters of educated men"—as outsiders to a British nation which, in her view, fails to repudiate the patriarchalism that structures both fascist states and the "private house": " 'For,' the outsider will say, '. . . as a woman, I have no country. As a woman I want no country. As a woman my country is the whole world' " (109).[14] In *Imagined Communities: Reflections on the Origins and Spread of Nationalism* (1983), perhaps the most influential study of nations and nationalism, Benedict Anderson notes "the formal universality of nationality as a socio-cultural concept" and proposes that "in the modern world everyone can, should, will 'have' a nationality, as he or she 'has' a gender" (14). Similarly, he characterizes the limited, sovereign nation as a "deep, horizontal comradeship, [a] fraternity" (16). He does not, however, explore the implications of his analogy or consider the situation of women with respect to a nation conceived as a brotherhood. Anderson's association of nationality with fraternity might relegate women to an ideological "outside," a kind of national elsewhere like the one that Woolf's outsider ostensibly occupies.

Recent work on women and nationality recuperates gender considerations that Anderson elides and revises Woolf's notion of the antagonism of women and nations.[15] A special issue of *Gender and History* delineates "the different ways in which women and men may become national subjects," while an issue of *Feminist Review* devoted to nationalisms and national identities challenges the traditional gendering of "national ideologies" in which "women are the *symbol* of the nation, men its *agents*, regardless of the role women actually play in the move-

[14] Caren Kaplan asks, "Can worlds be claimed in the name of categories such as 'woman' in all innocence and benevolence, or do these gestures mark the revival of a form of feminist imperialism?" ("Politics of Location," 137). Woolf takes care to specify which "woman" she is describing, in *Three Guineas* and elsewhere.

[15] See Jayawardena, *Feminism and Nationalism in the Third World*; Enloe, *Bananas, Beaches, and Bases;* and Yuval-Davis and Anthias, *Woman-Nation-State.* Much of this work is couched in a kind of critical future tense; it urges us, as Enloe says, to read histories of nationalisms as histories "filled with gendered debate" (59).

ment." [16] Anne McClintock points out that nations are "frequently figured through the iconography of familial and domestic space" and
that the "family trope . . . offers a 'natural' figure for sanctioning national *hierarchy* within a putative organic *unity* of interests." [17] Balibar
asserts that "nationalism . . . has a secret affinity with sexism: not so
much as a manifestation of the same authoritarian tradition but in so
far as the inequality of sexual roles in conjugal love and child-rearing
constitutes the anchoring point for the juridical, economic, educational
and medical mediation of the state." [18]

In this book, I focus on novels as a crucial site in which Balibar's "secret affinity" unfolds. I show how the novels of Stead, Lessing, and
Gordimer situate women in the national maps they draw and expose
the uneven articulations of power elided in Anderson's analogy between nationality and gender. Stead's *The Man Who Loved Children* and
Lessing's *The Fifth Child* (1988), for example, offer different versions of
McClintock's national family and suggest different ways that "having
a gender" might influence "having a nationality." Gordimer's *Burger's
Daughter* (1979) and Lessing's *The Golden Notebook* locate women in
public spheres conventionally gendered masculine; in different ways,
both novels explore the consequences of women's marginal or tangential relationship to the national and transnational political and cultural
formations they describe. *Burger's Daughter* places its young, white female protagonist in the struggle against apartheid and, in doing so, re-
thinks such traditional concerns of the feminine bildungsroman as
sexual awakening and the quest for autonomy. *The Golden Notebook* details the effects on its white, middle-class, British female protagonists
of an institutionalized misogyny that pervades the world it describes:
the dominant culture of postwar Britain and such putative but equally
masculinist alternatives as the Communist Party and the New Left.

In "DissemiNation," Bhabha proposes that the nation and its subjects are constituted in an opposition or split between the performative
and the pedagogical, between the invention or improvisation of nationness and subordination to the authority of always already existing
political and cultural traditions (145–46). The novels of Stead, Lessing,
and Gordimer participate in the conceptually ambivalent process that
Bhabha calls "writing the nation." These novels invent, improvise, and
inscribe themselves in national cultures under construction, yet they—
and, by implication, their performative nationality—are subject to ped-

---

[16] *Gender and History*, 159; *Feminist Review*, 1.
[17] McClintock, *Imperial Leather*, 357.
[18] Balibar and Wallerstein 102.

agogical imperatives, to contingencies of race, gender, genre, and geography. Gordimer identifies herself as a South African, but for much of her writing life, the very existence of a *national* literature is virtually foreclosed by the color bar, which, as she puts it in a 1974 essay, "prevents any real identification of the writer with his society as a whole, so that ultimately he can identify only with his colour." [19] In the 1970s, when Black Consciousness is the dominant ideology of the struggle against apartheid and its regime, Gordimer's whiteness puts her South African nationality in question. Similarly, *The Man Who Loved Children*, written and published in the United States by an Australian-born woman with left-wing affiliations, is an intervention in debates about American national culture in the late 1930s. Yet the American setting and subject matter that make up its manifest content and its self-presentation as an American novel are disturbed by eruptions in the novel itself of Australian themes and idioms and by Stead's insistence, much later in her life, that it is a literal, autobiographical account of her Australian childhood. [20]

These novels are not only performances in which, as Bhabha puts it, "national life is redeemed and iterated"; [21] they also explore the opposition between the performative and the pedagogical. Bhabha argues that the performative strategies whereby subjects construct their own national identities are disrupted by nationalist pedagogies. But for the most part, he does not distinguish between masculine and feminine subjects or subject positions. The trajectories of such characters as Rosa Burger, protagonist of *Burger's Daughter*, Anna Wulf, the main character of *The Golden Notebook*, and Louisa Pollit, in *The Man Who Loved Children*, show us how gender inflects pedagogical imperatives; thus, they expose the muting of gender constraints in Bhabha's analysis.

The nation, as Bhabha conceives it, is a "liminal signifying space that is *internally* marked by the discourses of minorities, ... heterogeneous histories ..., antagonistic authorities and tense locations of cultural difference." [22] In examining the novels of Stead, Lessing, and Gordimer, I consider gender as a component of the national ensemble, a determinant of "minority discourse," cultural difference, and heterogeneity. In other words, I explore the ways that gender influences and is influenced by the "nation split within itself." *The Fifth Child*, for example, exposes both residual elements and emergent possibilities in concerns traditionally gendered feminine. It suggests that a mother's feeling for

[19] Gordimer, "Literature and Politics in South Africa," 226.
[20] See Chapter 1 below.
[21] Bhabha, "DissemiNation," 145.
[22] Ibid., 148.

her children can be assimilated to, co-opted by, or subversive of dominant or hegemonic (national) formations. At the same time, in portraying the conflicting values of the father and mother in its version of a family that represents the British nation, it shows how the performative national identities of women may differ in significant ways from those of men and how gender difference might affect the construction of women and men as objects of national pedagogies.

In drawing on the work of Anderson and Bhabha, I also amplify the narrative of 19th- and 20th-century British and Anglophone women's writing constructed by British and American feminist critics over the past 20 years. In the late 1970s and early 1980s, Elaine Showalter, writing as a practitioner and theorist of gynocriticism, asserted that this kind of feminist criticism was limning the contours of women's writing, defining a female or feminine aesthetic, and identifying, tracing, or recovering particularly feminine literary traditions.[23] In much of this work, questions of form and filiation are treated as expressions of political agendas of one kind or another. Nancy K. Miller reads the apparently "implausible" or "excessive" ending of The Mill on the Floss as a sign of resistance to patriarchal ideological imperatives, which are reproduced in canonical notions of "plausibility."[24] Rachel Blau DuPlessis identifies in the work of modern women novelists an array of strategies that "delegitimate" and "displace"—disrupt—a romance plot that reproduces structures of male dominance.[25] Jane Marcus explores Woolf's revisionary dialogue with the "languages of patriarchy" and, in rediscovering Woolf's politics, rectifies the distorted image of Woolf as neurasthenic, unworldly aesthete.

For these critics and many others, poetics, like the personal, is political. They elaborate a textual politics that gives priority to stylistic innovation and especially to women writers' departures from formal conventions exposed, now, as representations of patriarchal norms. This work is bracing in its insistence that women's apparent failure to conform to acknowledged literary standards encodes responses to particular sets of experiences, including but not limited to what might be called an experience of gender. In other words, these critics show us how the writings of women encompass acquiescence in, resistance to, and subversion of specific material and ideological circumstances.[26]

---

[23] See, for example, Showalter, "Toward a Feminist Poetics" and "Feminist Criticism in the Wilderness."

[24] Miller, "Emphasis Added."

[25] DuPlessis, Writing beyond the Ending, xii and passim.

[26] The locus classicus of this sort of feminist criticism is The Madwoman in the Attic, Sandra Gilbert and Susan Gubar's study of the "anxiety of authorship" of nineteenth-century

In place of the plausibility, realism, breadth, and clarity praised by earlier generations of critics, men and women alike, these critics value implausibility, brevity, difficulty, lyricism, rupture. Their criteria of judgment and hierarchy of literary values elaborate Woolf's contention that women's writing "breaks the sentence" and "breaks the sequence."[27] The novels of Stead, Lessing, and Gordimer, however, are not clearly legible if judged by these criteria. Stead and Lessing, especially, tend to produce encyclopedic, sprawling, somewhat shapeless novels quite unlike the sleek, spare, lyrical narratives praised by Woolf and her successors. In fact, these texts are more productively illuminated by Benedict Anderson's notion of the novel as a "form of imagining" that "provided the technical means for 're-presenting' the *kind* of imagined community that is the nation" (30) than by critical notions of "women's writing" or "feminist fiction."

Anderson proposes that the narration of nationality is made possible by the particular ways that the novel represents time. An important feature of both novels and nations, he suggests, is "simultaneity-along-time...an idea of 'homogeneous, empty time,' in which simultaneity is, as it were, transverse, cross-time, marked not by prefiguring and fulfilment, but by temporal coincidence, and measured by clock and calendar" (30). Anderson is reflecting, here, on the emergence of both the novel and nationness in the 18th century: the specific genre he seems to be describing is the classical European political novel or novel of ideas.[28]

---

women writers. The sweeping, even universalizing claims implied in the subtitle, *"The Woman Writer and the Nineteenth-Century Literary Imagination,"* claims modified by later critics (e.g., by Denise Riley, who in *"Am I That Name?"* treats "woman" as a strategic category), do not obviate the connection made between poetics and politics. A different version of this connection underwrites Nancy Armstrong's insertion of the genre of domestic fiction, gendered feminine, in a larger history in which the "dissemination of a new female ideal" is connected to the "empowering of the middle classes in England" (*Desire and Domestic Fiction*, 9). See also the 1977 anthology titled *The Authority of Experience* edited by Lee R. Edwards and Arlyn Diamond. Toril Moi attacks a straw man or woman in her critique in *Sexual/Textual Politics* of the essentialist abstraction and bogus authenticity of "experience" in Anglo-American feminist criticism. Cf. Rita Felski's emphatic rejection of the notion of a female or feminine style: "By 'feminist aesthetics' I mean . . . any theoretical position which argues a necessary or privileged relationship between female gender and a particular kind of literary structure, style, or form. . . . There exist no legitimate grounds for classifying any particular style of writing as uniquely or specifically feminine" (*Beyond Feminist Aesthetics*, 19). Joan W. Scott offers a nuanced and thoughtful discussion of experience as a contested category "at once always already an interpretation *and* . . . in need of interpretation" ("Evidence of Experience").

[27] See Woolf, *A Room of One's Own*, 95, and DuPlessis, *Writing Beyond the Ending*, chap. 3.

[28] In Irving Howe's definition of this genre, "political ideas play a dominant role . . . [and] the political milieu is the dominant setting" (*Politics and the Novel*, 19). Bakhtin de-

The classical political novel, however, is a genre traditionally gendered masculine. Its best-known exemplars are male-authored novels with predominantly male protagonists. Yet most of the texts I discuss in this book, woman-authored and with female protagonists, can be classified as political novels, and Stead, Lessing, and Gordimer all associate their work with this genre. In the genealogies they construct for themselves, they invoke as precursors such figures as Cervantes, Stendhal, Balzac, Dostoevsky, and Conrad.[29] Tackling political issues such as nationality and exile, articulating sexual politics with other kinds, these writers refashion a European, traditionally masculine genre. Thus, their work not only enlarges our conception of the political novel but also urges us to reconsider what is placed under the rubric of "women's writing." At the same time, it raises questions about whether their thinking back through their fathers, as Woolf puts it, is accomplished through the exclusion of ostensibly "feminine" concerns or the repression of ties with the feminine literary traditions that Woolf invokes when she describes women writers as thinking back through their mothers.[30]

In suggesting that these writers transform our maps of women's writing or show us that these maps chart a domain that belongs to certain groups of women who wrote in English, I want to align my work with postcolonial feminist criticism.[31] Although Said focuses only occasionally on gender, his work on Orientalism and his discussions of the vexed, complex, and troubling relationship of (European) culture and imperialism opens up a space in which a postcolonial feminist critique might emerge. Gayatri Chakravorty Spivak shows us how the construction of Jane Eyre, as preeminent subject of British women's narrative and paradigmatic object of British and American gynocriticism, furthers the project that Spivak calls the "worlding of the Third World."[32] Françoise Lionnet develops the concept of *métissage,* an interweaving of heterogeneous traditions and languages. In métissage, which means, literally, "mixing," Lionnet finds a "dynamic model of

---

scribes the protagonist of this genre as an ideologue or "man" of ideas (*Problems of Dostoevsky's Poetics,* 78).

[29] See Stead, "Uses of the Many-Charactered Novel"; Lessing, "The Small Personal Voice," 4; and Gordimer in *What Happened to "Burger's Daughter,"* 19.

[30] Woolf, *A Room of One's Own,* 101, 79.

[31] See, for example, David, *Rule Britannia;* Raiskin, *Snow on the Cane Fields;* McClintock, *Imperial Leather;* Donaldson, *Decolonizing Feminisms;* Lanser, "Compared to What?"; and Mohanty, "Under Western Eyes." Cf. work scrutinizing the "whiteness" of white women, such as C. Hall, *White, Male, and Middle Class;* Ware, *Beyond the Pale;* and Frankenberg, *White Women, Race Matters.*

[32] Spivak, "Three Women's Texts," 263.

relationality" that is " 'universal' even if, in each specific context, power relations produce widely varying configurations, hierarchies, dissymmetries, and contradictions."[33] In this study of white women writers who move between different national cultures within the same global language area, I draw on and adapt the approaches of postcolonial critics who elaborate a critical perspective that attends to issues of identity, nationality among them, yet circumvents the impasses of identity politics.

In what follows, I treat the work of each writer as a set of strategies for moving between colonial and formerly colonial "margins" and metropolitan "center" and between national and transnational affiliations. Each chapter focuses on a particular novel (or, in one case, a fictionalized memoir), chosen for the exemplary way(s) it negotiates questions of identity. Reading these texts as narratives of nationality, I place them with respect to national and transnational literary traditions as well as the specific national cultures in which they were produced: I suggest that these novels inscribe national identity not only in their manifest content or subject matter but also in rewriting precursor texts and representing specific material and ideological circumstances.

In Part I, "Christina Stead: Buffoon Odyssey?" I consider Stead as a writer perpetually in exile. In the two chapters of this section, I examine Stead's construction of a hybrid, Australian American identity and her posture of exile from Australia. In Part II, "Doris Lessing: In Pursuit of the English," I treat Lessing as a British novelist. In the three chapters of this section I discuss Lessing's meditation on Englishness and self-fashioning as an English writer in the early postwar period, her anatomy of British cultural politics in the 1950s, and her representation of Thatcher's England and Thatcherism. In Part III, "Nadine Gordimer: Literature and Politics in South Africa," I consider Gordimer as a South African writer. In the three chapters of this section, I treat Gordimer's reflection on whether or how European beginnings can be transplanted and translated into South African culture, her inquiry into the place of whites in South Africa during an era she defines as an interregnum between the apartheid period and an as yet unspecified order, and her meditation on a nonracial South African identity in a future just emerging.

In different ways, the novels I discuss investigate the role of white,

---

[33] Lionnet 4; cf. Raiskin, who argues that creole subjectivity (*la créolité*, or "creoleness") offers a "national and political challenge" to the binary opposition between metropolitan and colonial (5).

middle-class women in an emerging postcolonial political and cultural order. My own exploration of this question began in the 1970s with my involvement in what was then called the anti-imperialist feminist movement. Alongside but distinct from radical feminism and with ties to the antiwar movement, anti-imperialist feminists saw as crucial the participation of women in global politics and rejected the claim that gender issues always had to be deferred until some unspecified future moment when other problems had been solved. But discussions of women and nationalism clearly have a different meaning now, as we enter an era of increasingly violent and virulently misogynist nationalisms, on the one hand, and, on the other, witness a new order in South Africa that I could only imagine in 1987, when I began work on what eventually became this book.

Part I
Christina Stead: Buffoon Odyssey?

1

Unsettling Australia:
The Man Who Loved Children
as National Family Romance

In 1928, Christina Stead, chafing at the restrictions of a provincial existence lived in the house of her repressive, overbearing father, left Sydney and went to London.[1] Not long after arriving there, she found a job as secretary to a man named William Blech (later changed to Blake), a cosmopolitan American economist, Marxist polymath, and writer who was working as associate manager in a grain importing and exporting firm. Early the next year, Stead agreed to accompany Blech to Paris, where he was to work in a private investment bank. By February 1929, the two had become lovers, beginning what was to be a lifelong relationship. (They were married in 1952, after his first wife finally agreed to divorce him.)

Throughout the 1920s and early 1930s, Stead and Blake lived in Europe, primarily in London and Paris. Stead, encouraged by Blake, became a writer, publishing three books in the early 1930s and sometimes also working in the bank where he was employed.[2] In 1935–36 they lived in New York, where they were involved in the left-wing culture associated with *New Masses*. They returned to Europe to write in 1936, living first in Spain and then, when Franco threatened the Spanish Republic, in France and later in Belgium. In 1937 they returned to New York, where they remained through the war years. (They left the United States in 1946, fleeing anticommunist persecution.) Throughout this period, Stead was affiliated with left-wing cultural institutions in both Europe and the United States. She was the secretary to the English

---

[1] The details of Stead's life are drawn from Rowley, *Christina Stead: A Biography*. Rowley says that Stead later denied that she had left Australia because of its cultural inferiority (64). Stead fictionalizes her exile from Australia in *For Love Alone* (1944); see Chapter 2, below.

[2] On Stead's early career, see "A Writer's Friends."

delegation to the First International Congress of Writers, held in Paris in June 1935, and she read manuscripts and wrote reviews for *New Masses*. Stead's European wanderings and her experiences working in the bank are reflected in *House of All Nations*, a Rabelaisian satire of capitalism published (in New York) in 1938.

In *The Man Who Loved Children* (1940), Stead shifts her setting from Europe to the United States and turns her focus from the public world of finance to the putatively private world of the family. The family is situated in a politicized landscape—the area around Washington, D.C.—that superimposes the United States in which the novel was written on the Australia of the author's childhood. As a novel about an American family written by an Australian woman with affiliations in the American and European Left, *The Man Who Loved Children* is a discursive site in which national identity is contested.

The Man Who Loved Children belongs to the genre of the family romance, which Marianne Hirsch defines, elegantly glossing Freud, as an "interrogation of origins . . . which embeds the engenderment of narrative within the experience of family."[3] The novel sets the trajectory of its protagonist, Louisa Pollit, age eleven when the novel begins, against the marriage of her father, Sam, and stepmother, Henny, antagonists in a battle between the sexes. Louisa's adolescence is punctuated by the increasingly violent quarrels of her parents, by Sam's intrusive attempts to assert control over his children, and by the poverty that follows when Sam loses his position as a naturalist in the Conservation Bureau. For much of the novel, Louisa is suspended between Sam and Henny, shifting her allegiances and antagonism from one to the other. Her zigzagging between maternal and paternal poles is abruptly brought to a close when she decides to free herself and her siblings by killing her parents. She changes her mind, but Henny, noticing that she has already put cyanide in a teacup, takes the poisoned drink and dies. The novel ends soon afterward when Louisa runs away to take "a walk round the world" (491).

This summary conveys the extravagant turn that resolves the plot of *The Man Who Loved Children*, but it does not do justice to the novel's portrait of a family at once ordinary and astonishing or the richness of the novel's language. More important, in its focus on the family story, the summary suppresses the significance of the novel's represented

---

[3] Hirsch, *Mother/Daughter Plot*, 9; cf. Lynn Hunt's definition of the family romance as the "collective, unconscious images of the familial order that underlie revolutionary politics . . . a kind of collective political unconscious . . . structured by narratives of family relations" (*Family Romance of the French Revolution*, xiii). See also Freud, "Family Romances."

world, the United States, and does not account for the way it grafts American onto Australian subject matter. In this chapter, I examine the novel's depiction of the Pollit family, its representation of an American scene, and its deployment of Australian discourses of race, class, and gender. The traces of Australian material that mark the novel's portrayal of an American family play out the hybrid, unstable national identifications of the author and inscribe *The Man Who Loved Children* in a genre I call the national family romance.

Patriarchal Pathologies: The Pollits as Polis

The Pollit family is represented in *The Man Who Loved Children* as a polis: a locus of conflicts between husband and wife, parents and children; a set of hierarchies of difference and domination.[4] At the head of this order is Sam Pollit, the novel's version of a paternal tyrant. Samuel Clemens Pollit, named for "Mark Twain" and Harry Pollitt, chairman of the British Communist Party during the years of the Popular Front, suggests white men's power over women, children, and colonized racial others.[5] Sam is challenged in the novel, chiefly by Henny and Louisa. But, like patriarchy itself, Sam is hardy, resilient, and capable of withstanding the threats he encounters.

Sam's position in the family is illuminated by Michel Foucault's notion of the family as a "microcenter" or "transfer point" in which relations of pleasure, power, and knowledge are organized.[6] Yet *The Man Who Loved Children* exposes slippages between sexuality and gender that Foucault frequently ignores. Sam treats all the members of his family as sources of pleasure and objects of power and knowledge. He appears to his sons and daughters alike as the personification of authority: "Their father was the tables of the law, but their mother was natural law; Sam was household czar by divine right, but Henny was the czar's everlasting adversary, household anarchist by divine right"

---

[4] The family has been the main focus of critical attention since 1965, when *The Man Who Loved Children* was reissued. See my "Fifty Years of Reading"; Boone, "Of Fathers, Daughters, and Theorists," and the expanded version of this essay in his *Libidinal Currents*, which appeared after I wrote this chapter; Brydon, *Christina Stead*; Gardiner, *Rhys, Stead, Lessing,* and "Male Narcissism"; Lidoff, *Christina Stead*; and Sheridan, *Christina Stead*.

[5] Stead, "Interview" (with Beston), 93–94. Gardiner, *Rhys, Stead, Lessing*, 134. Sam's beliefs and values resemble what Donna Haraway designates as the "Teddy Bear Patriarchy" of the American Museum of Natural History and Carl Akeley, doyen of its Africa Hall (*Primate Visions*, chap. 2).

[6] Foucault, *History of Sexuality*, 1:82–83, 92–93, 103.

(36). But he singles out his daughters as targets of his invidious notions of sexual difference. He infantilizes the compliant Evie, but his treatment of the resistant Louisa is ambiguous. On the one hand, he identifies her as an extension of himself.[7] On the other hand, he insists that she recognize sexual difference—sexuality itself—as a disability that renders women vulnerable to men's power and especially their erotic aggression.

Sam is a classifier: "child namer," cataloguer, record keeper, world maker, and system builder. He is based on Stead's father, the naturalist David Stead.[8] To Sam, Tohoga House, the family home, is a museum, an archive, a repository of things and persons to be described and categorized. As a naturalist, he resembles the early-20th-century primatologists that Donna Haraway describes. His obsession with taxonomy recalls the order of primatology that, as Haraway explains, "works by the negotiation of boundaries achieved through ordering differences."[9]

The continuities between patriarchal domination of women and colonial domination of feminized racial others are illustrated in an episode that describes Sam's trip to Malaya as a member of an anthropological mission. Sam's particular combination of racism and liberalism and his desire "to know my fellow man to the utmost . . . to penetrate into the hearts of dark, yellow, red, tawny, and tattooed man" (50) make him a latter-day comic echo of Joseph Conrad's Kurtz who belongs, initially at least, to the party of enlightenment. And, like Conrad's Marlow, Sam encounters in the colonial scene a test of his mettle and his manhood. Sam regards Malaya as a reflection of his own beliefs, values, and preconceptions and as an arena in which to realize his ambitions:

> In a short time he had fallen madly in love with Malaya and saw her as a great country, unplundered, untouched, undreamed of, brimming with natural wealth, which would make all of its soft-skinned people rich and happy. All that was needed was understanding and the eviction of the People of Greed. He himself was helping mightily the people, he believed, by getting to know them and finding out their different types and entirely addled strains. He could tell the indigenous Malays from the new imports from India, Hailam from Canton, Hohkien from Teochiew, and he

[7] Boone, ("Of Fathers, Daughters, and Theorists," 516 and passim, and *Libidinal Currents,* 328 and passim), and Gardiner (*Rhys, Stead, Lessing,* 137, and "Male Narcissism," passim) comment on Sam's narcissism.

[8] Stead reflects on her father's influence in "A Writer's Friends" and "A Waker and a Dreamer." See also Rowley, "How Real Is Sam Pollit?" 505.

[9] Haraway, *Primate Visions,* 10.

tried to have a friend in each of these and many other strains. He felt like
a kind of Livingstone going into the heart of the darkest unknown, as he
put it, the heart of man. (213)

Sam's version of "Malaya" resembles a figure in Orientalist discourse as Edward W. Said describes it. (It also recalls Australian versions of eugenics.) Sam conflates the biological and the cultural
("strains," "types") and confuses description and judgment ("ad-
dled"). He identifies Malaya—or Malayans—with "other peoples variously designated as backward, degenerate, uncivilized, and retarded,
. . . [with] elements in Western society (delinquents, the insane,
women, the poor) having in common an identity best described as
lamentably alien." [10] And he "Orientalizes" Malaya, producing it both
as an object of knowledge and as a passive, inert, feminized object of
desire. Soon afterward, he imagines himself as the husband of Chinese,
Indian, Malay, and Cingalese women and the father of a multiracial
"phalanstery" (219).

Sam's adventures in Malaya suggest the self-importance, muddle-
headedness, and irrelevance of ostensibly liberal, "scientific" versions
of the colonial project. He is defeated by the tropical heat and humid-
ity. He despises those he calls the "People of Greed," but he benefits
from their exploits. He compiles notes for a comprehensive report on
the mission, but he cannot complete the report without the assistance
of his Chinese secretary. By extension, Stead suggests, the liberal colonialism for which Sam speaks depends on the exploitation of native
subjects without whom he cannot realize his project of enlightenment.
Indeed, the letters he writes his family belong to the genre of imperial
travel writing, a genre in which, as Mary Louise Pratt explains, Europeans writing "about non-European parts of the world went (and go)
about creating the 'domestic subject' of Euroimperialism." [11] But Sam's
predicament also points to Stead's own situation, that of a white colonial intellectual at once critical of and complicit in the colonial order
that makes her career possible. [12]

Henny is Sam's principal antagonist. She challenges Sam's authority,
mocks the rationality he professes, and attacks his commitment to science and morality. As Julia Duffy points out, Henny incarnates what

---

[10] Said, *Orientalism*, 207.

[11] Pratt, *Imperial Eyes*, 4.

[12] Sam's letters are taken verbatim from a letter that David Stead wrote his family
while on a mission for the Australian government (Rowley, *Christina Stead*, 263, and
"How Real Is Sam Pollit?").

M. M. Bakhtin identifies as "the essential principle of grotesque realism, degradation, that is, the lowering of all that is high, spiritual, ideal, abstract." Her characteristic mode of utterance is the tirade, a torrent of abuse that dramatizes "carnival liberties and carnival truths."[13]

> "Look at me! My back's bent in two with the fruit of my womb; aren't you sorry to see what happened to me because of his lust? I go about with a body like a football, fit to be kicked about by a bohunk halfback, an All-America football, because of his lust, the fine, pure man that won't look at women. . . . To you he's something wonderful; if you know what he is to me, something dirty, a splotch of blood or washing-up water on my skirts." (253–54)

But Henny's linguistic fecundity does not enable her either to escape or to transform the "proliferating miseries" that make her marriage a "life sentence" (11).

In the impasses that she incarnates, Henny appears as the voice of abjection, as Julia Kristeva explains it. Henny's grotesque intensity dramatizes the "violence of mourning for an 'object' that has always already been lost"; here she suggests the mother who died when Christina Stead was an infant and was always already lost in (to) the conscious life of the author. Henny also evokes the archaic mother feared, Kristeva explains, for the "generative power" that "patrilineal filiation has the burden of subduing."[14]

Henny plays a part as well in the family seen as an economic unit. She lives on credit, subsisting and sustaining her family on her debts. In the very first episode of the novel, she discovers that her wealthy brother has refused the loan she has requested. The climax of the novel is set in motion by the loss of Tohoga House, the home that Henny and Sam have rented from Henny's father, David Collyer, believing that he will leave it to them when he dies. When Collyer dies broke, Tohoga House is sold to pay his debts, and the Pollits are forced to move from their beloved Washington to a seedy quarter of Annapolis. After Sam loses his government job, Henny tries unsuccessfully to patch up the

[13] Duffy, "Grain of the Voice," 50–51; Bakhtin, *Rabelais*, 19, 27–28. Henny is based on Stead's stepmother, Ada, David Stead's second wife, but Stead invented her language (Rowley, *Christina Stead*, 260). Lidoff links the grotesque imagery that describes Henny and the "domestic gothic" that defines Stead's own style (21, 38).

[14] Kristeva, *Powers of Horror*, 15, 77. Boone links Henny's "subversive if ambivalent power . . . to a repressed female history distorted by the lens of patriarchal vision" ("Of Fathers, Daughters, and Theorists," 528). Lidoff sees Henny as the powerful figure of the pre-oedipal mother (33).

holes in the family finances by pawning her few valuables, pilfering the meager savings of her son Ernie, and borrowing from a notorious usurer. But Sam cannot or will not admit that she is feeding the family.

As an unacknowledged foundation of the family's existence, Henny's debts signify her exploitation: that is, they link her and, by extension, the women she stands for to the proletariat whose exploitation supports the structure of capitalism. Here *The Man Who Loved Children* revises American, left-wing, 1930s configurations of class and gender whereby the proletariat is gendered masculine and the bourgeoisie seen as feminine or effeminate.[15] In addition, Henny's debts and the plot that flows from them inscribe *The Man Who Loved Children* in the tradition of Dickens and Balzac, novelists whom Stead consistently identified as influences.[16] In this respect, *The Man Who Loved Children* might be seen as Stead's homage—an acknowledgment of her debt—to her literary forefathers.

Unlike Henny, who wallows in abject femininity and dramatizes the power of passivity, Louisa exemplifies two distinct strategies of gender. On the one hand, she refuses the disabilities of women and claims the privileges of men. In response to Sam's meddling and prying, she thinks to herself, "I am triumphant, I am king" (320). On the other hand, she insists on the prerogatives of difference. When Sam praises her mother (his first wife, who died when she was an infant), she retorts, "What do you know about my mother? She was a woman" (488).

Louisa's self-identification as a woman coincides with the development of a tenuous bond between herself and Henny, a bond that expresses the "natural outlawry of womankind" (243–44). But this connection is fleeting, and their fragile solidarity entails Louisa's tacit acceptance of the common lot of "every woman" (13), vulnerability to sexual innuendo, harassment, and assault.

Another locus of Louisa's maternal identification is Harpers Ferry, West Virginia, home of her mother's family, the Bakens. In Louisa's personal mythology, the Bakens and Harpers Ferry summon up a maternal domain uncontaminated by the father's law. At the end of the novel, when Louisa runs away from home, her intended destination is Harpers Ferry. She is attempting to recover or recapture a place untouched by Sam. But the Baken family belongs to the same patriarchal regime as the Pollits. The head of the family is the stern and puritanical

---

[15] On the gendering of class in (male) Marxist writers in the 1930s, see Rabinowitz, *Labor and Desire*, 8, 22, 47.

[16] See Stead, "Uses of the Many-Charactered Novel" and "A Waker and a Dreamer."

grandfather Israel Baken, and all but one of Louisa's uncles tyranni-
cally dominate their submissive wives.

In addition to taking refuge in a female solidarity more imagined
than real, Louisa attempts to ignore the constraints of gender by appropriating the prerogatives of men. According to Diana Brydon, Stead,
too, refused to acknowledge her gender as a handicap: perhaps this
gesture of refusal reinscribed her affiliation with a Left in which gender was subordinated to class as an analytic category.[17] Louisa wants to
assert her claim to a heroism exempt from the disabilities of sex. If this
desire propels her to run away, the sequel, *For Love Alone*, suggests that
even women's wanderings make them vulnerable to the sexual power
of men.[18] In *The Man Who Loved Children*, however, the adolescent
Louisa evades some of the constraints of gender by being young
enough not to have to experience them.

Louisa's refusal of gender constraints is also conveyed in her relation to a bourgeois, patriarchal, predominantly European literary tradition like the genealogy that Stead fashioned for herself. Throughout
the novel, Louisa lays claim to the enabling narratives of "her" culture,
finding in them models she can emulate or fantasies that console her.
Louisa identifies mainly with male heroes. One important prototype is
Hans Christian Andersen's ugly duckling (59–60), a male creature
whose gender is not mentioned in *The Man Who Loved Children*.[19] Another is Friedrich Nietzsche, an important influence on Stead herself.[20]
Louisa also reads *The Pilgrim's Progress* and a biography of John Brown.
And she attacks Sam by quoting at him Byron's "Ode to Napoleon
Buonaparte": "The Desolator desolate, / The tyrant overthrown; / The
Arbiter of other's fate, / A Suppliant for his own!" (267). (Louisa sub-
stitutes "tyrant" for Byron's "Victor.")

Like Teresa Hawkins, the protagonist of *For Love Alone* who sees herself as an Australian Ulysses, Louisa puts herself in the place of men.
She rewrites the scripts that construct women as objects of men's desire or symbols of men's heroism and identifies herself with (male) heroes who are agents, not victims, of patriarchal cultural hegemony.[21]
But if identifying with male heroes is a fantasy that compensates for

[17] Brydon 4. See Rabinowitz 6 and passim, and Stead, "Writers Take Sides."
[18] See Chapter 2.
[19] Randall Jarrell describes *The Man Who Loved Children* itself as a "neglected masterpiece," that is, an ugly duckling only later recognized as a swan (Afterword, 492, 500).
[20] On the influence of Nietzsche in *The Man Who Loved Children*, see Rowley, "Christina
Stead: The Voyage to Cythera," 1; Walker, "Language, Art, and Ideas"; R. Baker,
"Christina Stead: The Nietzsche Connection"; and Stewart, "Heaven and Hell."
[21] Cf. Brydon: "The female artist learns to proceed through subterfuge, identifying her
models in male heroes conceived by men and seeing no irony in that identification" (70).

women's powerlessness, it does not enable Louisa, as an aspiring writer—or Stead, as an established one?—to transform the gendered cultural text she lays hold of.

Louisa's literary efforts dramatize the narrow compass in which she can assert herself. To celebrate her father's birthday, she attempts to rewrite Shelley's *The Cenci*, the story of Beatrice Cenci, executed in 1599 for the killing of her father, a brutal, corrupt count. Louisa's play, titled *Tragos: Herpes Rom* ("Tragedy: The Snake Man"), is written in an invented language; it is about a father who kills his daughter.[22] When Sam asks why her play is not written in English, she replies, in what might be the novel's finest moment, "Did Euripides write in English?" (377). But her protest against paternal despotism is ineffective because no one understands the invented language in which it is expressed. Whatever Louisa's intent, *Herpes Rom* reproduces the patriarchal script in which the mother cannot prevent the father's victimization of the daughter. Like Lucretia Cenci, who cannot save Beatrice from the collective power of father, state, and church, and like Henny Pollit, who cannot save Louisa from the onslaughts of Sam, the mother in *Herpes Rom* cannot help her daughter, who dies at the end of the play. Like Sam's letters home, Louisa's writings pose questions about Stead's own project, that of a colonial woman writer: Can Stead establish her own authority, or is her writing a mimicry of metropolitan and patriarchal originals?

The end of the novel replays Louisa's oscillation between her parents. In her rebellion against Sam, she identifies with Henny. She runs away, then, to escape Henny's destiny: confinement and unpaid labor in the patriarchal family.[23] But Louisa is a survivor, and her survival links her with the surviving parent, Sam. She is, after all, at least partly responsible for Henny's death. Is the daughter's freedom dependent on the destruction of the mother? Of what the mother represents? Or does Louisa's role in Henny's death signal her complicity in the male dominance—and especially the antifeminism—that pervades the Pollit polis, the patriarchal, misogynist Australian culture in which Stead was reared, and the international and American Left in which she later found a home in exile? Unresolved, these questions linger in Louisa's

[22] On the revisionary force of the play, see Gardiner, *Rhys, Stead, Lessing*, 135, and Arac 188. Sheridan argues that the play dramatizes a "nullification of female subjectivity" (48).

[23] Boone reads this ending as a revision of the "psychosexual dynamics . . . of oedipal narrative"; unlike Oedipus, whose patricide leads to union with the mother, Louisa's matricide leads to separation from the father ("Of Fathers, Daughters, and Theorists," 537).

resemblance to Sam and to the snake man, fathers who strangle, suffocate, or otherwise do away with the femininity incarnated in daughter and mother alike. They are prompted, too, by Stead's own affiliation with a masculine (European) novelistic tradition and with a Left in which feminist commitment and feminine identifications are devalued.

Civil Wars

Stead wrote *The Man Who Loved Children* in the late 1930s in the United States, where it was published before it was published elsewhere. The novel is set in an American scene contemporary with the moment in which it was written. Stead represents her novel as American literature and herself as an American writer by inserting her text into American cultural debates.[24] In other words, *The Man Who Loved Children* is an attempt to perform an American identity for itself and its author alike. But this performative project, enabled in part by the value that the Popular Front placed on Americanness, is disrupted by the pedagogical imperatives of Stead's Australian (colonial) history.

The American identity of *The Man Who Loved Children* is announced, at least implicitly, in the very first scene, in Henny Pollit's notion of her marriage as a "civil war" (11). Throughout, Stead presents the violent quarrels that divide the Pollit family as a retelling of the American national story. The Pollits' conflicts unfold in an area bounded by Washington, Baltimore, Annapolis, and Harpers Ferry. These places are not only sites of such important events in American history as John Brown's raid but also a crossroads, a microcosm of the entire national landscape, in which North and South intersect. Stead's version of the American national legend is based on an analogy between the husband and the victorious North and the wife and the defeated South, but these oppositions are undermined by her ambivalence toward North and South, husband and wife, and by ambiguities in her treatment of class as a conceptual category.

Throughout the novel, Sam is identified not only with the North but also with the artisan class from which he springs and with bourgeois liberal ideology. The Pollits' Baltimore, a domain of puritanical attitudes toward alcohol and culture, belongs to the North. Sam also ex-

---

[24] See my "Fifty Years of Reading" for a discussion of the national identities attributed to the novel by reviewers. In a 1941 application for a Guggenheim Fellowship, Stead described her project as an "addition to *American* literature" (quoted in Harris, "Interrogating Ideologies," 5; emphasis added). In the 1942 edition of *Twentieth-Century Authors*, she identified herself as Australian American.

emplifies an androcentric, racist liberalism at once universal and quintessentially American.[25] He sees himself as the great white father and as a representative of the "United States of mankind" (71, 202–3). And, at the end of the novel, he proposes to pull his family up out of poverty by spreading his message of cultural enlightenment on a radio show called the *Uncle Sam Hour*.[26]

In addition to the historical or legendary characters such as Franklin Delano Roosevelt and the Horatio Alger heroes that Sam himself explicitly takes as models, he evokes figures who represent diverse aspects of American culture. These include Artemus Ward, Herman Melville's Ahab (and Melville himself), and Mark Twain. Ward, a nineteenth-century journalist and humorist, wrote sketches in an idiosyncratic, pseudo-folksy dialect that sounds like baby talk. In Sam's incessant chatter, a pastiche composed of the "verbal tatters of Artemus Ward" (301), Stead simultaneously emphasizes his misogyny and trivializes it: "If I had my way no crazy shemales would so much as git the vote! Becaze why? Becaze they is crazy! . . . if they ain't got childer, they need childer to keep 'em from going crazy; en if they have childer the childer drive em crazy" (108).

Stead's allusions to Melville work in several different ways.[27] Toward the end of the novel, when the Pollit family is virtually starving because Sam has lost his job, he catches a marlin and decides to boil it for its oil, which he plans to use for cooking and heating the house (436–44). The minutely detailed description of Sam's elaborate preparations and the anticlimactic yield of just one gallon of oil make the marlin-boiling scene a travesty of Melville's "Try-Works" chapter.[28] In *Moby Dick*, the boiling of the oil in the Pequod's try-works occasions in Ishmael a vision of the "redness, the madness, the ghastliness of others" (354) and a meditation on sorrow and mortality (chapter 96). The boiling of the fish oil in *The Man Who Loved Children* produces a stench that permeates the house and occasions Henny's remark that "my life has been one blessed fish chowder!" (437). Substituting chowder for

---

[25] On Sam as a liberal, see Arac; Yglesias, "Marx as Muse"; and Stead, "Christina Stead in Washington Square."

[26] Late in her life, Stead expressly denied that Sam was intended to represent Uncle Sam ("Christina Stead in Washington Square," 73–74, and "Interview" [with Wetherell], 443).

[27] M. H., reviewing the novel in 1940, and Day Thorpe, reviewing the 1965 reissue, noticed the Melville connection.

[28] Stead said that this episode was based on an incident from her childhood and denied that she meant to parody Melville. ("A Waker and a Dreamer," 490; letter to Robie Macauley, 20 September 1965, Harry Ransom Humanities Center, University of Texas, Austin). The echoes of Melville illustrate Bakhtin's notion that an utterance encounters "alien words that have already been spoken about it" ("Discourse in the Novel," 276).

mortality, Henny punctures Sam's self-deluding optimism and undercuts Ishmael's metaphysical concerns.

Melville is not simply an object of parody but also a figure for Louisa's aspirations and, by implication, for those of the author herself. Soon after the fish-boiling episode, Louisa recites from *Moby Dick*, " 'Bear me out in this, thou great democratic God! who didst not refuse to the swart convict Bunyan the pale poetic pearl: Thou who didst clothe with doubly hammered leaves of finest gold, the stumped and paupered arm of old Cervantes' " (444). Here, Melville—along with the writers that he invokes, Bunyan and Cervantes—signifies the literary heritage to which Louisa lays claim. In identifying with Melville and his canon of male geniuses maimed, imprisoned, impoverished, or unappreciated in their own day, Louisa asserts her ambition and inserts herself into a tradition of "kingly commons" (*Moby Dick*, 105) at once democratic and patriarchal, European and American. Like her unspoken rejoinder to Sam, "I am triumphant, I am king" (320), Louisa's appropriation of Melville is an attempt to refuse her own subjection to hierarchies of difference.

In the novel's national allegory and its condensed American geography, the Pollits are identified with the North, and Henny's family, the Collyers, with the South. In Sam's ascendancy over Henny, the subordination of women is transcoded as the defeat of the South by the North. But ambiguities undermine the implied analogies and expose the Old South—a "residual" formation in Raymond Williams's terms—as a nostalgic myth.[29]

Henny's childhood home in Frederick, Maryland, is an estate with a name redolent of the Old South, Monocacy. (The Monocacy River runs through Frederick and Harpers Ferry.) Under the aegis of Henny's sharp-tongued mother and alcoholic, Faulknerian, ne'er-do-well brother, the now dilapidated estate emblematizes Henny's history: a belle who could not catch the kind of husband she was brought up to marry, she had to settle for Sam.

As Stead's identification of Sam with the North is amplified through echoes of *Moby Dick*, her identification of Henny with the South is elaborated through allusions to *Gone with the Wind*. Stead disliked Margaret Mitchell's novel. Her antipathy may have been reinforced by pressure from her agent and publisher to satisfy the tastes of the literary marketplace by writing popular romances.[30] Indeed, the one clear

---

[29] Williams, *Marxism and Literature*, 122.

[30] Stead complained that her agent represented John Steinbeck and *Gone with the Wind* and was pushing her to write books that sell. Letter to Stanley Burnshaw, 31 August 1942, Burnshaw Collection, Harry Ransom Humanities Center, University of Texas, Austin.

reference to *Gone with the Wind* in *The Man Who Loved Children* suggests that popularity—sales—requires a serious distortion of reality:

> [Henny] made herself some tea, and then got into bed, to try and read the saga of upland Georgian gentility, which she had three times abandoned because she, Henny, had "no fancy big buck niggers to wait on her and lick her boots": but once more she threw it away. Where, indeed, was she to find heroes to succor her and how could she succeed in business with her spendthrift ways. "I'm a failure all right," said Henny; "and why don't they write about deadbeats like me—only it wouldn't sell!" (414)

Here, Henny voices Stead's critique of Mitchell, a critique that associates *The Man Who Loved Children* with a tradition of novelistic realism that, from Cervantes onward, exposes the sentimental excesses and implausibility of romance. These excesses are conventionally coded as "feminine." [31]

The Man Who Loved Children has no equivalent of an Old South that dies, as does Scarlett's mother, Ellen O'Hara, or survives, as do Ashley and Melanie Wilkes, by accommodating itself to the rapacious commercial tendencies associated with the New South of Scarlett O'Hara and Rhett Butler. Scarlett thrives by working hard, by outright stealing, by exploiting the labor of convicts and former slaves, and by marrying three men whose money she puts to good use; Henny is destroyed by debts. Scarlett is virtually unaffected by motherhood; Henny, whose nicknames Moth, Mothering, Motherbunch, and Pet identify her with maternity, is dragged down by Sam's sexual demands and her children's insatiable needs. *The Man Who Loved Children*, set in the 1930s, exposes the era depicted in *Gone with the Wind*, the 1860s and 1870s, as a depression-era fantasy. [32]

But Stead reinscribes as well as revises the assumptions that underlie Mitchell's text. [33] She demystifies Mitchell's racist romanticization of the South, while she is, like Mitchell, skeptical about the virtues of the dominant (northern, liberal) culture. Both Stead's version of American history and Mitchell's dramatize the exploitation and victimization of women by men: for both writers, that is, gender is also a marker of class. The two writers—the white, Southern woman and the left-wing, Australian-born woman—conflate gender oppression and geographical marginality or subordination. In *Gone with the Wind* the defeat of the South is enacted in the marriages of white northern men (both,

---

[31] On romance and the feminine, see Langbauer, *Women and Romance*.

[32] Jane Tompkins historicizes the romance element of *Gone with the Wind* as "true to what so many were thinking and feeling at the time" ("All Alone," 195).

[33] I thank Margaret R. Higonnet for pointing this out.

ironically, former overseers of slaves) who take possession of white southern women ("white trash" and an impoverished plantation aristocrat) and symbolically of the South itself. Scarlett escapes the common fate of these two women, but Henny's situation resembles theirs. Unable to turn her marriage to account, she is proletarianized by her subjection to Sam, whose racism belies his liberalism, and to the imperatives of maternity.

Henny insists that Sam is not the self-made man that he claims to be. She declares that Sam's rise in the world is not the result of his own efforts but rather of his dependence on her father and thus of his exploitation of her:

> "You took me and maltreated me and starved me half to death because you couldn't make a living and sponged off my father and used his influence, hoisting yourself up on all my aches and miseries . . . boasting and blowing about your success when all the time it was me, my poor body that was what you took your success out of. . . . A brute, a savage, a wild Indian wouldn't do what you did." (136)

Henny elaborates Stead's class-conscious analysis of gender, but her parroting of racist platitudes undermines the critique of *Gone with the Wind*. Here, she describes herself as the victim of a man worse than a "wild Indian," but she also identifies with the "wretched beggars, Chinks and niggers" she was brought up to hold in contempt, regarding Sam as "the family carpetbagger" who imposes his hypocritical morality on all those he tyrannizes at will (253).

If Henny represents one model of opposition to Sam and the American cultural values that he exemplifies, Louisa's maternal kin, the Bakens of Harpers Ferry, represent another. Louisa's grandfather Israel is reminiscent of John Brown himself. The tiny library of Israel's gentle son Reuben is the source of Louisa's literary and political inheritance, *The Pilgrim's Progress, Paradise Lost,* and James Redpath's *The Public Life of Captain John Brown* (148). At the end of the novel, after Henny's death, when Sam tries to regain control over Louisa, she invokes the Bakens and the heritage they represent: " 'You remember when you used to take me to see the Lincoln Memorial, walking along the Reflecting Pool from your office on Saturdays. I learned from him, not from you. . . . When I was at Harpers Ferry, I only thought about John Brown. I always thought Israel Baken was just like him—my grandfather. Not a Pollit, thank goodness, not one of you' "(488).

Despite the palpable tyranny of Israel Baken, Harpers Ferry represents—to Louisa, at least—an imagined alternative to her father's authority. In giving Louisa Harpers Ferry as a maternal or matrilineal heritage, Stead presents the "walk round the world" on which Louisa embarks at the end of the novel as a daughterly declaration of independence that announces a third American revolution, following on John Brown's second and Thomas Jefferson's first. At the same time, Stead articulates a cultural politics that opposes both racism and the masculinist bias of an—"the"?—American cultural tradition that canonizes texts such as *Moby Dick* and, as Jane Tompkins rightly argues, refuses cultural authority to the devalued femininity inscribed in works such as *Gone with the Wind*.[34] *The Man Who Loved Children* negotiates an alternative to an antiracist tradition that is implacably patriarchal if not misogynist and a woman's tradition that is irretrievably racist.

In situating *The Man Who Loved Children* in debates about American culture, canonical and popular, high and low, Stead produces it as an American text. But the novel bears the marks of its origins, as if Louisa's declaration of independence—or Stead's—were inaugurating yet another revolution that remains to be fulfilled. In identifying with John Brown, Louisa imaginatively aligns herself with but also displaces the black slaves on whose behalf he raided the arsenal in Harpers Ferry. Suppressed, in this retelling of an American tale, are the stories of particular African Americans, the race plot that underwrites the colonization of America and Australia alike, and hence the Australian beginnings of this American novel.

Unsettling Australia

"Oh yes, I am an Australian. Of course I'm an Australian."
—Christina Stead quoted in Joan Lidoff, *Christina Stead*

The terrain on which the battle of the sexes unfolds is not only the family construed as microcosm, or polis, not only an American political landscape, but also an Australian milieu like the one in which Christina Stead herself grew up.[35] In some respects, Stead is always writing "about" Australia even when she sets her novels elsewhere, as she herself implies when she says that she set her novel in the United States to

[34] Tompkins 191.
[35] On the influence in *The Man Who Loved Children* of early-twentieth-century Australian intellectual life, see Walker; R. Baker; Stewart; Green, *"The Man Who Loved Children"*; and Reid, *Fiction and the Great Depression*. For Stead's reading of Australian authors, see "Interview" (with Wetherell), 446.

shield family members living in Australia.[36] "Australia" is a source of pressure on the manifest content of *The Man Who Loved Children*. This pressure remains for the most part beneath the narrative surface, but it erupts periodically, marking the novel or leaving traces in details that appear incongruous in the American scene that Stead portrays.

One of these eruptions occurs in a climactic scene in the novel, the family party held to celebrate Sam's return from Malaya. This gathering is described as a "family corroboree" (236), a word that, according to the *Oxford English Dictionary*, originates in the Port Jackson dialect of Australia and denotes a warlike or festive dance of Australian natives. In this episode, Sam chastises Henny, Louisa transfers her allegiance from father to mother, and a telegram arrives announcing the death of Henny's father. Immediately afterward, the last Pollit child is born, rumors circulate that Sam is not the child's father, and Sam loses his job. During the party, Sam's father, Charles Pollit, dramatizes scenes from *Great Expectations*, following the lead of his namesake, Charles Dickens.

Throughout *The Man Who Loved Children*, allusions to *Great Expectations* comment on the history of the Pollit family. *Great Expectations* also operates as a metonym for the story of Australian colonization in general and for Stead's history in particular.[37] In Dickens's novel, Pip has to confront the "criminal" source of his expectations in the wealth of the convict Magwitch, whose punishment for theft is "transportation" to Australia. In foregrounding Pip's connections to British crime and law, *Great Expectations* elides the Australian consequences of Magwitch's fortunate fall, the appropriation of aboriginal lands that makes possible the "sheep farming" that underwrites Pip's transformation into a "gentleman."[38] (Dickens also distorts the later history of those brought to Australia as convicts, very few of whom became rich.) The colonial racial script suppressed in *Great Expectations* also plays a part in Stead's own family history: her paternal grandfather—the model for Sam Pollit's father—was influenced to emigrate to Australia by Dickens's novel.[39]

The Pollits' family life is another instance of the eruption of "Australian" matter in the American environment of *The Man Who Loved*

---

[36] Stead, "Christina Stead: An Interview," 242; Rowley says that Stead changed the locale to make the book marketable in the United States (*Christina Stead*, 261).

[37] See Chapter 2 for a discussion of *Great Expectations* as an intertext in *For Love Alone*. Said discusses *Great Expectations* as part of a "history of speculation about and experience of Australia" (*Culture and Imperialism*, xiv–xvi.) Peter Carey, in *Jack Maggs*, published after I wrote this chapter, takes *Great Expectations* as his point of departure.

[38] Prior ownership by indigenous people of the land that became Australia was not recognized until June 1992 (Curthoys, "Citizenship and National Identity," 25).

[39] Stead, "A Waker and a Dreamer," 481–82; Lidoff 203.

Children. Henny apparently personifies an American cultural type, the déclassé Southern belle, and Sam's association with his namesakes, Uncle Sam and Samuel Clemens, makes him an exemplary American. But their marriage is not connected to the 1930s American scene. The depression is virtually unmentioned in the novel and, strangely, plays no part in Sam's losing his job. If we recover the Australian genealogy of Henny and Sam, however, we can account for apparently incongruous or idiosyncratic narrative details. The marriage of Henny and Sam belongs to the Australia of Stead's childhood and adolescence, and Sam and Henny themselves recall early-twentieth-century Australian articulations of race, class, gender, and family.[40] The novel's relentlessly binary vision of gender—"their father was the tables of the law, but their mother was natural law"—represents the rigid sexual division of labor and "gender apartheid" that Australian historians and sociologists have traced in this period.[41]

Henny's grotesque femininity and exaggerated, even parodic fecundity transcribes material and ideological changes in early-twentieth-century Australia. The sociologist Desley Deacon explains that during this period there was a decline in the situation and status of middle-class and elite women relative to those of men in the same classes.[42] Changes in the Australian economy led to policies and institutions that defined productive labor as the province of men, relegated women (identified as wives and mothers) to the home, and reconceptualized women's domestic labor as nonwork.[43] Married women in this era lacked legal protection. They had limited property rights but no guaranteed rights either in the guardianship of the children or to the family's accumulated wealth.[44]

In addition, this period saw what the sociologist Kerreen Reiger identifies as the "rationalization" of domestic life. As Reiger explains, "experts" attempted to extend "the principles of science and reason to the operation of the household and the management of personal relationships," while the infant welfare movement focused on maternal adequacy—or, more often, inadequacy.[45] Henny's helter-skelter notion of motherhood—"they grow up whether you look after them or not," she says (427)—makes her both target and victim of the ideological

[40] Rowley says that Stead set the novel in the 1930s because the America she knew was contemporary (*Christina Stead*, 261).
[41] Matthews, *Good and Mad Women*, 148.
[42] Deacon, *Managing Gender*, 153–54.
[43] Matthews 58.
[44] Rowley, *Christina Stead*, 27–28; Allen, "Breaking into the Public Sphere."
[45] Reiger, *Disenchantment of the Home*, 3; on the infant welfare movement, see Deacon, *Managing Gender*, 212; Matthews 78.

strategies that these Australian scholars describe. Similarly, Henny's conflation of marriage and maternity, her fatalistic sense of marriage as a life sentence, recalls the discursive construction of compulsory marriage and motherhood as the "cornerstone of femininity."[46] Judged in terms of the demand that the mother supervise all aspects of a child's existence or the idea of the home as a haven for men,[47] Henny will inevitably be found wanting. Yet these are precisely the criteria that guide Sam's "scientific" and managerial view of Henny's laissez-faire housekeeping.

Like Henny's abject domesticity, Sam's public spiritedness has an Australian provenance in the values of the new middle class. This class, consisting of workers "who depended on the sale of education, technical and social skills, or 'cultural capital,' " was consolidated in the late nineteenth and early twentieth centuries through the exclusion of women, Asians, and "other races."[48] Early in the novel, Sam lectures his children about his vision of an "ideal state," a "system" that he calls "Monoman or Manunity": "Monoman would only be the condition of the world after we had weeded out the misfits and degenerates. . . . People would be taught, and would be anxious to produce the new man and with him the new state of man's social perfection" (51).[49] (The children are not impressed.) The eugenic fantasia that Sam spins out reaccentuates early-twentieth-century Australian population ideology that articulates "the 'White Australia' immigration policy; . . . state intervention in matters of education [and] welfare, . . . religious debate over purity and decadence, scientific debate over evolution and degeneracy, [and] political debate over socialism and liberalism."[50] In addressing his children as potential citizens of his ideal state, Sam also echoes the exponents of the Australian infant welfare movement.[51]

Between 1913 and 1920—roughly the years of Stead's adolescence—the government was professionalized. Professional government workers attempted to reform the family by intensifying the sexual division of labor and the asymmetrical organization of gender. Sam Pollit's angle of vision and the rhetoric in which he expresses his beliefs in progress reproduce the idiolect of the new middle class, a "language of science, technology and expertise."[52]

[46] Matthews 112.
[47] Reiger 172, 38.
[48] Deacon, *Managing Gender*, 4 and chap. 4.
[49] Arac identifies Sam's vision of Monoman with United States imperialism (179).
[50] Matthews 74–75. On the "White Australia" policy, see also Ward, *Nation for a Continent*, 30–32.
[51] Deacon, *Managing Gender*, 212.
[52] Ibid., 210, quotation from 206.

The Australian beginnings of Stead's text can also be traced in what appears— to a late-twentieth-century American reader, at least—as a jarring depiction of families and children. The Pollit family is characterized by extreme violence, both physical and emotional, but the violence is presented almost dispassionately. This incongruity situates the novel at the juncture of two distinct historical moments. Between 1880 and 1940 there was a shift in Australia from criminal to family law in juridical attempts to resolve family violence. One consequence of this shift was the emergence of the "family" as an entity in need of treatment.[53] The conceptualization of childhood changed in similar ways. The old idea that a child is responsible for her or his behavior gave way to ideas of children as victims of either the environment or their families.[54] Louisa's emergence, apparently unscathed, from the clamor and violence she witnesses daily and the matter-of-fact attitude she takes when she decides to poison her parents are residues of earlier constructions.

In numerous interviews and in her own autobiographical writings, Stead acknowledges the Australian origins of her American story. Indeed, in her account, Australia takes priority over America, the novel's represented world. Susan Sheridan observes that Stead retrospectively legitimates her novels by asserting that they tell authentic, autobiographical truths.[55] The statements Stead makes about the Australian provenance of The Man Who Loved Children are instances of these assertions. Stead's claims of authenticity, Sheridan argues, sanction some ways of reading the novels and preclude others, notably those that interpret them as works of imaginative fiction (15–18). These claims attempt to foreclose the narrative or discursive construction of a hybrid—in this case, Australian American—national identity. At the same time, they prohibit reading practices that explore such constructions. The performative construction of American identity in The Man Who Loved Children is not subverted by exclusionary conceptions of "Australianness" or "Americanness"; rather, it is retrospectively prohibited by Stead's insistence on the literal truth of what she writes.

The authority that Stead assigns to the cluster Australia–autobiography–authenticity apparently forbids a reading that regards the Australian material I have been describing as subject to repression in The Man Who Loved Children. By extension, the claims of authenticity preclude readings that emphasize the "affinity," to borrow Balibar's term, between family and nation or between the family romance as Freud

[53] Allen, "Invention," 20.
[54] Reiger 168.
[55] Sheridan 15. See notes 22 and 24, this chapter.

and psychoanalytic critics and historians such as Hirsch and Lynn Hunt conceive it and the genre that I want to call the national family romance. Yet the word Stead uses to describe the Australian material in her novel invites just such a reading.

Stead presents the relationship between "Australia" and "America" as one of translation; she says she took experiences from her childhood in Sydney and dropped them, whole and entire, into the area around Washington, D.C. The word she uses for this operation, however, invites scrutiny: she says she "transported" Watson's Bay to the Chesapeake.[56] *Transportation,* presumably, is a metaphor. But unlike its synonyms *transposition* and *translation,* "transportation" is also a metonym, one that evokes an Australian colonial history and specifically the convict past that, as Robert Hughes argues, was subject to amnesia, repression, or distortion in the collective national consciousness of Australia in later years.[57] This distortion is reproduced in Stead's account of her grandfather's emigration: Samuel Stead is inspired by the story of Magwitch, but he omits—or his granddaughter sometimes does when she retells his story—the sentence of transportation and penal servitude that sent Magwitch to Australia.

The narrative of Australian colonization, a story of "transportation" in both the literal and the figurative senses, is absent from *The Man Who Loved Children,* yet it underwrites all the stories told in the novel. Like repressed material, like identities that are lost in cases of amnesia, and like the constellation of abjection that Kristeva delineates, "Australia," ostensibly privileged in Stead's account of her own literary production, also signifies what is forgotten or misremembered: the mother (the maternal origin) that is always already lost. "America," ostensibly devalued but narratively prominent, evokes the paternal or symbolic order to which other orders are subject.

In *The Man Who Loved Children,* then, "Australia" and "America" contend for dominance. This contention is grafted onto the family story that occupies the narrative surface of the novel. Louisa's oscillation between mother and father is played out in her identification with the "natural outlawry of womankind" and her assumption of kingly (masculine) prerogatives. This oscillation not only rewrites the family constellation of Stead's childhood but also inscribes the hybrid, contested national identity of the novel itself.

At the end of the novel, Louisa leaves her family. Her declaration of independence is an attempt to escape from mother and father alike.

---

[56] Stead, "Another View," 515.
[57] Hughes, *Fatal Shore,* xiv–xv.

Louisa's escape recalls Stead's exile from Australia, an exile that leaves behind what cannot be acknowledged and must therefore be forgotten. Reproducing the repression of the abject mother, Louisa's escape reinscribes Stead's allegiance to the father—the United States in the guise of the liberal/tyrannical Uncle Sam—and her identification, however equivocal, with the America in which she wrote *The Man Who Loved Children*. It also suggests Stead's continuing affiliation with a Left in which women's concerns were subordinate or secondary. But if, in allying itself with the liberal cultural politics of the Popular Front, *The Man Who Loved Children* reproduces the swerve toward the father that is the characteristic gesture of Stead's life and career, its sequel, *For Love Alone*, exposes the perils of male identification and exile alike.

2

"Buffoon Odyssey"?:
For Love Alone
and the Writing of Exile

For Love Alone (1944) is a sequel to *The Man Who Loved Children* in Stead's fictionalized autobiography. Like all Stead's published work, it is a product of her "wandering life."[1] Written in the United States and published in New York in 1944 and London in 1945 (it was not published in Sydney until 1966), *For Love Alone* tells the story of Teresa Hawkins, a young woman who leaves Australia, where she is born and grows up, and travels to England, where she falls in love and becomes a writer. Teresa's decision to leave Australia is motivated, at least in part, by a desire to escape the constraints of provincial Australian culture. But even before Teresa leaves Sydney, she is symbolically in exile, "alien and critical," as Virginia Woolf puts it.[2] She rebels against her tyrannical father and against the repressive sexual morality and rigid gender hierarchy that he exemplifies.

For Love Alone vividly depicts the frustrations Teresa encounters in an oppressive, misogynist culture and the grim determination that enables her to realize her plan to escape. Teresa's rebellion and, later, her exile make her the subject of a heroic quest:[3] she is an Australian Ulysses, as she herself puts it. But her quest is thwarted in ways that make her see herself as an object of ridicule.

In Teresa's trajectory, Stead raises questions about the authority of women and colonial subjects and, by extension, about the status of her novel as the work of a white, colonial woman who writes in exile from her place of birth.[4] Are this exile and the writing it engenders a means

---

[1] Stead, "On the Women's Movement," 272.

[2] Woolf, *A Room of One's Own*, 101.

[3] On the quest motif in *For Love Alone*, see Sheridan, *Christina Stead*, 55–81, and Higgins [Sheridan], "Christina Stead's *For Love Alone*."

[4] On the ambiguous meaning of the exile of colonial women writers, see Gardiner, "Exhilaration of Exile."

of evading colonial and provincial constraints, a way of inventing, or performing, an identity that overcomes or challenges colonial limitations and patriarchal hegemony? Or are they irrevocably shaped by patriarchal and colonial histories and economies?

Antipodean Epistemologies

> There is therefore in every present mode of writing a double postulation: there is the impetus of a break and the impetus of a coming to power, there is the very shape of every revolutionary situation, the fundamental ambiguity of which is that Revolution must of necessity borrow, from what it wants to destroy, the very image of what it wants to possess.
> —Roland Barthes, *Writing Degree Zero*

For Love Alone begins with a prologue, "Sea People," that explores questions of cultural authority. Stead attempts to describe the world from an Australian vantage point and to dismantle the European perspective that represents Australia as colonial, marginal, "peripheral," or provincial. But her text is constituted by the "double postulation" that, Roland Barthes argues, afflicts every "present mode of writing"; it "must of necessity borrow from what it wants to destroy."[5] Stead "borrows" some of the characteristic conventions of British and European literature, among them the figure of the antipodes, a rhetoric of comparison that describes Australia in terms of and thereby subordinates it to England, and a narrative perspective that effaces the indigenous peoples who were there before the Europeans arrived. In reproducing European ways of seeing and describing, the prologue calls into question its own narrative authority and that of the novel itself.

Stead compares Australia with a landscape familiar to her readers. The comparative narrative mode addresses an implied audience— Americans and Britons—unfamiliar with Australia: it therefore inscribes Stead's own history of exile. In addition, the rhetoric of comparison links *For Love Alone* with both British and Australian texts that explain the provincial, marginal, or peripheral in terms of the central, dominant, or metropolitan.[6] Stead's comparative narrative style puts in tension conflicting versions of Australia as an adjunct, subordinate, or colony of England and Australia conceived in its own terms. In other words, it evokes what Bill Ashcroft, Gareth Griffiths, and Helen

[5] Barthes, *Writing Degree Zero*, 87. .
[6] See Hughes, *Fatal Shore*, 3.

Tiffin see as the crucial issue for literature in settler colonies, that of "establishing their 'indigeneity' and distinguishing it from their continuing sense of their European inheritance."[7]

A similar tension is effected in a meditation on the figure of the antipodes. In the prologue, Stead at once describes Australia as the antipodes of Europe and attempts to undermine the figure of the antipodes and the Eurocentric, colonialist ideology it represents. This is the first of many instances in the novel in which Stead appropriates a traditional—European—figure, trope, or plot and inverts its terms (up/down, England/Australia, man/woman). This inversion is a gesture that might itself be called antipodean. But it reproduces as well as subverts European ways of seeing. As Ross Gibson, an Australian cultural critic, suggests, the "theme of antipodean inversion" was a myth that "rendered the South Land comprehensible to the European mind."[8]

Throughout the prologue, Stead at once adopts and adapts the perspective of the English settlers for whom the "island continent" was terra incognita. But at the same time, she reproduces the hierarchies of high and low, north and south, absolute and relative, fixed and variable that the image of *antipodes* inscribes. Stead apparently displaces the European point of view by designating Europe as "the other world" and identifying England as "a scarcely noticeable island." The image of a world "shown on maps drawn upside-down by old-world cartographers" (1) likewise seems to reflect an Australian angle of vision and to decenter the fixed points of reference on British or European maps. But the motif of the world turned upside down has a long history in European literature as a figure of moral disorder, carnivalesque transgression, and political upheaval.[9] This history is invoked in nineteenth-century texts that characterize Australia as an upside-down, topsy-turvy land.[10] Thus, the image of the antipodes raises questions about the authority of Australian modes of perception and representation.

Similarly, Stead's description of Australia uses some of the same colonial and imperial rhetorical strategies it ostensibly attempts to displace. In a study of narratives of Australian exploration, Paul Carter

---

[7] Ashcroft, Griffiths, and Tiffin, *Empire Writes Back,* 135. On the conflict between the European inheritance and Australian experience, see Docker, *Australian Cultural Elites,* and R. White, *Inventing Australia.*

[8] Gibson, *South of the West,* 10.

[9] See Hill, *World Turned Upside Down;* Bakhtin, *Rabelais,* chap. 3, esp. 219–20, 255; Curtius, *European Literature and the Latin Middle Ages,* 94–98; and Davis, *Society and Culture in Early Modern France,* 100, 107, 130–31.

[10] R. White 9, 16; Hughes 95.

suggests that they belong to the genre of "imperial history," which "reduces space to a stage . . . [and] rather than focus on the *intentional* world of historical individuals, the world of active, spatial choices . . . has as its focus facts which, in a sense, come after the event." [11] Stead's prologue offers a panoptic view like that of Carter's imperial history. This panorama (mis)represents as the empty site of "nothing" an "interior" uninhabited by white settlers. Individual historical actors are invisible except as generic "people" or "men": the women are not distinguished from the men, the children from the adults, or the convicts from their keepers. Aborigines are altogether absent from the scene. In effacing them, Stead reenacts their annihilation by the Europeans who began arriving in 1788. [12] Teresa's story, as introduced in the prologue, is founded on exclusion, on repressed class and racial scripts that resurface in the depiction of the exaggerated racism and class resentment of Teresa's father and the man she follows to England.

As we saw in Chapter 1, *Great Expectations* operates in *The Man Who Loved Children* as a metonym for the history of Australian colonization. In *For Love Alone*, too, *Great Expectations* is both enabling pretext and underlying subtext. Here, Stead borrows from the critique of ideology set forth by Marx and Engels in *The German Ideology* in order to revise Dickens's conception of the world upside down as a symbol of illusions and misperceptions at once egoistic and socially produced.

In the first chapter of *Great Expectations*, the convict Magwitch seizes Pip and turns him upside down, so that Pip sees the churchyard and village as if they were actually upside down. In this inaugural episode, the image of the world upside down suggests the infantile psychic and cognitive organization that makes Pip experience the world as a projection of himself. This image also represents the world as it appears under the distorting lens of ideology: "If in all ideology men and their circumstances appear upside down as in a *camera obscura*, this phenomenon arises just as much from their historical life-process as the inversion of objects on the retina does from their physical life process." [13] At the same time, the image of the world upside down prefigures the antipodean exile of Magwitch, who is transported to Australia. The rest of *Great Expectations* rectifies Pip's flawed and undeveloped perceptions. Although Dickens emphasizes Pip's personal, moral debt to Magwitch, it is Magwitch's Australian fortune that makes possible

---

[11] Carter, *Road to Botany Bay*, xvi.

[12] On white Australian responses to Aborigines, see Curthoys, "Identity Crisis," 171. Stead herself refers to the history of Australian peoples before the arrival of Europeans at the end of *Seven Poor Men of Sydney*.

[13] Marx and Engels, *The German Ideology*, 14.

Pip's transformation into a "gentleman." The same colonial economy authorizes Teresa's trajectory.

Stead's prologue undermines the Enlightenment assumptions and Eurocentric perspectives of *The German Ideology* and *Great Expectations* alike. In this, Stead writes as an Australian confronting European culture and as a woman confronting patriarchal literary and political traditions. She also destabilizes the opposition of English home and colonial exile that structures *Great Expectations,* among other British novels. Australia in *For Love Alone* is neither home nor exile, or it is both at once: the point of departure for Teresa's journey through life, it is a place of origin from which she already feels estranged when the novel begins.[14]

Stead attempts to subvert European modes of representation, but she cannot quite dispense with the repertory of traditional (European) tropes and topoi. An analogous case can be made about gender. In the prologue and throughout the novel—indeed, throughout her career and especially in interviews she gave late in life—Stead repudiates the limits of gender.[15] But gender, as limit, threatens Teresa's project, exile, and therefore calls into question the notion—Stead's and Teresa's— that women can overcome the patriarchal constraints against which they struggle.

Stead associates Australia with Ithaca and Teresa with Odysseus. In putting Teresa in the place of Odysseus, Stead rejects the feminine limits associated with Penelope and claims for her protagonist such traditionally masculine prerogatives as mobility, specifically the ability to travel or go into exile.[16] Teresa says that "each Australian is a Ulysses" (222), including herself in the category *Australian* and identifying herself with Ulysses. This identification challenges constructions of Australian identity in the colonial and early national period as white, male, and working or lower middle class. Among the principal character types associated with Australianness were the "bushman" who herded sheep in the outback, the larrikin (urban youth known for their jaunty, antiauthoritarian spirit), and the digger (World War I trench soldier). These versions of Australian identity exemplified a homosocial ethos of "mateship"—a working-class, Australian version of Benedict Anderson's "deep, horizontal comradeship [or] fraternity" (16); they

[14] Cf. Gardiner: "Being a colonial-in-exile puts into play an oscillation whereby no place is home" ("Exhilaration of Exile," 134).

[15] See, for example, Joan Lidoff, *Christina Stead*, 208, and Chapter 1, this volume.

[16] See K. Lawrence, *Penelope Voyages*, for a critique of patriarchal cartographies that map "women as space" and a corrective treatment of women as "self-movers" (18).

excluded women and devalued femininity.[17] Teresa's self-identification as an Australian is undercut and her rejection of gender constraints accordingly vitiated by the self-doubts that make her wonder whether she is a "detestable thing, an ugly, rejected *woman*" (emphasis added) and whether her journey of exile from Australia to England is a "rigmarole of [a] buffoon Odyssey" (348).

In dramatizing the tenuousness of Teresa's authority, moreover, Stead calls into question her own rejection of patriarchal constructions of gender. Teresa's doubts, rendered in the multivoiced discourse that is for Bakhtin a hallmark of the novel, reaccentuate traditional (epic) notions of heroism: in other words, they constitute Teresa as an exemplar of novelistic character as Bakhtin conceives it.[18] At the same time, these doubts associate her with such classic novelistic wanderers and doubters as Leopold Bloom and Don Quixote (Stead takes the novel's epigraph from Cervantes) and connect *For Love Alone* with the encyclopedic, satiric, carnivalesque European tradition that Stead reveres.[19] In these male-authored carnivalesque texts, women are usually presented as symbols of or obstacles to the realization of men's desire: in other words, as the passive, feminine objects of active, masculine subjectivity. In invoking this tradition, then, Stead raises the very questions that Teresa's identification with Ulysses is apparently meant to foreclose. She makes us ask whether the literary tradition she inherits, borrows, appropriates—a tradition exemplified by *The Odyssey* and Joyce's *Ulysses*—is capable of representing women's subjectivity or whether it makes women, as Karen Lawrence puts it, "a place on the itinerary of the male journey."[20] Throughout the novel, gender, disregarded or suppressed in Teresa's identification with Ulysses, erupts in a specifically sexual vulnerability that raises questions about her capacity to wander, travel, or go into exile. And the fate of Teresa's writings raises similar questions about the cultural authority of women and colonial subjects.

Sydney to London

Although there isn't a woman alive who . . . is not perfectly aware of the ignominy, detestation, and social death that awaits her if she does not

---

[17] See Ward, *Nation for a Continent*, 127, 144; Summers, *Damned Whores and God's Police*, 34, 36; Deacon, "Politicizing Gender," 2; and Schaffer, *Women and the Bush*, 8.

[18] See especially Bakhtin, "Epic and Novel" and "Discourse in the Novel."

[19] See Stead, "Uses of the Many-Charactered Novel."

[20] K. Lawrence, *Penelope Voyages*, 2.

conform, there are a lot of women who cannot conform. The refractory
spirit is in them. If they could they would take a pack and go out on the
roads, looking for the strange new country which is over every hill and
which is seen in the delirium of hunger and the hatred of communities.
　　　　　　　　　　　　　　　　　　　　—Christina Stead, 1940s

For Love Alone delineates the geographical and emotional contours of
the journey projected at the end of *The Man Who Loved Children*. At the
beginning of *For Love Alone*, Teresa Hawkins, age nineteen, is trapped
in Sydney in the home of her oppressive father, Andrew. In the course
of the novel, Teresa exiles herself from this environment literally—in a
series of escapes from Sydney that culminate in her journey to London—and symbolically—by resisting the sexual constraints enforced
by the provincial, puritanical, misogynist culture in which she grows
up. In representing the discrepancies between Teresa's heroic quest
and the obstacles to its realization, Stead dramatizes the limits on
women's ability or that of colonial subjects to challenge the hegemonic
culture.

For Love Alone begins not with Teresa but with her father, successor
to Sam Pollit. In the first chapter, Andrew Hawkins vaunts his power
over his rebellious children and lectures his daughters on the virtues of
feminine submissiveness. Teresa refuses her father's notion of sexual
difference as disability and claims for herself a value—honor—that he
reserves for men. Later, she similarly ponders her own situation as a
"woman and freeman" (224). In appropriating traditionally masculine
prerogatives, Teresa attempts a kind of antipodean inversion of sexual
asymmetry, but this inversion cannot resolve the question of what kind
of power women might have or whether they continue to be subject to
the power and authority of men.

Teresa's quest for self-definition is also shaped by her opposition to a
culture in which gender constraints are intensified by economic
scarcity. During the depression in Australia, a declining marriage rate,
an economy increasingly stratified by gender, and substantial unem-
ployment, especially among women, contributed to a perception that
there was a "surplus" of single (white) women.[21] In Teresa's aunts,
cousins, and friends, Stead makes palpable the predicament of "these
unfortunate women and girls, . . . a miserable mass writhing with desire and shame, grovelling before men" (18).

Teresa refuses to acquiesce in the sexual status quo; she insists on her

---

[21] Deacon, *Managing Gender*, 152–59 and passim; Reid, *Fiction and the Great Depression*,
100–101; Matthews, *Good and Mad Women*, 48, 58–63; Kingston, "Lady and the Australian
Girl," 38; and Summers 406.

own authority. But this insistence is as equivocal as her self-identification with Ulysses. On the one hand, Teresa claims the active role traditionally ascribed to men (75). On the other hand, she conceives herself as a passive object of male desire, an inert site in which the "work of passion was going on" (73).

> The things [Teresa] wanted existed. At school she first had news of them, she knew they existed; what went on round her was hoaxing and smooth-faced hypocrisy. Venus and Adonis, the Rape of Lucrece, Troilus and Cressida were reprinted for three hundred years, St Anthony was tempted in the way you would expect; Dido, though a queen, was abandoned like a servant-girl and went mad with love and grief, like the girl in the boat outside. This was the truth, not the daily simpering on the boat and the putting away in hope chests; but where was one girl who thought so, beside herself? Was there one who would not be afraid if she told them the secret, the real life? Since school, she had ravaged libraries, disembowelled hundreds of books, ranged through literature since the earliest recorded frenzies of the world and had eaten into her few years with this boundless love of love. . . .
> . . . At each thing she read, she thought, yes, it's true, or no, it's false, and she persevered with satisfaction and joy, illuminated because her world existed and was recognized by men. But why not by women? She found nothing in the few works of women she could find that was what they must have felt. (75–76)

Teresa insists on the power, immediacy, and authenticity of desire. Yet her own desire exists for her only insofar as it is mirrored or mediated in the writings of men.[22] Because these writings represent women as sexually passive or subordinate to men, Teresa either reads herself into an active-masculine-sadistic role—she "ravaged libraries"—or sees herself not as sexual agent but as sexual object, "ravished, trembling with ecstasy" (76).

Teresa rejects the notion of sexual difference as disability. But in affirming her own autonomy and authority, she reproduces colonial constructions of race, gender, sexuality, savagery, and the primitive. In her fantasy of sexual fulfillment, for example, she imaginatively overcomes the restrictions of a "northern" civilization by identifying with "wild animals in the bush," with "Australian savages," and with the women of Italy and Spain, ancient Greece and ancient Rome (75): that

---

[22] Stead said in a letter that the "long literary tradition . . . had enabled men completely to express themselves, while women feared to do so" (quoted in R. G. Geering, afterword to *Ocean of Story,* 546).

is, with the racial, sexual, and cultural others of the "civilization" she rejects.

Teresa affirms her sexual agency not only by identifying herself with cultural "others" but also by emphasizing her difference from them. When she decides to leave Sydney and go to London, she contemplates paying for her journey by doing office work in outposts of empire:

> She saw the significance of the maps of the British Empire showing the world strung on a chain of pink, all the pink was Britain's. In every one of those pink patches, no matter what the colour or kind of men there, nor the customs of the native women, she could get a job, she was a citizen there. There were advertisements in the Sydney papers for typists to go to Nauru, Cocos, Shanghai, British Columbia, and these could be just jumping-off places. (83)

Teresa authorizes herself as imperial agent and subject, potential "citizen" of all of the places represented by pink patches on the map. The word *citizen* is apparently unmarked by race or gender, but its implicit signification of race and gender migrates to the explicitly marked terms "native women" and men of whatever "color" or "kind."

The constraints—men's power, women's powerlessness—against which Teresa chafes in the first place are intensified in her first sexual encounters. Before Teresa goes to England, she runs away to the country, her destination a remote country place called Harper's Ferry. This episode recalls a similar incident in *The Man Who Loved Children*. In the earlier novel, Harpers Ferry represents both a maternal domain and the site of actual historical struggle; Louisa's flight is an attempt to recapture the former and ally herself with the latter. The Australian Harper's Ferry is a fictional place, unlike its American namesake,[23] so that the political force and racial dimension of the allusion in *The Man Who Loved Children* are absent from *For Love Alone*. But Teresa's flight to Harper's Ferry still carries a heavy figurative weight.

In this part of the novel, Teresa wanders through a landscape that is both a projection of her desire and a revision of Wordsworthian notions of nature. Teresa imagines Harper's Ferry as a Gothic place populated by shadows and unidentifiable mad voices. Her journey there takes her through a pastoral, romantic scene. As in such nineteenth-century British novels as *Jane Eyre*, *The Mill on the Floss*, and *Tess of the d'Urbervilles*, nature—whether as a signifier of (absent) mother or of the heroine's desire—is neither pristine nor free but subject to the

---

[23] Higgins 434.

power of money and men. But Stead intensifies British Victorian revisions of Wordsworth's passive, feminized, and maternal nature.

On the way to Harper's Ferry, Teresa stops at the home of her cousin, where one evening a young man who lives nearby seizes her and kisses her in an "affront, . . . a kind of debauch which she scarcely understood" (155). Soon afterward, she is frightened by men's shouting voices and accosted by an old man who taunts her and exposes himself in an "idiotic dance" (165). These encounters induce Teresa to return to the dubious shelter of Sydney and her family. She never does reach Harper's Ferry, for she turns back, forced to acknowledge as a kind of reality principle the sexual vulnerability of women and the sexual power of men.

Eventually, Teresa again takes up her plan to go to Europe, where she intends to study in a university, but now cognizant of the dangers of *solitary* wandering, she attaches herself to her Latin tutor, a mean-spirited, cruel young man named Jonathan Crow who is about to depart for London on a fellowship.[24] Stead's treatment of Teresa and Jonathan inverts the romantic (male) literary convention whereby women are portrayed as erotic objects that symbolize men's desire, beliefs, values, and ambitions, for Teresa actively pursues Jonathan, who represents both an erotic object and the possibility of exile from Sydney.[25]

Diana Brydon argues that *For Love Alone* "turns romantic conventions upside-down, rewriting them from an antipodean point of view—the woman's rather than the man's."[26] Stead employs a set of narrative strategies—resistance, ironic de-emphasis, exaggeration—that in Rachel Blau DuPlessis's terms delegitimate romance and valorize quest, or *Bildung*. Teresa's pursuit of Jonathan appears to be a symptom of romantic thralldom, which DuPlessis defines as "an all-encompassing, totally defining love between apparent unequals."[27] But it actually enables Teresa to leave Sydney and go to London, where she hopes to realize ambitions that she cannot fulfill in Australia.

Teresa's infatuation with Jonathan also signifies her subjection to provincial (colonial) culture and her acquiescence in ideologies of racial superiority and male dominance. Jonathan is identified with

[24] Jonathan Crow is based on a man named Keith Duncan; Stead followed Duncan to England but was more interested in "what he represented: wider horizons, the experience of European culture" (Rowley, *Christina Stead*, 59, quotation from 65).

[25] Ian Reid sees Jonathan as a "symbol of what [Teresa] wants but not the object of her quest" (107).

[26] Brydon, *Christina Stead*, 81.

[27] DuPlessis, *Writing beyond the Ending*, xi, 3–4, 66.

Australian appropriations of Friedrich Nietzsche, Charles Darwin, and turn-of-the-century eugenics. Teresa contests Jonathan's version of his genealogy, asserting her own claim to the cultural traditions he represents.[28] Jonathan promotes Nietzsche's misogyny but misses or suppresses Nietzsche's iconoclasm. Teresa repudiates Jonathan's Nietzsche and insists on her own, conceiving her journey as the voyage of a Nietzschean wanderer. But Teresa's career asks, too, whether women can be wanderers or whether, in Nietzsche's terms, they are consigned to the role of "shadow."

In addition to Nietzsche, Stead gives us in Jonathan a pastiche of early-twentieth-century Australian discourses on sex and race.[29] Jonathan is the novel's exponent of a local variant of eugenicist ideology that advocates "racial hygiene," part of an ensemble of discursive practices that construct "Australian" identity in this period as white, lower middle class, and male.[30] In Jonathan, then, Stead critically exposes the racism and sexism implicated in early-twentieth-century Australian self-representations. Like Teresa's father, Andrew Hawkins, and like Sam Pollit in *The Man Who Loved Children*, Jonathan represents an intellectual current that Teresa must supersede: specifically, the trap of subjection to ideologies of male dominance and racial superiority.

But if Stead does not give Nietzsche or his Australian epigones the last word, she does not give it to Teresa either. The last word—or, more precise, the penultimate one—belongs to Marx, and it is spoken by a character based on Stead's husband, William Blake. Reversing the journey of the grandmother who left England and of such Dickens characters as Magwitch and the Micawbers and Mr. Peggotty of *David Copperfield*, Teresa does eventually get to London, where she finds work as a secretary to a man named James Quick, the novel's antithesis to Jonathan Crow. Jonathan says there is "no such thing as love" (340); Quick soon falls in love with Teresa, and she with him. Jonathan represents the impoverished colonial culture of Australia; Quick is identified with England, especially London as it appears in the poems of

[28] On Stead's use of Nietzschean themes in *For Love Alone*, see Modjeska, *Exiles at Home*, 16–25; Reid 109; Rowley, "Christina Stead: The Voyage to Cythera"; and Summers 42.

[29] These discourses include Australian versions of eugenics; the "White Australia" policy limiting the immigration of nonwhites; and "basic wage" legislation that set women's wage as a percentage of men's and defined women's productive labor as a temporary expedient. See Schaffer 129; Matthews 60–63, 74; Ward 30–32; and Reiger, *Disenchantment of the Home*, 122, 178, 194–97, 200.

[30] On racial hygiene, see Reiger 194–97; for Australian identity in the early twentieth century, see above, pages 42–43, and note 17, this chapter.

William Blake and the novels of Dickens, with the cosmopolitan literary culture of Europe, and with the theoretical authority of Marxism.

Jonathan's potted Nietzsche is not subdued by Teresa's self-affirmation but by Quick's Marx. Quick subjects Jonathan and his thesis to a Marxist reading that decodes them as assemblages of tattered ideologemes.[31] Quick's interpretation—an old-fashioned class analysis—of Jonathan's thesis exemplifies Stead's affiliation with the Marxist cultural critique that developed in the era of the Popular Front. But Quick's materialist hermeneutic cannot adequately account for Teresa's aspirations or the thwarted desires of the novel's "writhing mass" of wretched women. Quick-Marx dislodges Jonathan-Nietzsche from Teresa's affective life and her intellectual pantheon. In effect, a mediated, cosmopolitan, European version of patriarchal ideological hegemony is put in place of the nasty, brutish, Australian variety.

Quick's considerable intellectual power is echoed in the erotic power that makes Teresa feel she is giving him an "awful empire" over her (447). Quick is companionable and generous; he "loved women as equals . . . as men loved friends" (364). When Teresa and Quick finally become lovers, they experience the world, if only momentarily, as a utopia. Yet even Quick regards love as an arena in which he can exercise his power. Not surprisingly, Teresa finds his embrace "suffocating" and, thinking she can "master men," wishes to "try men" (464).

The end of *For Love Alone* revises the resolution of nineteenth-century novels such as *Jane Eyre*, with its "Reader, I married him," by launching Teresa at virtually the same time in marriage and adultery. Soon after Teresa goes to live with Quick, she has her first affair. This affair involves an eruption of "illicit" desire that, in DuPlessis's terms, writes beyond the ending of marriage. It also marks a conflict between feminist quest—the expression of women's agency, ambition, and desire—and Stead's left-wing affiliations.

Teresa's lover, Harry Girton, is based on Ralph Fox, a British Communist with whom Stead was in love in the 1930s.[32] His name also recalls Harry Bloom, an American with whom Stead was involved during the years when she was writing *For Love Alone*.[33] Girton, like Fox, is a revolutionary who is about to fight with the Loyalists in

---

[31] An "ideologeme" is a "minimal unit" of a "larger class discourse" never fully present in any one utterance (Jameson, *Political Unconscious*, 87).

[32] On Stead's relationship with Fox, see Rowley, *Christina Stead*, 167–69, 223–29, and C. Williams, *Christina Stead*, 77–86. On Fox's influence on Stead's thinking, see Rowley, "Christina Stead: Politics and Literature," 151, 155–56.

[33] Rowley, *Christina Stead*, 286.

Spain. The love affair is consummated in Oxford, a setting that, along with the name "Girton," alludes to *A Room of One's Own*, originally written as lectures on women and fiction delivered at Newnham and Girton Colleges.[34] The character of Harry Girton, however, belongs to the Marxist Left in which the gender concerns that preoccupy *A Room of One's Own* are subordinated to the politics of class and the ethos of fraternity. Stead claimed to prefer the class politics of the Left to what she regarded as Woolf's elitist feminism. But the name "Girton," given to a character with whom Teresa betrays her Marxist lover and champion, James Quick, suggests the exigent, if unacknowledged, pressure of gender—that is, of women's desire for authority and autonomy—on the class politics that the novel ostensibly espouses.

When Quick encourages Teresa to go off with Girton, she feels that the men are "offering and counter-offering her love to each other, as a proof of their love for each other" (480). Similarly, in the scene in which Quick dissects Jonathan's thesis, Teresa appears to be little more than a pretext. In other words, even as Stead describes Teresa as a "freebooter," a hero of desire who is "stalwart, excellent and full of glory" (495), the ascription of (feminine) heroism is undermined by the (masculine) gender marking of such terms as "freebooter" and by the positioning of Teresa between two men whose bonds of love and rivalry she mediates—Jonathan and Quick, and Quick and Girton.[35] In the novel's ironic version of the quest plot and the echoes of a feminist text that Stead intensely disliked, *For Love Alone* lays bare the conflict between women's self-realization and patriarchal constructions of heterosexual love.

Writing and Exile

If *For Love Alone* locates Teresa between men, it also presents, at least tentatively, a way out of this impasse through writing. As the antithesis of Sydney and the site of Teresa's exile, London is not only the place in which she realizes her erotic ambitions but also the place where, like Stead, she becomes a writer or, more precise, a published writer. Like the realization of Teresa's desire, however, the disposition of her writing

[34] Sheridan reads "Girton" as an ironic suggestion of Teresa's college education (79). Stead was hostile to Woolf and particularly disliked *A Room of One's Own* and *Three Guineas*. See her venomous notes for a review, never completed, of Quentin Bell's biography of Woolf. I thank Hazel Rowley for sending me photocopies of this material.

[35] This positioning replicates the patriarchal narratives in which women's stories are absorbed into those of men. See Sedgwick, *Between Men*.

is equivocal. The vicissitudes of Teresa's writings in *For Love Alone* variously suggest the tenuous status of women's and antipodean cultural production, the perils of reception by the dominant culture, and the difficulties that colonial subjects encounter in affiliating with, appropriating, or opposing metropolitan cultural traditions. But the very existence of the novel points to a provisional resolution of these problems.[36]

Stead's description of Teresa's first creative effort, made while she is still in Sydney, represents women's cultural work as alienated labor. Stead gives this effort a pretext in an odious letter in which Jonathan Crow announces to the apparently lovestruck Teresa his intention to "live without . . . love" (237). Taken in by his declaration of his own misery, Teresa attempts to console him by making the "Legend of Jonathan," a "design" depicting Jonathan's life: "All these were pictures of incidents Jonathan had talked about, his sorrows and longings, while the last two were a picture of what Jonathan said was his present loneliness. She had a little skill in drawing, a wooden, naïve, but energetic skill, like a vigorous man talking in a foreign language, strangely, upside down and yet so full of ideas that even aesthetes listen to him" (238). As the maker of this design, Teresa is neither an author nor an artist. Rather, energetic, vigorous, and full of ideas, she is a kind of artistic primitive or *lusus naturae*. At the same time, she is a cultural worker alienated from her medium—a foreign language—and from her product—a "legend" that mystifies Jonathan's cruelty and emotional poverty as "sorrows and longings." In the figure of the *"man talking in a foreign language . . . upside down"* (emphasis added), moreover, Stead evokes the situation of Australian women writers in the early part of the twentieth century: exile in England, in male pseudonyms such as Henry Handel Richardson and Miles Franklin, and at "home."[37]

The reception of Teresa's early writings exemplifies the vulnerability of women's works in a literary economy that values masculine concerns and treats feminine concerns with contempt. When Jonathan goes to London, Teresa writes him numerous letters, but uninterested in her thoughts and feelings, he does not even open them. Eventually, though, Teresa becomes a writer, and she finds in James Quick the eager and appreciative reader every writer wishes for.

Like Stead's husband Blake, Quick is identified with the left-wing

[36] Cf. Gardiner, who sees writing as "both home and exile" for writers such as Stead ("Exhilaration of Exile," 146).

[37] Miles Franklin and Henry Handel Richardson, the best-known Australian women novelists, wrote in England. In the 1930s, the women whom Drusilla Modjeska refers to as "exiles at home" remained in Australia.

culture that flourished in the 1930s and 1940s. He accordingly represents a historical moment in which Stead herself found sympathetic readers. After Teresa arrives in London and while she is still pining after Jonathan, she begins writing a novel, so that she will have something to leave behind (422). Stead's first published novel, *Seven Poor Men of Sydney*, was written in similar circumstances.[38] In Teresa's fragmentary manuscript, *The Seven Houses of Love*, Stead translates her own lyrical, psychosexual, and sociological study of working-class women and men into a meditation on desire that secularizes the visionary writings of Saint Teresa of Avila and reworks the erotic imagery of Watteau's *Embarkation for Cythera*.[39]

If "The Legend of Jonathan" is the work of a colonized subject who lacks cultural authority, in *The Seven Houses of Love* Teresa appropriates, recycles, and thereby asserts her own claim to the "old heritage" that European culture represents to her (83). In this text, she grafts this heritage onto an Australian tradition of writing in exile. The resulting hybrid, like the novel's antipodean epistemology and its portrayal of Teresa's exile itself, is inflected by hegemonic cultural modes.

Stead describes Teresa's manuscript not as she writes it—that is, not as an outpouring of subjectivity—but as Quick reads it, apprehends it, and subjects it to his own interpretation (419). By representing Teresa's writing as always already transformed—read and rewritten—by the Marxist hermeneutic that dominates the novel and the left-wing culture with which Stead herself was affiliated, Stead dramatizes the constraints on full, self-conscious expression. She suggests, too, the limited compass within which subjects can perform or invent new identities or exercise their own authority. Yet, at the same time, she represents Teresa's life and writing, and by extension her own, as ways of struggling against the same constraints.

At the end of *For Love Alone*, when Teresa glimpses Jonathan, she says, "It's dreadful to think that it will go on being repeated for ever, he—and me! What's there to stop it?" (502). By producing neither another "Legend of Jonathan" nor another version of *The Seven Houses of Love* but the novel we actually read, Stead attempts to "stop it," to break the chain of repetition that Teresa finds so dreadful. That the results of this attempt are equivocal situates Stead's text in her own time and place, or Teresa's. But *For Love Alone* also reaches toward contemporary readers; it invites us to refuse, as Stead and Teresa did, to trade

---

[38] Brydon 9.
[39] On Teresa of Avila, see Sheridan 75; on the motif of the voyage to Cythera, see Rowley, "Christina Stead: The Voyage to Cythera," 3, and Brydon 2, 15.

"exile," however ambiguous, for a settled domesticity or stable nation-ality. Yet it also suggests that the state of exile, like nations themselves, is an imagined community in which women are not at home in the same way as are men.

In 1946, not long after the publication of *For Love Alone*, Stead left the United States, where she had lived for more than a decade. For the next twenty-five years or so, she and Blake lived in England and Europe, never settling anywhere and never quite belonging where they hap-pened to find themselves. Stead continued to write, but beginning in the mid-1950s and into the early 1960s, she could not get her novels published. Then, in 1965, *The Man Who Loved Children* was reissued, through the joint efforts of Stead's friend Stanley Burnshaw and Ran-dall Jarrell, who thought the novel a masterpiece. At home virtually nowhere but in her marriage, Stead lived on the margins of all the cul-tures she traversed. After Blake's death, she returned in the 1970s to Australia to live. She thought of herself as Australian despite her years abroad, although as late as 1967, she was turned down for the Britan-nica Australia Award for Literature because she neither lived in nor wrote about Australia.[40] Eventually, but only after she had effectively ceased writing, Stead was accepted as an Australian writer.

Christina Stead's career, like that of Teresa Hawkins, asks whether, in writing, one can make an alternate life (identity) or remake the life (identity) one is born into. Benedict Anderson says that in the modern world, everyone "can, should, will 'have' a nationality, as he or she 'has' a gender" (14). Stead's career of writing in exile—from Australia and from patriarchal and feminist constructions of gender alike—asks us to examine the meaning of Anderson's observation and to test it against her attempts to discard, disregard, or refashion both gender and nationality. There is something discomfiting about Stead's inabil-ity or unwillingness to settle down or settle in, but at the same time, it reflects a spirit of improvisation that is salutary and bracing, especially now, in this era of excessive nationalist fervor.

[40] Rowley, *Christina Stead*, 462–63.

Part II
Doris Lessing: In Pursuit of the English

3

The Englishing of Doris Lessing

Doris Lessing was born in Persia in 1919 and grew up on a farm in Southern Rhodesia. In 1949 she left Rhodesia and went to England, where she has lived ever since. She began writing in southern Africa and published poems and stories in Rhodesia and South Africa. Her first novel, *The Grass Is Singing* (1950), was written in Rhodesia but published in London.[1] Thus, Lessing's career as a published novelist nearly coincides with her residence in England. Lessing is an English writer not only because she lives in England and her novels have been published there but also because she self-consciously identifies as an English writer.[2]

In this chapter, I examine Lessing's self-invention as an English writer in *In Pursuit of the English: A Documentary* (1960). This text enters into postwar debates about British culture and refers to character-istically English and British literary traditions in its exploration or "pursuit" of Englishness. Yet Lessing's self-fashioning as an English writer—her textual performance of her own English identity—is com-plicated both by her colonial beginnings and by fault lines running through definitions of Englishness itself.

In Pursuit of the English, at once memoir, travel writing, satire, and ethnography, dissects English culture or, more precise, a small segment of English culture located in London just after the Second World War. In this text, Lessing investigates the meaning of the term "English," scrutinizing binary oppositions such as those between home and exile,

---

[1] *The Grass Is Singing* was bought by a Johannesburg publisher, but Lessing's agent urged her to withdraw it, and she sold it to Michael Joseph in London on more favorable terms. See *Under My Skin,* 404–5.

[2] Jenny Taylor argues in "Memory and Desire on Going Home" that Lessing's national identity is unstable and hybrid.

Englishness and foreignness, in which English identity is constructed.[3] At the same time, the text describes a year (1949–50) in which its narrator, an avatar of the author who is named on the last page as "Doris," leaves Rhodesia and goes to England.[4] It belongs—by virtue of its subtitle, "A Documentary," and its narrative stance—to the tradition of British documentary writing exemplified by George Orwell's *The Road to Wigan Pier*. As in *Wigan Pier*, a middle-class narrator-observer describes working-class subjects and, in doing so, offers a narrative of English (or, in Orwell's case, British) identity across differences of class and gender.[5]

The narrator of *In Pursuit of the English* is an observer whose relationship to England changes over the course of the year described in the text. Initially, as a colonial subject migrating from the British settler colony in Southern Rhodesia, she is both an outsider and an insider, at once English and foreign.[6] Her observation is rendered from this double vantage point. Eventually, unlike most ethnographers, travel writers, and documentarians who return to and write from their places of origin, she settles in England and into an English identity. Thus *In Pursuit of the English* performs a maneuver that I want to call the Englishing of Doris, or Doris Lessing. As a white, middle-class, colonial immigrant, Doris—or Lessing—occupies a privileged position, one that inflects her English identity and, by extension, the English identities explored in the text. *In Pursuit of the English*, then, raises questions about whether, or how, colonials can become proper Englishmen and -women and about what the implications of such a transformation—or "Englishing"—might be.

The interrogation of Englishness needs to be set in the context of postwar redefinitions of English (British) national identity. And the journey that takes "Doris" from Salisbury to Cape Town to London—from colony to metropole—needs to be placed in a larger history of postwar immigration into Britain. The most significant dates in *In Pur-*

---

[3] See Gikandi, *Maps of Englishness*, and Gorra, *After Empire*, on the ways these oppositions structure concepts of British identity.

[4] Knapp classifies *In Pursuit* as autobiography (*Doris Lessing*, xvi). Lessing describes it as "biography in a comic mode" (*Under My Skin*, 407). Whether "fictional" or "factual," *In Pursuit* is self-consciously literary. To emphasize its textual construction of identity, I refer to the character in the text as "Doris" or "the narrator" and to Doris Lessing as "Lessing", "Doris Lessing," or "the author."

[5] British documentary shares some of the features of imperial travel writing, notably the relation of "radical inequality" between European or middle-class narrator-observers and colonial or working-class subjects (Pratt, *Imperial Eyes*, 6).

[6] Lessing herself lost her British nationality when she married Gottfried Lessing, a German refugee who spent the war years in Rhodesia. Both she and Gottfried were naturalized as British citizens in 1948 (*Under My Skin*, 404).

suit of the English are 1949–50, the year in which the narrator arrives in England, and 1960, the year in which the text was published. The intervening decade saw important changes in definitions of British nationality. Beginning in 1948, immigrants—persons of color—from the New Commonwealth nations in the Caribbean, South Asia, and, later, Africa entered England in increasing numbers.[7] Initially, immigration from New Commonwealth countries was considered as a temporary solution to a perceived postwar shortage of skilled labor, but once in England, the immigrants who came to fill the demand for labor encountered racism in the form of discrimination in employment and housing and violence directed against them.[8]

In part in response to immigration from New Commonwealth nations, British nationality was redefined in the postwar years in increasingly restrictive and exclusionary ways. The 1948 British Nationality Act distinguished two classes of British subjects: citizens of the United Kingdom and its colonies—in effect, white colonials—and Commonwealth citizens. It granted both groups the right to enter, settle, and work in Britain. The Commonwealth Immigrants Bill, which was passed in 1961 and took effect in 1962, attempted to control the entry of black Commonwealth citizens into the United Kingdom by subjecting them to immigration control unless they were born in the United Kingdom, held United Kingdom passports, or were included in the passport of a person exempt from immigration control. Thus, the 1962 act restricted immigration on the part of black Africans, West Indians, and South Asians but not on the part of white former colonials.[9]

The 1948 British Nationality Act and the 1962 Commonwealth Immigrants Bill mark off a period punctuated by episodes of racial violence

[7] "New Commonwealth" refers to colonies gaining independence, beginning with India and Pakistan, in or after 1947, in contrast to the older Commonwealth nations such as Canada, Australia, and New Zealand that began as settler colonies. The black population of Britain was approximately 74,500 in 1951, 336,000 by 1959, and nearly half a million by 1962 (Waters, " 'Dark Strangers,' " 209).

[8] See Layton-Henry, *Politics of Race*, chaps. 2–3, and Solomos, *Race and Racism*, chap. 3. See also Paul, *Whitewashing Britain*, chap. 5. Paul's book was published after I completed the revisions of this book.

[9] Solomos 44, 51–52; Layton-Henry 13. Subsequent acts further restricted the entitlement of citizens of Commonwealth countries, that is, persons of color, to British citizenship. The 1968 Commonwealth Immigrants Act, intended to control immigration by East African Asians who held British passports, made any citizen of the United Kingdom or its colonies subject to control unless she or he or a parent or grandparent was born, adopted, naturalized, or registered as a citizen of the United Kingdom and colonies in the United Kingdom. The 1981 British Nationality Act distinguished between "patrials," citizens of the United Kingdom and colonies who had the right of abode in Britain, and "nonpatrials," who did not; white Commonwealth citizens could enter as "patrials," whereas black Commonwealth citizens could not (Solomos 54, 57–58).

culminating in 1958 in riots in Notting Hill and Nottingham in which black immigrants were attacked by whites. Throughout this period, the idea of immigrants as members of an "inferior race" or as "strangers" who did not know "how to behave" was used as an explanation of racist violence and as a justification for increasing restrictions on immigration.[10]

During this same period, the conception of British national identity underwent a crucial shift. Harry Goulbourne suggests that "traditional" nationalism, whose main project is "to effect a society in which political authority (the state) and the nation (the community) are coterminous," was displaced by "ethnic nationalism," in which race, culture, and ethnicity play a primary role. The resulting redefinition of the British national community, along with the "racialised construction of 'Britishness,' " increasingly excluded from membership recent non-white immigrants or accorded them only formal recognition.[11] (The culmination of this transformation in the late 1960s, 1970s, and 1980s was the white ethnic nationalism, or "new racism," of Enoch Powell and, later, Margaret Thatcher.)[12]

In Pursuit of the English elides the racialized discourse on immigration, the exclusion of racial minorities from definitions of Britishness, the debate about racial violence, and evidence of racial violence itself in part—but only in part—because it is set in 1949–50, when violent episodes were sporadic and opposition to the immigration of blacks and Asians was not yet as organized as it would later become.[13] Under any or all of the acts restricting immigration into Britain, Doris would be considered British. After 1948, moreover, white British women won the right to retain their nationality on marriage.[14] But in the years between 1949–50, when the events *In Pursuit of the English* describes took place, and 1960, when it was published, "Englishness" or "Britishness" became an identity denied to New Commonwealth—that is, black or South Asian—immigrants. Both the trajectory of Doris and the inquiry into "Englishness," then, need to be set alongside a history of race and immigration that *In Pursuit of the English* largely ignores.[15] This is not to

[10] Solomos chap. 3; Miles and Phizacklea, *White Man's Country*, chap. 2, esp. 21; Waters 223.

[11] Goulbourne, *Ethnicity and Nationalism*, 1–2, 55–63; Solomos 47; Waters esp. 221.

[12] See Chapter 5.

[13] On incidents of hostility toward New Commonwealth immigrants before 1958, see Layton-Henry 111. In 1949 there were riots in Deptford in July and attacks on an industrial hostel housing Indian workers near Birmingham in August.

[14] Klug, " 'Oh to Be in England,' " 22.

[15] I am arguing here for a "contrapuntal reading" along the lines that Edward W. Said suggests: "We must . . . read . . . to draw out, extend, give emphasis and voice to what is silent or marginally present or ideologically represented" (*Culture and Imperialism*, 66).

say that Lessing's exploration of what it means to be English should be invalidated but rather to note that the angle of vision from which it is conducted occludes an ongoing social and cultural debate and significantly distorts the historical record.

As a narrative, *In Pursuit of the English* has two movements. The first takes Doris from Rhodesia to Cape Town to London; the second situates her in London. In the first movement, Lessing authorizes her own enterprise by suggesting that those who don't quite belong to English culture or own it are the most astute observers of it: "For real perception into the side-channels of British culture one has to go to a university in Australia or South Africa" (35). Here, the narrator delineates the subject matter and approach of *In Pursuit of the English*, an effort of "perception into the side-channels of British culture."

Race is neither mentioned nor marked in this section of *In Pursuit of the English*, but the "perceptive critique" that issues from colonial locations such as Australia and South Africa seems to be voiced by observers who, like Lessing, are white. This is implied in the narrator's representation of herself as someone uniquely capable of understanding the English: "It is . . . because of my early and thorough grounding in the subject of the English character that I have undertaken to write about this business of being an exile. First one has to understand what one is in exile from" (8).[16] This passage undermines the distinction between home and exile, and like the prologue of *For Love Alone*, another narrative about a colonial woman who travels to the metropole, it decenters fixed points of reference. The destabilization of European, colonial binaries works differently here than in Stead's text, however.

Lessing suggests that "exile"—which I take to designate a social location distant from the British metropole—induces in the white colonial subject a need to "understand what [she or he] is in exile from": England or the English. The narrator's "grounding in . . . the English character" is paradoxically a sign of her condition of exile, a condition that she will remedy by a journey to England, her putative home. (Teresa Hawkins, in contrast, does not think of England as home.) "Exile" might also be regarded as a figuration of the narrator's experience in an England that is far away from the colonial home she leaves behind. But whether "exile" is a metaphor for the narrator's life in Africa or in England or the trajectory of her journey from one to the other, her exile is a privileged state of being in which she is English

[16] On exile as a theme of the literature of settler colonies, see Ashcroft, Griffiths, and Tiffin, *Empire Writes Back*, 27, 29. On "exile" in Lessing, see Gardiner, "Exhilaration of Exile," 133, 145–46, and Greene, *Changing the Story*, 17–18. Winifred Woodhull distinguishes the exile of "émigré" writers—Lessing or Doris—from that of culturally and economically marginal "immigrants" ("Exile," 7).

even if she has never been to England: "exile" marks her distance from or habitation in a home that belongs to her (to which she belongs) even though she has never lived there.[17]

The narrator demonstrates her grasp of the English character by enumerating the attitudes, styles of behavior, class traits, and temperamental quirks that define white, English-speaking inhabitants of Southern Rhodesia and Cape Town as English. Her father, who owns a farm in Rhodesia, exemplifies an Englishness constituted by traits of punctiliousness, racism, and violence and by the middle-class status that sets him and her mother apart from their working-class neighbors (14). In differentiating her parents from other members of the English-speaking community, the narrator does not mention the speakers of Afrikaans who live in the area or the black Africans who labor on her father's farm. The two women she meets in a Cape Town boarding-house identify themselves—or she defines them—as English by their exaggerated notions of propriety, excessive attention to decorum, and class snobbery. Yet in England, the narrator discovers, "middle-class" is not equated with "English" in quite the same way.

In the first movement of the text, which takes place in southern Africa, "English" means what exiles or colonials believe it to mean. But the rest of *In Pursuit of the English* suggests that in England, to be English is to be some kind of foreigner or to be thought of or to think of some other English person as foreign. Among the determinants of foreignness (or Englishness) are class, race (ethnicity), and region, although the foreignness of white colonials such as Doris is different from that of New Commonwealth immigrants perceived as truly foreign. The class position, race, ethnic identity, or regional provenance of a subject causes her or him to regard those in a different class (race, and so on) as not (quite) English.

In *Nation and Narration*, Homi Bhabha proposes a paradigm of national identity that encompasses difference: "The 'other' is never outside or beyond us; it emerges forcefully, within cultural discourse, when we *think* we speak most intimately and indigenously 'between ourselves.' "[18] Lessing, too, imbricates Englishness and otherness. Her deconstruction of identity categories asserts the narrator's authority to write about the English and *as* an Englishwoman. To define "English" in terms of what exiles or colonials—white colonials—think it means authorizes the narrator as a critic of English culture and, by extension,

---

[17] Lessing describes her background as "English, Scottish, Irish compost, nurtured by Kent, Essex, Suffolk, Norfolk, Devon, and Somerset" (*Under My Skin*, 419).
[18] Bhabha, "Introduction: Narrating the Nation," 4.

as a producer of English literature. To propose that the English are also "foreign" advances the claims of the narrator, an Englishwoman who is an exile and also, perhaps, a foreigner, to be considered "English."

The debate about English identity is dramatized in *In Pursuit of the English* in the depiction of the boardinghouse where the narrator rents a room soon after arriving in London. This house is a satiric, urban, dystopian version of one of the constitutive figures of English literature and one that is associated with a particularly English literary tradition, that of the house—usually a country estate like Ben Jonson's Penshurst or Jane Austen's Mansfield Park—that stands for England.[19] In using this figure, even if ironically, Lessing inscribes her text in a literary tradition in which, historically, English national identity has been debated; thus, she presents herself as an English writer.

The boardinghouse in *In Pursuit of the English,* run by one Flo and her husband, Dan, suggests London in the immediate postwar period. Seriously damaged in the Blitz, it is purchased by Dan with money made in shady wartime and postwar dealings. The tenants are a collection of working-class eccentrics who regard one another with suspicions customarily reserved for foreigners. The narrator describes them in a satirical manner that sets her apart. One object of her ironic gaze is a tenant named Rose, who comically illustrates working-class xenophobia. Rose warns the narrator that Flo "won't take foreigners" and, conflating Flo's views with her own, explains, "We're not having blacks. . . . We don't take Jews either" (42). Yet Rose also contradicts her own (or Flo's) definition of "foreign"; she considers the English different from themselves or the same as (some) foreigners. In Rose's view, Dan isn't English because he's from Newcastle, Flo isn't English because her grandmother is Italian, and she herself isn't English because she's from London (60). Difference, for Rose, is constitutive of sameness or identity. Thus Rose gives us a way of conceiving of a nation or national culture that encompasses different groups or difference itself.

The house where Rose lives is a microcosm of the nation, a liminal space, to borrow from Bhabha, in which "the national subject splits in the ethnographic perspective of culture's contemporaneity and provides both a theoretical position and a narrative authority for marginal voices or minority discourse."[20] In Lessing's text, however, the marginal voices and minority discourses in the boarding house that stands

---

[19] On the country house in British literature, see Williams, *Country and the City.* See Chapter 5, this volume, for a discussion of the house as a contested national space in the Thatcher period.

[20] Bhabha, "DissemiNation," 150.

for England do not achieve narrative authority. Rather, they are subordinated to the satirical eye and ironic voice of the narrator and to the authority of the would-be English writer, Doris Lessing.

In Pursuit of the English looks back at the immediate postwar period from a vantage point established by critiques of English culture and of the welfare state launched in the 1950s by writers such as Richard Hoggart and John Osborne.[21] Running through the text like a kind of refrain are the comments of various characters on whether or how the war has changed their lives and whether or how England after the war is substantially different from what it was before. One potentially significant agent—or symbol—of cultural change is television. Lessing's treatment of Flo's television conveys the homogenization and commercialization of popular culture; the displacement of local, working-class customs and traditions; and the moral impoverishment of the working class. Here, *In Pursuit of the English* recalls Hoggart's critique of the mass media and particularly his notion that "the older, the more narrow but also more genuine class culture is being eroded in favour of the mass opinion, the mass recreational product and the generalised emotional response."[22]

In actuality, the mass-mediated culture symbolized by Flo's television makes little substantial difference to most of the characters, whose lives are pretty much the same after the war as before. Lessing suggests that the "authentic" working-class culture whose demise Hoggart laments has long receded or may never have existed at all. Thus, *In Pursuit of the English* exposes his attempt to recuperate a genuine working-class culture as a pursuit of a chimerical working class (12).

In Pursuit of the English suggests that the postwar social transformation envisaged as early as the Beveridge Report (a proposal for a comprehensive welfare system) in 1942 and promised by the Labour government elected at the end of the war is merely superficial: Flo's boardinghouse is renovated, but the improvements are largely cosmetic; similarly, the changes in the lives of the tenants are insubstantial. The betrayal of the promise of postwar reconstruction is sketched in the story of two lodgers who seem more English and less foreign than the others. An elderly couple, poor, filthy, and unwilling or unable to pay their rent, they have lived in the house since before Flo bought it—in fact, since before the war (159, 182). Flo wants to evict them, raise the rent, and renovate their rooms for a new tenant. Claims

---

[21] See, for example, Hoggart, *Uses of Literacy,* and Osborne, "They Call It Cricket" and *Look Back in Anger.*
[22] Hoggart 280.

and counterclaims, suits and countersuits issue in a court case, and eventually the judge rules that the lodgers must leave.

This couple recall the typical working-class subjects of British documentary writing, like the people Orwell describes in *The Road to Wigan Pier* or the denizens of Henry Mayhew's London or Friedrich Engels's Manchester. They might command the sympathy of readers who share the narrator's "tint of social responsibility" (12), but a sympathetic response is foreclosed, or defused, because they are presented in the manner of music hall or farce: that is, in the genres of the "authentic" working-class culture catalogued, nostalgically, by Hoggart.

These lodgers evoke an older, working-class London culture defined by networks of kin and community.[23] Unlike the other tenants, they are significantly affected by the war and its aftermath. They live in a house that is nearly destroyed in the Blitz. They are displaced not by black immigrants, as the racist myths of the 1950s might suggest, but by Doris, a white, middle-class, colonial newcomer. Subsequently, they are dispossessed by the legal system and turned into clients of a welfare state that does not serve their needs. The vision of a welfare state inimical to the working class is similar to that in Osborne's *Look Back in Anger* (1956). In other words, like the Hoggartian analysis of the mass media echoed in Lessing's treatment of Flo's television, the treatment of the welfare state belongs more nearly to the mid- or late 1950s than to the late 1940s scene that *In Pursuit of the English* ostensibly describes.

In Pursuit of the English also stresses continuities between inter-and postwar constructions of gender, especially of motherhood. Most of the women in Flo's boardinghouse are seen and see themselves through the lens of the pronatalism—the identification of women's vocation with motherhood—that Denise Riley traces through different and competing ideological agendas in this period.[24] Pronatalism, as Riley explains, is not monolithic. In Lessing's book it is differently directed at and espoused by women (mothers) in different classes. Doris is relatively immune to pronatalist pressures, or at least evades them more successfully than do the working-class women in the house. She sends her son Peter to nursery school so she can spend her days writing unhindered. In fact, Peter is mentioned only infrequently; his apparent unimportance might be read as a sign of resistance to the hegemony of pronatalism.[25]

---

[23] For a depiction of networks of kin and community among the working class in the East End during the interwar period, see Gibson, "London."

[24] See Riley, *War in the Nursery*.

[25] Lessing says that she was "saved" from the misogyny of 1950s bohemia by the responsibility of having a child (*Under My Skin*, 409–10). The children of Anna Wulf and

In addition to the lodgers, the narrator encounters two other characters—men—who cannot be classified as foreign and might therefore be
considered authentically English. One of these is a Dickensian con man
known as Andrew McNamara, Alfred Ponsonby, and Bobby Brent. His
monikers make him variously Irish, stiff-upper-lip-English, and Cockney, but as a con man, he cannot be regarded as authentically anything,
even himself. The other is a retired military man, Colonel Bartowers,
who is presented as a pastiche of literary allusions: his very name
echoes the title of that quintessentially English text, Anthony Trollope's
Barchester Towers. Bartowers's Englishness is the product of an imperial
history in Southern Rhodesia that encompassed such exploits as "taking potshots at the nigs" (76). If the inhabitants of the boardinghouse
are simultaneously English and foreign and accordingly undermine
conventional categories of identity and point to the postwar transformation of the national culture, Bartowers and Ponsonby (aka Brent and
McNamara) signify an Englishness produced on the one hand by cultural genres both high and popular and on the other hand by imperial
and colonial adventures in Africa and elsewhere.[26] In this, they parody
the narrator's own claim to Englishness.

The narrator initially represents herself as a colonial who travels to
the metropole, an exile who is at the same time an Englishwoman (8,
14). Over the course of her first year in England, she assumes an English identity, like that of Colonel Bartowers, that is dependent on a
colonial history. Her impressions of England and the English are conveyed through rhetorical strategies that represent her as a colonial
writer. Throughout, colonial experience apparently takes precedence
over the English scene portrayed in this text. "Home"—England—is
described as being like or, occasionally, unlike colonies that are geographically peripheral or secondary but experientially, logically, and
discursively prior or primary, a standard of comparison for a metropolitan "center" therefore represented as ineluctably secondary. Thus, *In
Pursuit of the English* inverts the predominant mode of figuration of *For
Love Alone*, which describes provincial or colonial unknowns in terms
of a standard defined by a metropolitan known. In English documentary, too, socially marginal locales such as Wigan and Manchester are
compared with sites presumed to be familiar to middle-class readers.

Here, the narrator compares her room in the London boardinghouse

---

Molly Jacobs in *The Golden Notebook* are more visible than Peter, but the greater weight
given in that novel to love affairs and work than to maternity suggests resistance to
pronatalist imperatives. See Chapter 4, this volume.

   [26] Gikandi comments on the "invention of a British identity" that "depended on imperial possession" (29).

to an anthill in southern Africa: "Under the roof it was *like* sitting on top of an anthill, a tall sharp peak of baked earth that seems abandoned, but which sounds, when one puts one's ear to it, with a continuous vibrant humming. Even with the door shut, it was not long before the silence grew into an orchestra of sound" (80; emphasis added). The priority of the colonial scene, however, turns out to be a mirage. Like Colonel Bartowers, "Africa" in *In Pursuit of the English* is composed of intertextual allusions that reach back through Olive Schreiner's *The Story of an African Farm* to *Middlemarch.* The motif of an apparent silence that becomes an "orchestra of sound" recalls a famous passage in *Middlemarch:* "If we had a keen vision and feeling of all ordinary human life," the narrator remarks, "it would be like hearing the grass grow and the squirrel's heart beat, and we should die of that roar which lies on the other side of silence." The image of sounds that lie on the other side of silence must have powerfully affected Doris Lessing, for it reverberates in the title of *The Grass Is Singing,* in *Martha Quest,* in *The Golden Notebook,* and in *Under My Skin.*[27]

Like the prologue of *For Love Alone,* this passage exemplifies a problem faced by white European settlers in the Americas, Australia, New Zealand, and southern Africa, that of "establishing their 'indigeneity' and distinguishing it from their continuing sense of their European inheritance."[28] The colonial landscape, although apparently the ground of comparison in *In Pursuit of the English* and in Lessing's other works, does not establish an "indigeneity" distinct from an English cultural inheritance but rather is apprehended through allusions to English literature. In making these allusions, the narrator, or the author, affiliates herself with English literary traditions and enrolls herself in the ranks of English writers, although not, perhaps, on her own terms. Like Stead in *For Love Alone,* she must "borrow . . . the very image of what [she] wants to possess."[29]

To be English, for white colonials such as Doris or Lessing, is not only a matter of race privilege but also of class prerogative. Race and class sometimes work at cross-purposes but often reinforce each other, as in the narrator's account of the renovation of Flo's house. Watching the negligible progress of the construction workers sent by "War Damage" to repair the house, the narrator is distracted by colonial memo-

---

[27] Eliot, *Middlemarch,* chap. 20, 226. In *The Golden Notebook,* a character remarks, transposing Eliot's *keen vision* to ears, "If we had ears that could hear, the air would be full of screams, groans, grunts and gasps. But as it is, there reigns over the sunbathed veld the silence of peace" (370).
[28] Ashcroft, Griffiths, and Tiffin 135.
[29] Barthes, *Writing Degree Zero,* 87.

ries and grows "homesick" for her "country" of "accomplished idling" (205):

> A black labourer, hoe in hand, commanded to dig over a flower bed. . . . Leaning on the handle he gazes into the distance, thinking of that lost paradise, the tribal village where he might be lounging at that moment, under a tree, watching his women work in the vegetable garden while he drinks beer. Another shout of rage from the house. Again he stiffens, without actually hearing. . . . "Can't you go any faster than that?" demands the white mistress from the verandah of the house. "What do you think I pay your wages for?" Why? Well, of course, so that I can pay that stupid tax and get back home to my family . . . this thought is expressed in the sullen set of the shoulders. By the end of the day he has achieved the minimum amount of work.
>
> [The construction foreman], lazily allowing his chisel to slide over the cracked putty that held the cracked glass in place, remarked: "When we put the Labour Government in, we thought things would be better for the working people. But the way things work out, what's the difference?" (206)

Here, narratives of race, class, gender, and nationality compete, collide, and collapse. The narrator remembers or imagines a black (male) laborer who longs for a lost paradise where women work and men idle unmolested. Are readers—implied readers constructed here as white and English—supposed to regard the race and class exploitation that he suffers as mitigated or invalidated by the fact that in his utopia, women do the work? Or, are readers directed to excuse his patriarchal nostalgia as an attempt to compensate for his exploitation or to interpret it as a displacement of his understandable resentment of the race and class power of the "white mistress"?

In the narrator's fantasy, the black, male African laborer is fused with the white, male English construction workers. Does the foreman's complaint about the Labour government invite readers to consider his slack work habits, like those of the African laborer, as a sign of passive resistance to oppression? Perhaps the narrator, self-described as socially responsible, sympathizes with the foreman and urges readers to do so as well. But the chain of associations set in motion also connects the "white mistress," who berates the black laborer, to Flo and Dan, who regard the construction workers as malingerers; to "War Damage," the government office that hired them to do the job; and to the narrator, whose own work—writing—they interrupt.

The narrator subtly presents herself in this episode as a woman bothered by the unwelcome attentions of men, thereby transcribing class relations in gender terms. In doing so, she manages to deflect, at least slightly, the antagonism that readers sympathetic to the working class might direct at her as a member of the middle class. In this incident, the narrator's authority, her self-fashioning as a writer, is disrupted by class relations represented here in her silent conflict with the workers, in the annoyance she expresses only to the reader. These class relations operate as a surrogate for the colonial racial system evoked in her memory of the black laborer.

Any potential for the solidarity—brotherhood?—of the oppressed is dispelled by the foreman's resentment against "all these blacks coming in" (208). His antagonism, like the xenophobia of Rose, Flo, and Dan, is an instance of a phenomenon that historians identify as "working-class racism," but there were relatively few blacks in Britain in 1950.[30] The foreman is portrayed from a retrospective vantage point (1960) that looks back on a history of white, working-class antagonism toward black immigrants and racial violence that was just beginning to take shape in 1949–50. Perhaps the foreman, or the white English working class for which he speaks, expresses a racism that is pervasive throughout English society. This racism, as Colonel Bartowers's boasting about his imperial adventures reminds us, is an important element of the Englishness that this text seeks to discover or define and that it realizes ironically in the "Englishing" of its narrator.

The oscillation between Englishness and foreignness is not resolved in *In Pursuit of the English*. Nor is the meaning of "English" normalized or stabilized. Yet in the course of the year that the text describes, the English identity of Doris is established, and she, like the author Doris Lessing, becomes an English writer, as an advance on a previously written book enables her to begin work on a new one. Toward the end of *In Pursuit of the English*, the construction workers paper over the cracks in the walls of Flo's house, but they cannot repair its rotting structure. A habitation for transients, exiles, those without a proper home—but not for the New Commonwealth immigrants that, Chris Waters explains, the discourse of race relations constructs as "dark strangers"—the house is the site of a transitional phase in the life of the narrator. When she leaves it, she is already launched on her career as an English writer.

The "Englishing" of Doris, or Doris Lessing, then, exemplifies the situation of white, former colonial writers, or the transformation of

---

[30] On "working-class racism," see E. Lawrence, "Just Plain Common Sense," 48; Layton-Henry 50; Solomos chap. 3; and Miles and Phizacklea chap. 2. For figures on the black population of Britain, see note 7 above, this chapter.

white middle-class colonials into proper Englishmen and -women. Exploiting those less advantageously positioned in the English national community, what I have been calling Englishing is founded on the very structures and privileges it seeks to leave behind. The English identity of Doris Lessing, guaranteed by the British Nationality Act, is consolidated in such essays as "The Small Personal Voice" and the 1971 preface to *The Golden Notebook* that locate the author in a specifically British (English) tradition of cultural criticism. This English identity is anatomized in *The Golden Notebook* itself.

4

"Integrated with British Life at Its Roots": The Construction of British Identity in *The Golden Notebook*

The representation of the nation in Doris Lessing's *The Golden Notebook* exemplifies Homi Bhabha's conception of a "contested cultural territory" in which people are at once "historical 'objects' of a nationalist pedagogy . . . [and] 'subjects' of a process of signification that must erase any prior or originary presence of the nation-people."[1] This representation is undertaken from the perspective of the novel's protagonists, Anna Wulf and Molly Jacobs, who are at once British subjects and objects of a nationalist pedagogy. In anatomizing the national culture, Lessing produces *The Golden Notebook* as a British text. But this performative construction of identity is complicated by exclusions and by the pedagogical imperatives of the national culture itself. In this chapter I arrive at the construction of identity in *The Golden Notebook* by first considering two essays that define a space in which the novel's investigation of Britishness unfolds.

Before and After: Representing *The Golden Notebook*

"The Small Personal Voice" (1957) is an intervention in British cultural debates in the aftermath of 1956 and 1957: the Suez crisis, the Hungarian revolt, the revelations at the 20th Congress of the Soviet Communist Party of Stalin's brutal excesses, and Britain's explosion of a hydrogen bomb.[2] The 1971 preface to *The Golden Notebook* belongs to a later period when feminism had altered the literary and political ter-

---

[1] Bhabha,"DissemiNation," 145.

[2] On Lessing's place in British cultural debates in the 1950s, see Greene, *Changing the Story*, 115–16, 124; Hite, *Other Side of the Story*, 57–59; Jenny Taylor, "Introduction"; and Sinfield, *Literature, Politics, and Culture*, chap. 11.

rain.[3] But both essays attack the inadequacies of contemporary British culture. In the two essays, Lessing affiliates herself with a European (male) novelistic tradition that she describes in "The Small Personal Voice" as "realist" and in the preface as "philosophical"—the tradition that Stead claims as her literary genealogy and that Gordimer also invokes.[4] Unlike Stead and Gordimer, however, Lessing also places herself in a particularly English tradition of cultural criticism.[5] In aligning herself with both European and English precursors, Lessing represents herself as a writer at once English and cosmopolitan, and her work, as an alternative to an intellectually impoverished British culture.

"The Small Personal Voice" was first published in a collection entitled *Declaration*.[6] In this piece, Lessing praises the vitality of the Angry Young Men but takes aim at their provincial outlook (15). Lessing attacks British provincialism in terms that recall Matthew Arnold's essay "The Function of Criticism at the Present Time." But unlike Arnold, she offers as a remedy a perspective that reflects both a woman's critical stance and a colonial upbringing: that is, a doubly marginal position—like that of the English/exile in *In Pursuit*—that decenters the viewpoint of the English in England.

Lessing's vision of the writer (novelist) borrows from William Wordsworth and Jean-Paul Sartre.[7] Echoing Sartre, Lessing defines the role of the writer as responsibility. But her sense of the writer's vocation more clearly recalls Wordsworth than the European novelists she praises. "The novelist talks," she says, echoing Wordsworth's preface to the Lyrical Ballads, "as an individual to individuals, in a small personal voice" (21). Like Richard Hoggart's critique of "mass entertainment" in *The Uses of Literacy*, Lessing's attack on committee art, a concomitant of the value she places on voice, develops Wordsworthian notions of poetry. But Lessing—like Hoggart, F. R. Leavis, and Raymond Williams—transvalues Wordsworth's generic hierarchy, making the novel the bulwark against a commercialized popular culture.

The 1971 preface represents *The Golden Notebook* as part of an emer-

---

[3] On the differences between the two essays, see Hite, 55, 62–64, and Kauffman, *Special Delivery*, 133, 169.

[4] See Stead, "Uses of the Many-Charactered Novel," and Gordimer's description of *Burger's Daughter* as a "political novel" and as a "novel of ideas," in *What Happened to "Burger's Daughter,"* 19. Hanson sees Lessing's advocacy of realism in "The Small Personal Voice" as a camouflage for her postmodern turn ("Doris Lessing in Pursuit," 64).

[5] See Sinfield on a "left-culturism" in the late 1950s "compatible with . . . Matthew Arnold and F. R. Leavis" (243).

[6] Most of the essays in the collection are the work of writers identified as Angry Young Men or associated with an emerging left-liberal intelligentsia.

[7] See Draine, *Substance under Pressure*, chap. 4, on Sartre's influence on Lessing.

gent inter- or transnational literary culture and at the same time as English literature. Taking issue with "belittling" reviewers who averred that the novel was simply about the sex war (Preface, 25), Lessing seems to be resisting the domestication of her text under the sign of "women's writing."[8] Rather, she presents *The Golden Notebook* as a corrective for the deficiencies of nineteenth-century *British* novels hampered by Victorian notions of propriety, as an alternative to the official culture, and as a contemporary version of the philosophical novel. Retrospectively representing *The Golden Notebook* as a translation of a nineteenth-century, European, masculine genre into a twentieth-century English idiom that renders a woman's point of view, Lessing treats it as an international text and, at the same time, naturalizes it as an English novel, if not the English novel of its era.

The Golden Notebook consists of a frame narrative, "Free Women," a conventional novel, and five notebooks that, as Lessing explains, contain the "material that went into making" the conventional novel.[9] Near the beginning of "Free Women," Anna says to Molly, "The point is, that as far as I can see, everything's cracking up" (9). Near the end, Anna announces that she will be doing marriage counseling, teaching a class for delinquents, and joining the Labour Party, and Molly, who is about to be married, responds epigrammatically, "So we're both going to be integrated with British life at its roots" (568). The terms of the conversation between Molly and Anna situate the novel in the cultural climate of 1956 and 1957.

The Golden Notebook occludes a different aspect of the issue of "integration," and one that certainly commanded some public notice in the 1950s: that of the integration into British society of immigrants from Britain's colonies and former colonies.[10] The relative invisibility of New Commonwealth immigrants in *The Golden Notebook* and the resulting suppression of race as a constituent of British identity during this period are in part a function of the novel's being set in and retrospectively narrated from the vantage point of 1957, with the notebooks recording earlier events reaching back to 1950.

As we saw in Chapter 3, "race," in the guise of a racialized discourse on immigration, was present in the public consciousness throughout the 1950s but erupted with particular force in 1958—that is, the year

---

[8] See notes 53 and 54, this chapter, on the attempt by U.S. feminist critics to read Lessing's work as an expression of women's experience.

[9] Lessing, Preface, 23; Lessing, "A Talk with Doris Lessing" (interview with Florence Howe), 81. On the structure of *The Golden Notebook* as a deconstruction of conventional narrative, see Kauffman 165 and Schweikart, "Reading a Wordless Statement," 274.

[10] See Chapter 3.

after the events described in the novel take place—following riots in Notting Hill and Nottingham.[11] Yet, as in *In Pursuit of the English*, narrative chronology isn't entirely responsible for the treatment of race in the novel. In its construction of British identity, *The Golden Notebook* reproduces an emerging discourse of nationality in which Britishness is increasingly conflated with whiteness.[12] The Commonwealth Immigrants Bill, which subjected nonwhite immigrants from Commonwealth countries to restrictions and gave preferential treatment to whites, took effect in 1962, the same year that *The Golden Notebook* was published.

During the mid-1950s, British cultural critics sought to dissect and repair a crisis identified as a fragmenting of the body politic. The preoccupation with division and its corollary, the search for connection and meaning, appear most powerfully in the work of Raymond Williams.[13] In *The Long Revolution* (1961), Williams links struggles for democracy in the West, the Third World, and Eastern Europe; he sees these struggles, along with a democratization of culture, as potential remedies for a global, not just a national, crisis. The preoccupation with division and the representation of cultural crisis as social and moral fragmentation also figure in Hoggart's *The Uses of Literacy* (1957), Leavis's *The Great Tradition* (1954), and many of the essays in Tom Maschler's *Declaration*. Anna Wulf, too, values connection. She laments her inability to write a novel that can make connections like those made in the nineteenth century by the European novelists praised in "The Small Personal Voice" or in the twentieth century by Thomas Mann (59).[14]

Anna's response to Molly's declaration that they will be integrated with British life—"I was carefully avoiding that tone" (9), she says— directs us to read Molly's statement ironically. Anna puts into play a counternarrative that emphasizes the marginal location of these two women in the national culture being constructed or reconstructed in

[11] On race in Britain in the 1950s, see Jacobs, *Black Politics and Urban Crisis*; Layton-Henry, *Politics of Race*; Miles and Phizacklea, *White Man's Country*; Solomos, *Race and Racism*; Paul, *Whitewashing Britain*; and Waters, " 'Dark Strangers.' " On the riots in Notting Hill and Nottingham in summer 1958, see Layton-Henry 35–36; Solomos 48; Jacobs 32; Miles and Phizacklea 24–37; and Paul 155–59.

[12] Goulbourne, *Ethnicity and Nationalism*; Waters.

[13] See Brenkman, "Raymond Williams and Marxism."

[14] Hite reads *The Golden Notebook* as a woman's critique of Williams (59); Abel sees Anna's inability to write a philosophical novel as a sign of Anna's repudiation of a male canon and masculine literary values *("The Golden Notebook")*. Taylor ("Introduction," 13–15, 24–39) and Greene (*Changing the Story*, 124) stress continuities and resemblances between Lessing and Williams. Sprague places *The Golden Notebook* at the end of the tradition outlined by Leavis (*"The Golden Notebook:* In Whose or What Great Tradition?" 83).

the years the novel describes. The antagonistic relationship between Anna and Molly and "British life" is grounded in a specific moment: it inscribes the resistance of white, middle-class, intellectual and professional women, especially those affiliated with the Communist Party, to the postwar gender system.[15]

The Golden Notebook oscillates between the two poles represented by the integration of the protagonists into the national culture, on the one hand, and their remaining at least ambiguously resistant to it, on the other. In the rest of this chapter, I examine what is suppressed, conscripted, or transformed in the construction of Anna and Molly as British subjects and explore the question of whether or how white, middle-class, heterosexual women can be integrated into British national culture "at its roots."

Colonialism and Decolonization

The Golden Notebook is poised at a pivotal moment in the history of decolonization: India and Pakistan became independent in 1947, Ghana in 1957, and other Asian, African, and Caribbean nations followed in turn. The novel looks back at the colonial and imperial past and ahead to the future. It asks whether the order ushered in by the independence of former colonies will differ substantially from the imperial order or rather be a repetition of it: that is, whether the emerging global political and cultural order will be more accurately characterized as post- or neocolonial. More important, *The Golden Notebook* dramatizes the articulation of colonial and imperial economies with British (metropolitan) culture.[16] Critically rewriting British texts, both "high" and popular, in which this articulation occurs, *The Golden Notebook* also calls into question its own revisionary strategies.

The colonial production of British identities is represented in the early installments of the black notebook, which concerns Anna's career as an author and global politics in the era of decolonization. In these entries, Anna revisits the events portrayed in "Frontiers of War," her best-selling novel about colonialism in central Africa during the Sec-

[15] In a comment on a version of this chapter presented at the Columbia University Seminar on Women and Society, January 1994, Susan Pennybacker linked Molly and Anna to women in and around the Communist Party. These women were often hostile to feminism, which they regarded as a bourgeois movement, yet their resistance to gender imperatives sometimes coincided with feminist agendas.

[16] Cf. Gikandi's project in *Maps of Englishness:* "to read Englishness as a cultural and literary phenomenon produced in the ambivalent space that separated, but also conjoined metropole and colony" (xii).

ond World War. Appalled by the nostalgia that, she now believes, infects her novel, she attempts to rid her writing of sentimentality.

As Anna now tells the story, during the war, she joins a group that is forming a Communist cell. They spend a great deal of time at the Mashopi Hotel, owned by a British couple named Boothby. One member of the group, Paul Blackenhurst, befriends the Boothbys' African cook, Jackson. The relationship of Paul and Jackson raises a question that recalls such modern novels of empire as E. M. Forster's *A Passage to India:* it asks whether, in a colonial society, there can be anything like "friendship" between a black man and a white man. Paul stages his "friendship" with Jackson in a series of gestures intended to provoke the Boothbys. He is unaware that George Hounslow, an associate of the group, is having an affair with Jackson's wife, Marie. Mrs. Boothby, enraged at Paul, expresses her anger by firing the cook. Jackson lands a job in the city, but his wife and children cannot stay with him as they did at Mashopi, so he sends them to Nyasaland (134).

This exemplary colonial tale consists of a set of stories in different genres. Paul, who is killed when he walks into the propeller of the plane that is about to take him to the North African theater of war, is the protagonist of an ironic narrative. George Hounslow's story is a ludicrous parody of *Oliver Twist,* with the role of Oliver, the orphan who turns out to be a member of the family, played by the son Marie bears him. Jackson might be the protagonist of an African novel that has not yet been written. But the victim of all these stories is Marie, the African woman. Forcibly severed from her life at Mashopi and dispatched to Nyasaland, she literally disappears from Anna's text—that is, from the purview of British and colonial culture alike.

The colonial construction of British (female) identity is also dramatized in allusions to *Brief Encounter* (1945), a film written by Noel Coward and directed by David Lean. *Brief Encounter* portrays the adulterous attraction of Laura Jesson, an upper-middle-class housewife, and Alec Harvey, a married doctor. Released in November 1945, just after the war had ended, *Brief Encounter* participates in the ideological transformation of gender that makes up a crucial element of postwar reconstruction.[17] Its resolution juxtaposes the containment of middle-class women's desire at home—in England, in the family—with the displacement of middle-class men's ambition to the colonies. At the end of the film, Laura apparently rededicates herself to the familial and

---

[17] On *Brief Encounter,* British identity, and postwar reconstruction, see Lant, *Blackout,* and Dyer, *Brief Encounter.*

especially maternal obligations she neglected during her infatuation with Alec. In this scenario, the agency of middle-class white women is almost entirely occluded: Laura's final turn or return to her husband and children is ensured by Alec's decision to take a position in Johannesburg, and Alec's wife, who accompanies him to Johannesburg, is absent from the narrative altogether.

The Golden Notebook comments both explicitly and implicitly on *Brief Encounter*'s imbrication of gender, class, and colonial themes. *Brief Encounter* is revised in "The Shadow of the Third," a novel that Anna is writing about a woman named Ella, who is involved in a tortured affair with a married man named Paul Tanner. Eventually, Paul grows bored with Ella. He ends their affair when he is offered a position in Nigeria and, without consulting her, decides to accept it (189). The theme of the empire, or the former empire, as an outlet for angst-ridden, upper-middle-class, male British talent is also reflected in the plan of Richard, Molly's capitalist former husband, to send their hapless son Tommy to run his office in Ghana (222).

In *The Golden Notebook* and in Anna's novel, Ghana and Nigeria are put in the place occupied by Johannesburg in *Brief Encounter*. Colonial or formerly colonial sites are interchangeable. A colonial or neocolonial escape hatch enables British or European men to realize ambitions thwarted at home, but the illicit, extravagant, adulterous desire of women such as Ella and Laura is confined, literally and figuratively, in England. The settler wife, represented in the spouses of Alec and Paul, is erased both in the film and in *The Golden Notebook*'s rewriting of it, and black Africans—colonized subjects, men and women alike—are effaced altogether.

The Golden Notebook cautions (white) readers in the British metropole against drawing conclusions about black Africans from the ways they are depicted in texts written by white colonial authors: that is, in the kinds of stories Anna parodies in her notebook descriptions of the Mashopi episode. The novel critically marks the representation of black Africans in white-authored texts as figures in colonial discourse. Anna records a dream in which the Mashopi story is made as a television film shot by an all-black crew. She notes that the director "was changing the 'story' " (449). His treatment of the Mashopi incident is simply added on to those that Anna has already given; there is no explanation of the relationship between the different versions of the story. But their juxtaposition raises the question of whether the perspectives of Africans such as the film director can be recuperated in the writings of colonial, former colonial, or even anticolonial British whites—including Lessing, Anna, and their avatars in the novel?—or whether the power of capitalist mass media and the hegemony of colonial modes of representation inevitably conscript them in the production of British identities.[18]

A related question underlies a series of dreams and fantasies that Anna has in the second half of the novel. In these dreams and fantasies, the manifest content changes, but the latent content, the power of one group over another, remains constant. As Anna shifts her focus from colonialism in the 1940s to anticolonial struggles and decolonization in the 1950s, her fantasies, dreams, and memories migrate from colonial central Africa to North Africa, specifically Algeria, and then to Cuba, China, Eastern Europe, and the Soviet Union. The dreams all ask different versions of the same basic question: Is transformation of the order of knowledge and power possible? Or is change just an exchange, a substitution of one group for another? Does independence or decolonization—or de-stalinization, for that matter—make a significant difference? Or is it rather a repetition or imitation of an authoritative colonial original—a post- or neocolonial mimicry—that substitutes one order of oppression for another? These questions also reflect the concerns of an emergent British New Left in the late 1950s. Having left, or left behind, the Communist Party and its affiliates, those in the New Left (a group that included Lessing) debated what kind of socialist movement could be formed and whether it would differ from or revert to the politics of the Communist Party, on the one hand, or the Conservative (and Labour) reaction to postwar reconstruction, on the other.[19]

The question of whether the postcolonial order simply repeats or significantly alters the colonial one is also raised by the newspaper clippings about African liberation struggles that Anna collects and tacks on her walls and by the depiction of a new cultural type, the African intellectual in the era of decolonization. This type is embodied in two characters, the saintly Tom Mathlong and Charlie Themba, who is driven mad by the pressure of the liberation struggle. Mathlong, Themba, Paul Blackenhurst, Jackson, Marie, and many others all make possible Anna's British female subjectivity. Their articulation and inscription in the character named in the novel as Anna Wulf points to the implication of British identity in the colonial order it variously appropriates, incorporates, and transforms.

[18] Cf. Spivak's examination in "Can the Subaltern Speak?" of "how the third-world subject is represented within Western discourse" (271).
[19] See Hall, "The 'First' New Left," 23–24.

Communism: In and Out of the Party

Anna's career as a Communist in and out of the Party is plagued by the same sense of inexorable division and motivated by the same longing for wholeness that virtually defines her character (142) and that Raymond Williams identifies in the national culture as a whole. Anna herself is ambivalent about both lower- and upper-case Communism. Her ambivalence is reflected in the novel's undermining of the idea of political agency and mirrored in the portrayal of a Communist Party that is itself disintegrating.

When Molly remarks, "We're both going to be integrated with British life at its roots," she ends an episode or period in the political histories of herself and Anna—and England. *The Golden Notebook* gives us the story of Anna's involvement in Communism in light of the ending that Molly imposes on it. In Anna's narrative, too, and especially in the notebooks, incidents that might appear aleatory or haphazard as they unfold are given a shape that is a textual effect of a retrospective narration that orders or reorders the events described or of apparently arbitrary choices such as Anna's decision to write down everything that happens on a particular day. In other words, the novel represents the making of political decisions not as a matter of will, self-determination, or conscious belief but rather as a reflex of other factors. Thus, it calls political agency into question.

The representation of Anna's life in the Communist Party exemplifies rupture, division, and doubleness. Like Anna, each member of the Mashopi group experiences an ambivalence that undermines her or his politics. The internal disintegration of the group members and the external pressures that fracture the group prefigure the psychic breakdowns of particular Communists and the fragmentation of the Communist Left in London in the 1950s. The group is dissolved, however, not by divisions within or between its members but by the explosive denouement of the Mashopi episode ("colonialism") and by Paul's death ("mortality"). The juxtaposition of conflicting explanations might be seen as a version of overdetermination, the assigning of multiple causes to single events, but it also works to foreclose any explanation, and especially the materialist explanation—"class analysis"—that featured in Communist Party writings about culture. The eschewing of explanation is one way that Lessing, or Anna, repudiates the Communist Party in the aftermath of 1956.

A similar reluctance to rehearse left-wing (Communist) protocols of interpretation underlies the description, in the red notebook, which is devoted to Anna's reflections on Communism, of her decision to join the British Communist Party. In this narrative of political conversion, neither politics nor conversion appears meaningful. Affirmative political beliefs, which play at least a small part in Anna's account (in the black notebook) of becoming a Communist in central Africa, play virtually no part here. Rather, in this account, Anna's Communism is motivated by her alienation from postwar British culture. Echoing the Angry Young Men, Anna attacks the "prissy, maiden-auntish, class-bound" literary world (136). At the same time, she internalizes the Angries' misogyny and reproduces the slippages between anger at middle-class complacency and anger at women that prominently mark their writings in *Declaration* and elsewhere.[20] In this account, gender is muted as a determinant of Anna's alienation from the dominant culture, but it resurfaces, in a return of the repressed, as an influence on her disaffection with the Communist Party itself. As in the culture at large and in the work of the Angries, the Communist Party is a locus in which class resentment is translated into anger at women. Male Communists attack Anna by vaunting their working-class origins, whether real or imagined, and impugning the middle-class status that, they claim, renders her communism inauthentic.[21] As we shall see in the next chapter, Lessing levels the same charge at the spurious communists in *The Good Terrorist* (1985).

Yet *The Golden Notebook* does not entirely discredit Communism or all Communists. Jack, who works with Anna in the Communist Party publishing house, is fair-minded, thoughtful, and compassionate. He argues with Anna, listens to her, confides in her, and takes her seriously—until she decides to leave the Party. He is one of the very few men in the novel who does not despise women and virtually the only political person whose actions are not chiefly motivated by bad faith.

[20] Cf. Lessing, "The Small Personal Voice," 15–16. The writers Lessing praises in this essay are all men. On the conflation of class and gender in the Angries, see Segal, "Silence of Women in the New Left," 115.

[21] The depiction of the misogyny in the Old Left must have resonated with the experience of second-wave feminists who read the novel in the 1960s and early 1970s with vivid memories of sexism in the New Left. Perhaps this resonance led these women to claim that *The Golden Notebook* influenced them to become feminists or helped create the feminist movement. See the comments by Linsey Abrams, Eleanor Broner, Vivian Gornick, and Ann Snitow in "Opening *The Golden Notebook*," a report of a 1991 symposium at PEN. I thank Rachel Blau DuPlessis and Elizabeth Janeway for bringing this symposium to my attention. On the novel's influence on feminists, see also Greene's paper presented at the 1992 MLA convention and her *Changing the Story*, 57; Drabble, "Doris Lessing," 186, 188; Louise Bernikow, conversation with author, spring 1993; DuPlessis, "Reader, I Married Me," Greene, "Looking at History," and Miller, "Decades," all in Greene and Kahn, *Changing Subjects*; and Adrienne Rich's interview with Elly Bulkin.

The value he places on work distinguishes him from most of the novel's Communists.[22] Yet as a "good man betrayed by history" (301), Jack so closely resembles the protagonists of Anna's parodies of socialist realist fiction that commitment itself seems to be little more than a prelude or invitation to betrayal.

Lessing was actively—although, as Jenny Taylor notes, ambiguously—involved in the New Left. She was a member of the editorial boards of the *New Reasoner* and, later, *New Left Review;* she was involved in the Campaign for Nuclear Disarmament (CND) and was a member of the organizing committee of the first Aldermaston march for nuclear disarmament.[23] But the New Left has a relatively minor role in *The Golden Notebook*, except, perhaps, as a harbinger of the "integration," however partial, of Anna and Molly into British life. Anna's decision to leave the Party is a move that, at least potentially, might repair the breach between herself and British culture. But such a repair is not identical to the "integration" that Molly proclaims or even to the connection envisioned by Raymond Williams, in part because of the difficulty of integrating women into a misogynist culture or the terms on which such integration might occur. The novel suggests that misogyny (sexism) is as endemic on the left (new and old alike) as elsewhere; in this, it anticipates Juliet Mitchell's feminist revision of *The Long Revolution* in "Women: The Longest Revolution" (1966) and elaborates a radical critique of gender.

The Organization of Gender

The gender system represented in *The Golden Notebook* has several components: male dominance; the ideological confinement of middle-class women, as mothers and wives, in a reconstituted "family"; women's attraction to misogynist, powerful men and, implicitly, to the power they wield; and compulsory heterosexuality or, seen from another perspective, institutionalized homophobia.[24] These components are elements in the reciprocal reconstruction of gender and society that

[22] It also links him to the grass-roots organizers described in the accounts of historians such as James Hinton ("Coventry Communism") and in the memoirs of such activists as Arthur Exell ("Morris Motors in the 1940s").

[23] See J. Taylor, "Introduction," 26; S. Hall, "'First' New Left," 22; and Sinfield chap. 11. On the development of left-wing cultural formations, see Oxford University Socialist Discussion Group, *Out of Apathy*, and the essays by Anderson, Tynan, and Osborne in Maschler, *Declaration*.

[24] In a discussion of *The Golden Notebook* published after I completed this chapter, Boone notes that homosexuality is "an absent theme" in criticism of the novel; he reme-

preoccupied Britain in the 1940s, 1950s, and into the 1960s. To say this is not to imply that ideologies of gender are monolithic. Rather, it is to follow the practice of *The Golden Notebook* and to isolate gender as one element in a larger ensemble.

The novel's account of gender tends to obscure race. *The Golden Notebook* treats whiteness as racially unmarked and presents Anna and Molly not as white women but as "women."[25] Race is glimpsed in its effects—in the traces it leaves in a colonial (imperial) and then in a decolonizing culture. Similarly, the novel's account of gender elides class: it conflates the situation of Anna and Molly with those of women who occupy different class positions. Anna and Molly displace working-class women by taking center stage in the novel and its milieu. These very elisions and occlusions reproduce the ways that white, middle-class, heterosexual women are positioned as British subjects—"integrated with British life"—through the reconstruction of gender in the postwar period.

Historians have amply documented the massive ideological effort to "return" women to the family after the Second World War. Denise Riley suggests, as we saw in Chapter 3, that the postwar reconstruction of women as wives and full-time mothers was the product of competing ideological agendas, among which were British psychoanalytic explanations of the experience of children in wartime and the exigency of finding employment for men leaving the military.[26] Films such as *Brief Encounter* played a part in this reconstruction, as did the novels of sensibility written by Rosamond Lehmann, Rose Macaulay, and others.[27] In the mid-1950s, the Angry Young Men attacked the feminizing assaults on working-class masculinity by the postwar welfare state: "She devours me whole," says John Osborne's Jimmy Porter as he lashes out at Alison, the wife he identifies with the national culture and with her mother, his exemplar of the moral corruption of an empire in decline.[28] *The Golden Notebook* occupies a cultural terrain left vacant by the opposition between the "sensibility" of women writers and the Angries' misogyny.

---

dies the absence in a brilliant exploration of its interweaving of misogyny, homophobia, and racism. See his *Libidinal Currents*, 364, 389–418.

[25] On whiteness as a racial marker, see Ware, *Beyond the Pale*; Frankenberg, *White Women, Race Matters*; Dyer; and Catherine Hall, *White, Male, and Middle Class*.

[26] See Weeks, *Sex, Politics, and Society*, chaps. 12–13; Finch and Summerfield, "Social Reconstruction and the Emergence of Companionate Marriage, 1945–59"; Riley, *War in the Nursery*; and Field, "Perspectives on the Working-Class Family." I thank Geoffrey Field for sharing with me his work in progress on the reconstruction of gender during and after the Second World War.

[27] O'Rourke, "Doris Lessing: Exile and Exception," 215.

[28] Osborne, *Look Back in Anger*, 37.

Historians Janet Finch and Penny Summerfield argue that women's "confinement" in domestic space was represented in the ideology of "companionate marriage" as it was elaborated in the late 1940s and 1950s. The construction of women as the "companions" of their husbands mystified the material circumstances of married and single women alike. On the one hand, it distorted the asymmetrical organization of gender that mandated the economic dependence of married women on their husbands and treated their work as "supplementary" and their wages as a way to purchase luxuries rather than a means of survival for their families. On the other hand, it was predicated on ideas of women's essential difference from men. The domestication of women was reinforced by the pronatalist ideology of postwar British psychoanalysis. In different ways, psychoanalysts such as Anna Freud, D. W. Winnicott, and John Bowlby asserted the need of children for full-time maternal care and redefined maternity as a vocation. Yet their claims about the ill effects of "maternal deprivation" were often based on the observation of evacuees whose experiences of wartime dislocation were anomalous as well as extreme. The pronatalist ideology that underlies Winnicott's idea of the good-enough mother, like the conception of sexual difference that underwrites "companionate marriage," intensified the constructions of gender that existed before and during the war.[29]

The treatment of gender and sexual politics in *The Golden Notebook* represents and reacts against this postwar ensemble.[30] Molly's and Anna's self-identification as "free women" and their attempt, however compromised or attenuated, to live without or independent of men, enact their resistance, or opposition, to the sex/gender system they inhabit, the reconstructed heterosexualist bourgeois patriarchy of the postwar British welfare state. Resistance to the ideological imperatives of the dominant culture might also explain the relatively insignificant part that Molly's son, Tommy, and especially Anna's daughter, Janet, play in the novel.[31] In different ways, both Anna and Molly resist incorporation into what Riley identifies as "the 'family' of immediately postwar family policy, the fiscal man and the reproductive woman and

---

[29] See Riley, *War in the Nursery,* 171; the memoirs of Reed and Isserlis, both in Johnson, *Evacuees;* the chapters on evacuees and the working-class family in Geoffrey Field's work in progress, "The British Working Class during the Second World War"; and Winnicott, *Playing and Reality.*

[30] Greene places *The Golden Notebook* in a group of British and American feminist texts published in 1962–63. Novels such as Sylvia Plath's *The Bell Jar* and Sue Kaufman's *The Diary of a Mad Housewife* and Betty Friedan's *The Feminine Mystique* explore the ideological confinement of women in the family (*Changing the Story,* 33, 58).

[31] Gardiner sees Anna's maternal values as "profoundly ambiguous" (*Rhys, Stead, Lessing,* 148–49).

the stock of children."[32] The apparent lack of concern that mothers—Molly and Anna, like Doris in *In Pursuit of the English*—show for their children might be read as opposition to the pernicious emphasis of "experts" and popular culture alike on maternity as the sole or principal vocation of Riley's "reproductive woman." (Molly, Anna, and Doris belong to a different cultural time and place than Stead's Henny Pollit, whose laissez-faire maternity is shaped by and against ideological changes in the years of Stead's youth.) But the critical force of this opposition is defused by the representation of women's collusion in their own oppression, a collusion that militates against the idea that women—or feminism—might be a force for change in the world.[33]

Throughout *The Golden Notebook*, Anna notices with distaste the confinement of women—of wives—in the family. Yet the fear of autonomy is pervasive among women in the novel, both married and single.[34] It extends even to Anna and Molly, who resist the domesticating constraints of gender. As Anna explains, after reflecting on her relationship with her lover Michael and identifying Ella, a character in her novel in progress, with herself and Ella's lover Paul with Michael: "Paul gave birth to Ella, the naive Ella. He destroyed in her the knowing, doubting, sophisticated Ella and again and again *he put her intelligence to sleep, and with her willing connivance,* so that she floated darkly on her love for him, on her naivety, which is another word for a spontaneous creative faith" (183; emphasis added). But why, the novel makes us ask, does Ella "connive" in her own moral and intellectual somnolence? Why should Paul or Michael or any man be held responsible for "put[ting a woman's] intelligence to sleep"?[35] At the same time, the novel suggests, women are not wholly responsible for their own situation. In Anna's novel, Ella remarks that being left in the lurch (or left altogether) by men is the price they pay for "having chosen to be free women," and her friend Julia replies, "Free! What's the use of us being free if they aren't?" (392).

Throughout *The Golden Notebook*, women are attracted, almost inexplicably, to powerful, misogynist men or to the power they wield. This attraction is produced by and reproduces women's complicity in male

[32] Riley, *War in the Nursery*, 155.

[33] Lessing's analysis of gender resembles Friedan's, but *The Golden Notebook* stresses the obstacles to feminist transformation, whereas *The Feminine Mystique* looks toward change through collective action. Lessing's retrospective repudiation, in the 1971 preface, of feminist intent crystallizes a tendency inchoate in the novel itself.

[34] On women's fear of autonomy in Lessing, see Rubenstein, *Novelistic Vision of Doris Lessing*, 81, and Boone, *Libidinal Currents*, 398, 405.

[35] Kauffman suggests that Lessing "historicizes desire by examining fascism's capacity to make subjects desire their own subjection" (133).

domination and hence in their own oppression.[36] Anna's relationships with men in the last third of the novel represent extreme or exaggerated versions of this same pattern. The most disturbing instance of her attraction to eroticized, infantile, seemingly gratuitous male aggression is her involvement with Saul Green, who subjects her to a "brutal sexual inspection" (471).[37] Anna regards Saul as a "real man." The rhetoric of "real manhood" raises the question of whether real—authentic?—manhood is misogyny, domination, or the protest of a fragile, infantile ego against the perceived encroachment of engulfing, maternal femininity.[38] In other words, the novel represents Saul's predicament as a version of Jimmy Porter's. During the time when Anna is involved with Saul, her analyst, whom she calls Mother Sugar, directs her to experience "joy-in-destruction" (508). In effect, the analyst is urging her to collude, and even to revel, in Saul's sadistic treatment of her. Here, the novel asks whether psychoanalysis, or the attachment of daughter to mother that is invoked in Anna's pet name for her analyst, is a source of women's erotic investment in the protest of the (male, infantile) ego motivated by aggression against them, that is, in the maintenance and reproduction of male domination.

Throughout the novel, Anna counterposes the "real manhood" of Saul Green to what she considers the meretricious manhood of homosexual men. Ivor, who rents a room in her flat, and Ronnie, his lover, are hostile to femininity, both in the abstract and as it is incorporated in actual women, notably in Anna herself. Their hostility is staged as a performance, an extravagant parody of femininity that, like Bhabha's mimicry, is "constructed around an ambivalence" and "produces its slippage, its excess, its difference."[39] Judith Butler suggests that performative constructions of gender destabilize the idea that sex and gender are fixed.[40] (This idea underlies the rhetoric of real manhood.) The performances or acts that Butler describes, with their "dramatic and contingent construction of meaning," playfully produce utopian sexual possibilities, but Ronnie's parody is intended to wound the audience it mocks: women, especially Anna. Later, Anna examines her body through what she characterizes as a homosexual literature of disgust

[36] Greene defines a feminist novel as one that shows "gender as socially constructed" and suggests that "change is possible" (*Changing the Story*, 2). *The Golden Notebook* represents gender as socially constructed but resistant to change.

[37] Kauffman says that Lessing identifies Saul with Anna and "portrays aggression as a force that transcends gender" (160).

[38] On "real manhood," see Hite 77; Greene, *Changing the Story*, 121; and Boone, *Libidinal Currents*, 358.

[39] Bhabha, "Of Mimicry and Man," 86.

[40] See Butler, *Gender Trouble*, 128–41.

(524). Her self-loathing—a reflex of Ronnie's hatred of women, or Saul's—exemplifies the way that a patriarchal order devalues the female body. It points to the limits of poststructuralist epistemologies that attempt to dispense with such categories as "patriarchy" or "experience." Yet Anna's homophobia—reflected in her notion that Ivor and Ronnie are not "real men"—implicates her in invidious patriarchal constructions of the feminine and vitiates her critique of misogyny and that of the novel as a whole.

Anna regards lesbianism, like the inauthentic manhood of the male homosexual, as a parody of femininity, a disease born of bitterness and desperation. Not only erotic attachment but also solidarity and community between women are virtually unimaginable. Claire Sprague reads the novel's homophobia as a reflection of a specific moment.[41] But historicizing *The Golden Notebook* does not change the way that homophobia infects its critique of gender. Absent from the novel are the debates about homosexuality during the 1950s that led to the issuing in 1957 of the Wolfenden Report. This report advocated the decriminalization of homosexual acts between consenting males but ignored lesbian sexuality altogether.[42] The novel's rhetoric of "real manhood" excludes homosexual men, but it also leaves all women out in the cold.

Everything's Cracking Up

Gayle Greene observes that *The Golden Notebook* "registers the loss of the systems—social, moral, philosophical, political—that once gave life meaning."[43] This loss is presented as both product and symptom of the nuclear age. As Lessing explains, "An epoch of our society, and of socialism, was breaking up at that time. It had been falling apart since the Bomb was dropped on Hiroshima. . . . I feel as if the Bomb has gone off inside myself, and in people around me. That's what I mean by cracking up."[44] In *Declaration*, John Osborne, Kenneth Tynan, and Lindsay Anderson all link the crisis of the national culture to Britain's explosion of a hydrogen bomb in 1957.[45] Hoggart, too, remarks on the loss of

[41] Sprague, *"The Golden Notebook:* In Whose or What Great Tradition?" 83. On lesbianism as reflex of the battle of the sexes in *The Golden Notebook,* see Rich 182. "Opening *The Golden Notebook,*" 12–13, quotes Jan Clausen, Eleanor Broner, and Mary Gordon on the novel's homophobia.

[42] See Weeks chap. 12.

[43] Greene, *Changing the Story,* 120. On the crack-up, see also Rubenstein; Draine; Hite; Kauffman; and Boone, *Libidinal Currents.*

[44] Lessing, "Doris Lessing at Stony Brook," 65.

[45] Osborne, "They Call It Cricket," 66; Tynan, "Theatre and Living," 111–12; Anderson, "Get Out and Push!" 175.

"order, values, limits"; he seeks in the personal (authentic feeling) a remedy for the disintegration of community.[46]

In the first two-thirds of *The Golden Notebook*, the theme of the crack-up or breakdown is elaborated in the novel's representation of national and global politics. Soviet-inspired Communism, European colonialism and imperialism, British society, and national liberation struggles in the Third World are disintegrating, collapsing, crumbling, fragmenting under pressures both internal and external. The last third of the novel relocates the crack-up in the person, or psyche, of Anna herself.[47] Anna's crack-up is provoked by and enacted in her relationship with Saul Green. Saul induces in Anna an anxiety "like a crack in a substance through which something else pours through" (478). Anna fuses with Saul, as they struggle "to refuse entrance to alien personalities wanting to invade [them]" (532). The trope of invasion by aliens is a staple of the paranoid rhetoric of cold war popular culture in such films as *The Invasion of the Body Snatchers* (1956): it marks Anna as a product of her time.

The painful episode of the crack-up abruptly comes to an end when Anna and Saul each write the sentence that begins the other's novel. Anna gives Saul a sentence about a soldier in Algeria; Saul orders Anna to write what we know to be the first sentence of "Free Women": "The two women were alone in the London flat" (547–49). The novel that each goes on to produce loosely conforms to conventions of gender and genre in which war is a male province and "private life" is a female domain; these conventions are destabilized by the feminine genealogy of his text and the masculine genealogy of hers.[48] The exchange of sentences and the novels produced by the exchange effect an equivocal resolution of the crack-up. Writing, as process, might be a means of healing a wounded psyche or a fragmented society, but the written products—Anna's notebooks, her novel "Free Women," and Saul's novel about Algeria—reflect fundamental divisions that cannot be healed.

The end of *The Golden Notebook* represents Anna as a citizen of the British welfare state, a middle-class, heterosexual, female British subject. Because it treats Anna as Anna-Molly and as Anna-Saul, it constructs a self who is always also other than or other to herself. At the same time, it dramatizes the process of subject formation theorized by Louis Althusser. At the end of the novel, Anna is "interpellated"—or, as Althusser explains this word, hailed, called into being, recruited by

[46] Hoggart, *Uses of Literacy*, 161, 165.

[47] On the relationship between personal (psychosexual) and global versions of the crack-up, see Hite 62; Kauffman 140–41; and Greene, *Changing the Story*, 120.

[48] See Kauffman on gender in the novel as a "writing effect" (151).

and hence transformed—as a subject of ideologies of (British) identity.[49] The "individual" known as "Anna Wulf" is produced as a split subject at once integrated with British life and profoundly alienated from the national culture anatomized in the novel we have just read.

As a Woman, I Have No Country

I want now to shift my focus to the novel's placement of women in the political landscape it describes. The location or dislocation of Anna (and her stand-ins) is not just a sign of the ruptured subjectivity called into being by the working of ideology. Nor is it simply a product of the "double narrative movement," the conflict between the performative and the pedagogical, that Bhabha characterizes as "dissemination." Rather, it inscribes women's marginal position in a political—and discursive—space in which men realize, frustrate, or are otherwise associated with the ambitions of a nation or of transnational geopolitical entities such as "Europe."

There are three episodes in *The Golden Notebook* that dramatize the radically divergent places of men and women in national (and transnational) polities. In all three episodes, men identify themselves with national or transnational political cultures. Women, in contrast, are situated in a chronotope—a narrative articulation of time and space—defined by gender.[50]

In the first of these episodes (284–85), Anna's lover Michael lists the family members, friends, and political associates he has lost to the Nazi gas chambers and the Communist purges in Czechoslovakia. Attempting to explain his tangled emotions, Michael describes himself as "the history of Europe over the past 20 years." Anna's response is an anger that she defines as "the disease of women in our time . . . the woman's emotion: resentment against injustice, an impersonal poison."[51] Michael connects himself with a particular political history and geography; Anna situates her anger in a discursive space that is a-local, entirely congruent with gender. The two poles of the binary opposition—"the history of Europe," "the disease of women"—are incommensurable, conceptually asymmetrical.

Anna's interchange with Michael is replayed in a conversation with

[49] See Althusser, "Ideology and Ideological State Apparatuses," 173–76.

[50] M. M. Bakhtin defines chronotope "(literally, 'time-space') [as] the intrinsic connectedness of temporal and spatial relationships . . . in literature" ("Forms of Time," 84).

[51] Greene says that *The Golden Notebook* names " 'the disease of women in our time' as a political 'disease' " (*Changing the Story*, 110).

Saul Green (494). Saul asserts that his "character was formed by Armstrong, Bechet and Bessie Smith" and says that what happened to it "is what has happened to America." Anna counters: "You say, I am what I am because the United States is such and such politically, I am the United States. And I say, I am the position of women in our time." Once again, the man identifies himself with a nation or a national culture (the United States, jazz), and the woman defines herself as coterminous with a gender that cuts across or erodes national boundaries.

The third episode appears in Anna's unfinished novel, "The Shadow of the Third." When Ella shows Paul the novel that she is writing, he says, "Don't you know what the great revolution of our time is? The Russian revolution, the Chinese revolution—they're nothing at all. The real revolution is, women against men" (184). The politics of class and nation, figured here in the Russian and Chinese Revolutions, is once again set against the sexual politics that pits "women against men." But the opposition between women and nationality is undermined by the regress of text within text within text and by Paul's ironic tone.[52] This irony invites us to ask whether the "revolution of women against men" substitutes for, trivializes, or repeats—that is, mimics—revolutions such as the Russian and Chinese that have (always) already been corrupted.

The antagonism between woman and nation dramatized in these episodes is also called into question in *The Golden Notebook*. The novel explores the circumstances that integrate women with or divide them from "British life"—it delineates the pedagogical imperatives of which women are the object—and it speculates about the consequences of integration and alienation alike. In the process, it inscribes itself in contemporary debates about the national culture and the crisis of postwar reconstruction and produces itself as an instance of performative nationality, a British (women's) novel.

Integrated with British Life?

This reading of *The Golden Notebook* as an intervention in national debates attempts to recuperate women as actors on the national scene. It exposes critical lacunae—the invisibility of women, the erasure of gender—in traditional treatments of nationalism such as Benedict Anderson's *Imagined Communities* and E. J. Hobsbawm's *Nations and Nationalism*. At the same time, it re-places *The Golden Notebook* in a political context from which it was perforce severed when it was read and

[52] On Paul's irony, see Sprague, *Rereading Doris Lessing*, 74–76.

discussed in the academy—in the United States, at least—as a feminist text.[53]

Since the early 1970s, in panels at conferences, in the work of the Doris Lessing Society, in the *Doris Lessing Newsletter,* and in essays and books, including the Kaplan and Rose volume on *The Golden Notebook* in the Modern Language Association's "Approaches to Teaching" series, scholars and critics have considered the novel from several perspectives that treat it as a woman writer's representation of women's experience.[54] The canonization of *The Golden Notebook,* in the name of a feminism grounded in unexamined ideas about women's experience and a feminist criticism that takes as its object feminine style, is ironic, given Lessing's repudiation of feminist intent and her reluctance to identify *The Golden Notebook* as women's writing. Yet the novel does offer a powerful critique of gender. A similar critique underwrites the conservatism of the novels—*The Good Terrorist,* the pseudonymous *Diaries of Jane Somers, The Fifth Child*—that Lessing wrote and published during the Thatcher period. These novels remind us that the recovery of gender as a category of analysis sometimes involves the suppression of narratives of race, class, sexual orientation, and nationality.

But the same can be said of national affiliation. Lessing has recently described herself as a British—not postcolonial, "Commonwealth," transnational, or woman—novelist.[55] As we shall see in the next chapter, *The Good Terrorist* and *The Fifth Child* affirm this identity by examining Britain in the 1980s.

[53] On the reception of Lessing, especially by feminists, see Kaplan and Rose, "Genealogy of Readings" and "Power of the Common Reader."

[54] These critics examined the novel through the protocols of "gynocritics," "models based on the study of female experience" (Showalter, "Toward a Feminist Poetics," 131). See, for example, "Opening *The Golden Notebook,*" and Kaplan and Rose, "A Genealogy of Readings." On experience as a constructed historical category, see J. Scott, "Evidence of Experience."

[55] See Sprague, "Doris Lessing at the New School."

5

Reading Doris Lessing with Margaret Thatcher: *The Good Terrorist, The Fifth Child,* and England in the 1980s

The established framework of British politics has, since the mid-sixties, been steadily eroded. The expressions are numerous: the precipitous decline of Britain as an international power including the collapse of the Empire and imperial role together with consequent realignments, the emergence of new national tensions within Britain, powerful working-class militancy, persistent and chronic economic crisis, a new social challenge from women and now a growing threat to the post-1945 achievements of full employment, the welfare state, and the nationalised sector. These developments have weakened the previous class and social alignments, provoked a growing crisis of hegemony, and challenged the established structures, assumptions, and ideologies of the right and left in British politics.

—Martin Jacques, "Thatcherism: Breaking Out of the Impasse"

The Good Terrorist (1985) and *The Fifth Child* (1988) explore a perceived crisis in British national culture in the Thatcher era. Both novels challenge the "established structures, assumptions, and ideologies of the right and left in British politics." In both novels, some women— white, middle-class, heterosexual women—are moral agents who oppose the most venial aspects of a corrupt and corrupting national culture. Yet in presenting these women as defenders of a nation under siege by enemies intent on destroying it, the two novels rehearse some of the constitutive features of Thatcherism and reproduce the "crisis of hegemony" that Martin Jacques describes. The ideological and narrative incoherence of both novels raises questions not only about their representation of Thatcher's England but also about the larger consequences of Thatcher's dismantling of the postwar consensus described in *The Golden Notebook* and *In Pursuit of the English.*

The Daughter of the (Not-)Good-Enough Mother; or, Margaret Thatcher through the Looking Glass

The Good Terrorist, like *In Pursuit of the English*, is an urban, dystopian updating of the house-as-England genre. Once again, England is represented by a house in London, specifically a "squat" that is occupied by an obscure left-wing sect. Like Joseph Conrad's *The Secret Agent*, Henry James's *The Princess Casamassima*, and Fyodor Dostoevsky's *The Possessed*, *The Good Terrorist* is a political novel or, more precise, a novel about politics that calls into question the authenticity of political beliefs, the efficacy of political actions, and the possibility of agency. At the same time, it recalls such woman-centered novels as *Mansfield Park* and *Howards End*, in which the female protagonist suggests a potential alternative to a morally bankrupt national culture. These two traditions are spliced together in *The Good Terrorist*, in which the alternatives to Thatcherism are virtual imitations or mirror images of the thing itself and in which once significant distinctions—between the Left and the Right, anarchist and communist, middle class and working class—break down.

Stuart Hall has argued that the crisis of the British state in the 1980s takes the form of a "fracturing of traditional ideologies" and a "crisis of political representation" that find their fulfillment in the "authoritarian populism" of Thatcherism.[1] *The Good Terrorist* is both a response to and a symptom of this crisis of representation. It exposes the devastating effects of Britain's economic decline on what remains of its working class and the deformation of men and women alike by misogyny in particular and by the ideological hegemony of patriarchy in general. Yet it distorts the political landscape of Britain in the 1980s by ignoring or discrediting the new social movements of gays, blacks, and women that arose during this period in opposition to policies identified with Thatcher.[2]

The main character of *The Good Terrorist* is Alice Mellings. Middle class in origins, college educated, downwardly mobile, and emotionally arrested in a state of perpetual adolescence, Alice is a member of

[1] Stuart Hall defines "authoritarian populism" as a form of the capitalist state that "retained most . . . formal representative institutions in place, and . . . construct[ed] around itself an active, popular consent." Thatcherism "condense[s] at the negative pole statism, bureaucracy, social democracy, and 'creeping collectivism' " and values individual initiative. See "Great Moving Right Show," 22, and "Popular-Democratic vs. Authoritarian Populism," 142.

[2] I thank Catherine Hall for urging me, in a response to a version of this chapter presented at the Berkshire Conference of Women Historians at Vassar College, June 1993, to consider the novel in the context of new social movements.

the Communist Centre Union (CCU), a minuscule, would-be militant sect whose political program is not spelled out. Lessing's Alice, like Lewis Carroll's, is passive—things happen to her—but she is also assertive, although her assertiveness does not result in meaningful action.[3] Alice's life in the squat is a bizarre parody of bourgeois domesticity and "feminine" (maternal) nurturance. She cleans, repairs, and renovates the house; furnishes it by stealing money from her wealthy father and recycling the detritus of her mother's life; cooks wholesome food for the group; and drifts aimlessly from one political project to another.

As Flo's boardinghouse symbolizes a nation in the process of being reconstructed after the war, the squat represents England in the Thatcher period. The very existence of the squat might be seen as the result of Thatcher's policy of privatization in the field of housing. This policy enabled some in the middle class to purchase council houses they had previously rented, while rendering many homeless.[4] The consequences of Thatcher's housing policy are illustrated in films of the period. In Mike Leigh's *High Hopes* (1988), a gentrifying, upper-class couple buy and renovate a council flat after displacing its working-class occupants. They urge an old woman who lives next door— Leigh's version of the traditional working class in its death throes—to fix up her house or sell it, but she has nowhere else to go. In the Hanif Kureishi and Stephen Frears film *Sammy and Rosie Get Laid* (1987), squatters are violently removed from an area slated to be bulldozed for development. Lessing's CCU claims to be occupying the squat in protest against the housing shortage created by Thatcher's policies. But its protest, like most political discourse in the novel, is more an eruption of sheer rage than a substantive demand for justice.

The inhabitants of the squat are a polyglot, multiethnic group. In Homi Bhabha's conceptualization of "dissemination," the national narrative encompasses cultural hybridity, minority discourse, and difference itself. The squat, though, is a grotesque parody of identity politics and cultural diversity.[5] Its dominant ethos is a competitive individualism that, despite the CCU's professions of communist solidarity, pits each against all.

[3] On echoes of Carroll in Lessing, see Lurie, "Bad Housekeeping," and V. Scott, "Doris Lessing's Modern Alice in Wonderland."

[4] On Thatcher's housing policy, see Murie, "Housing and the Environment," and Gough, "Thatcherism and the Welfare State," esp. 152–53.

[5] I am following Bhabha's distinction between cultural diversity, "an epistemological object . . . an object of empirical knowledge," and cultural difference, "the process of the *enunciation* of culture as 'knowledge*able*' " ("Commitment to Theory," 34).

Members of different identity groups—gays, lesbians, the white working class, women, blacks—barely coexist. There is no sense that they might actually cooperate or work as a coalition, as, for example, in *Sammy and Rosie Get Laid*, in which politics across difference is dramatized in protests against police brutality and urban renewal and envisioned in extravagantly utopian scenes of interracial sexual coupling. The different groups represented in *The Good Terrorist* have little in common except for the fact that they all see themselves as victims of a system that they cannot explain. The working-class characters, especially, seem to be blinded by a "false consciousness" that makes them incapable either of understanding their situation except as it appears in the eyes (ideology) of the dominant culture or of changing it.[6]

The novel's treatment of class is ambiguous. On the one hand, *The Good Terrorist* represents class as the master narrative of social relations; on the other, it laments the demise of class as a conceptual category and of class consciousness as a motivation for political action. Lessing seems to be directing her irony at "revolutionaries" in thrall to obsolete notions of class; thus, the novel satirizes the bogus class politics of the CCU. But she also presents class as the only possible signifier of political authenticity and as the object of nostalgia for an earlier era. In the England of *The Good Terrorist*, class has little or no meaning, yet there is no formative concept or category other than class, no narrative to give shape to experience, and no new "structure of feeling" in which people might understand themselves and their place in society. The oscillation between satire and nostalgia is responsible for the narrative incoherence of the novel's represented world.

One of the working-class inhabitants of the squat is a young black man named Jim. As if in a travesty of British imperial relations, the CCU members attempt to subject him to the discipline of the group, but he resists their efforts of colonization. Unlike the inhabitants of Flo and Dan's boardinghouse or the New Commonwealth immigrants in the immediate postwar years, Jim is the real thing, a "genuine cockney" (32). In presenting Jim as a cockney, Lessing challenges the equation of Britishness with whiteness that underpins Enoch Powell's "new racism."[7] But the novel also belies the experience of black Londoners in the 1970s and 1980s who were, as Paul Gilroy observes, "Cockney by birth and experience (technical Cockneys)" but "denied . . . access to the social category established by the language which real (i.e. white) Cockneys spoke."[8] Jim experiences the working-class identity

---

[6] Lessing's earlier Marxism leaves traces in the rendering of the characters' "false consciousness."

[7] See A. M. Smith, *New Right Discourse on Race and Sexuality*, esp. chaps. 1 and 4.

[8] Gilroy, *There Ain't No Black in the Union Jack*, 194–95.

that makes him a "genuine cockney" as a source of his victimization. Presented as the pawn of middle-class individuals such as Alice and as the passive victim of impersonal social forces that disempower and dispossess him, Jim is exploited equally by those, like Alice's father, Cedric, who grew wealthy under Thatcher and by those who claim to represent him—Alice, the CCU, the bankrupt Left. Throughout, Jim plays forlornly on his "Caribbean drum." The drum might be a token of the black expressive culture that Gilroy documents, but in *The Good Terrorist*, it is a sign of his powerlessness and a shabby substitute for meaningful politics or a real job.[9]

Another working-class occupant of the squat is a chronically unemployed and essentially unemployable laborer named Philip. In the novel's schematic mapping of the nation, Philip exemplifies the deskilled worker made redundant, in the telling British phrase, by the decline of British capitalism and the collapse (or Thatcherite restructuring) of the economy. Philip might be the son, or grandson, of *In Pursuit of the English*'s construction workers. Like them, he is supposed to be shoring up a rotting structure, a house that stands for England. But while they resist hard work, he is incapable of it, and he utterly lacks their camaraderie. The emotional isolation and passivity of Philip and Jim appear highly tendentious when juxtaposed with the portrait of casual labor in London in Ken Loach's *Riff Raff* (1993). In this film, men from Glasgow, Bristol, Dublin, Liverpool, and Nigeria and a Londoner who was born in Jamaica forge ties of solidarity and friendship across differences of race, religion, regional or national location, and generation.

A third working-class inhabitant of the house, and the only working-class member of the CCU, is Faye, a lesbian who seeks in her lover, Roberta, the mothering of which she was deprived as a child. Like the male Communists in *The Golden Notebook*, Faye petulantly uses her working-class background to manipulate the middle-class leftists with whom she associates. Suicidally depressed, Faye bungles her part in a CCU bomb plot, perhaps intentionally, and causes it to go awry.

Alice is the main target of the novel's attack on a politics waged—by do-gooding members of the middle class—on behalf of a disappearing working class. Her ineffectual schemes suggest the failures of the "social responsibility" about which the narrator of *In Pursuit of the English* is ambivalent and of the "welfare work" undertaken by Anna at the end of *The Golden Notebook*. Alice herself comes from a proper middle-class home, yet she trashes the bourgeois tendencies and origins of her

---

[9] Ibid., chap. 5. See also Baker, Diawara, and Lindeborg, eds., *Black British Cultural Studies*.

"comrades" and touts an illusory working-class solidarity. She sympathizes with Philip and Jim, whom she sees as "victims," but at the same
time, she disdains their inaptitude for hard work and lack of political
commitment.

Like Jim and Philip, virtually everyone in the house is dominated by
the middle-class men and women, ersatz communists, who make up
the "leadership" of the CCU. Insofar as most of the house's inhabitants
are oppressed by those who claim to speak and act for them, the house
is a mirror image of the dominant (national) culture that it purports
to be opposing or a metaphor—a microcosm—of the nation itself.
Lessing's most scathing satire is directed at the male "heavies" in the
organization, middle-class men who take up working-class accents as
a way of demonstrating their political bona fides.[10] Alice is smitten
with one of these men, Jasper, and supports him by giving him her
dole. She puts up with his physical cruelty and emotional brutality and
craves attention, sexual and otherwise, which he takes a sadistic pleasure in withholding from her. Uninterested in Alice, Jasper gets his
kicks by cruising the gay underworld or attaching himself to self-
styled revolutionaries, to the Irish Republican Army, or to real Communists from the Soviet Union.

The CCU, like Benedict Anderson's nation, is a "deep horizontal comradeship . . . a fraternity" (*Imagined Communities*, 16) that women wish
to join as equal partners but cannot. Alice's relationship with Jasper recalls Anna's involvement in *The Golden Notebook* with male Communists
and with Communism. As in the earlier novel, Lessing takes aim at
women who collude in male-dominant political organizations and thus
in their own oppression. Like *The Golden Notebook*, *The Good Terrorist* exposes the conscription of women's desire in the reproduction and maintenance of male domination. But, once again, the critique of women's
infatuation with patriarchal misogyny and their emotional dependence
on misogynist men is undermined by homophobia. Conflating misogyny with homosexuality, Lessing elides the misogyny pervasive in patriarchal constructions of (male) heterosexuality and mutes the critique
of women's complicity in their own oppression.[11]

Lessing's treatment of the CCU rewrites political commitment as
psychopathology and, ironically inverting the feminist slogan "the
personal is political," stresses the degeneration of the political into the

---

[10] On voice and accent in *The Good Terrorist*, see Scanlan, "Language and the Politics of
Despair."

[11] The depiction of Jasper as a misogynist homosexual is a residue of the 1950s, when
Lessing's own English identity was consolidated. The predominant form of homophobia
in the Thatcher era is "queer bashing." See A. M. Smith 18 and chap. 5.

merely personal. Most of the novel's so-called radicals lack ego boundaries and appear to be fixated in the early stages of infancy that Melanie Klein describes in "Love, Guilt, and Reparation" or in Freud's anal phase. They are literally living in excrement until Alice makes them clean it up or cleans it up for them.[12] The arrested emotional development of the CCU members literalizes V. I. Lenin's metaphorical formulation of left-wing communism as an infantile disorder. Next door to the squat where Alice lives is another house, inhabited by a mysterious Russian, possibly a Soviet agent. But, in another instance of the pattern in *The Good Terrorist* whereby significant differences devolve into dull sameness and political concepts and categories are drained of meaning, the Leninists in one house are virtually indistinguishable from their infantile communist clones in the other.

Absent from the novel, foreclosed by the presentation of politics as the pathological result of inadequate object relations, is a substantive sense of what these self-proclaimed leftists oppose. Unlike other cultural texts from this period, the novel de-emphasizes or ignores altogether those features of the national scene that could be said to have caused the situation it describes.[13] In *High Hopes* and *Sammy and Rosie Get Laid*, among other films, and in two condition-of-England novels, A. S. Byatt's *Possession* (1990) and David Lodge's *Nice Work* (1988), the characters are situated in a sociopolitical terrain whose contours are delineated. These works prominently represent the Yuppie ascendancy, gentrification, urban renewal, racism in the form of panics about mugging, and attacks on trade unions in particular and the working class in general.[14] But in *The Good Terrorist*, these constituents of Thatcherism's dismantling of the postwar settlement are not specified.[15] Or, they appear dimly refracted through the rages of pseudo-communists who are just like real ones.

Alice's compulsion to mother everyone she encounters is an extreme case of psychological regression or failure to thrive. An exemplar of her

[12] Moira Ferguson, in a response to a version of this chapter presented at the 1993 Berkshire Conference, related the novel's excremental vision to Lessing's Sufi mysticism, which identifies the material world as excrement. Boschman reads the excremental vision through Freudian notions of anal fixation ("Excrement and 'Kitsch' "). The slang word *squat*, frequently repeated, also evokes the characters' infantile psychosexual organization.

[13] Perhaps this is what prompts Schor ("Homelessness in the Novel") and Hite (*Other Side of the Story*, 102) to classify *The Good Terrorist* as "postrealist."

[14] On mugging as a racial signifier, see Gilroy, *There Ain't No Black*, chap. 3, and "Police and Thieves"; Solomos, *Race and Racism*, chap. 7; and A. M. Smith 176–77. On Thatcherism's attack on labor, see Stuart Hall, "Great Moving Right Show," 27, and Lane, "Tories and the Trade Unions."

[15] See S. Hall and Jacques, Introduction, 11, and Biddiss, "Thatcherism," 1.

entire generation, Alice represents postimperial Britain as pre-oedipal fixation: she is an agent of Kleinian reparation or the anxious, delinquent child of maternal neglect that John Bowlby and D. W. Winnicott describe. In *The Golden Notebook,* Molly's and Anna's apparent indifference to maternal obligation is also a sign of resistance, on the part of characters and author alike, to the ideological imperatives of pronatalism. In *The Good Terrorist,* however, Lessing's attitude toward maternity is much more ambivalent, perhaps because she focuses on the daughter and not, as in the earlier text, on the mother.

One manifestation of this ambivalence is a shifting or instability in the tone of the novel. Alice is generally depicted through a distancing irony. But in some episodes, the irony collapses, and Alice's perspective fuses, more or less, with that of the novel itself. In one such episode, Alice is "invaded" (261) by memories of the parties that her Labourite parents gave during the boom years of the swinging sixties. On these occasions, she felt cruelly neglected by her parents, especially her mother, Dorothy. As the distance between the narrator's perspective and Alice's disappears, Alice, the needy child unable to separate or grow up, is seen as a victim of Dorothy's not-good-enough mothering, which is presented as a function of her self-indulgent immersion in the swinging London scene.

Here, ironically, the novel makes its closest approach to such staples of Thatcherite ideology as the return to Victorian morality; the assertion of "family values"; the repudiation of the sexual revolution; and the attack on the welfare state for, on the one hand, coddling the nation's citizens and, on the other, robbing the nation and its children of their inheritance.[16] Throughout this episode, Alice's parents, beneficiaries of the economic boom of the 1960s, are identified with the London scene of that decade. In Alice's fragmentary recollections, they follow their own pleasures. Alice—representing her entire generation—is the victim of their greed, dispossessed of her rightful inheritance by their selfish squandering of the nation's wealth. The dismantling of the postwar consensus that extended into the 1960s here takes the form of the fragmenting of the body politic and the disintegration of the national psyche. The site in which this process of disintegration occurs is Alice, who is an image, or incarnation, of England in its postimperial decline.[17]

[16] On Thatcherism as a return to "Victorian" values and a repudiation of the permissive 1960s, see Jenkins, *Mrs. Thatcher's Revolution,* 67; S. Hall, "Great Moving Right Show," 28, and "No Light at the End of the Tunnel," 83; and Crewe, "Values: The Crusade That Failed," 243. For Thatcher's attack on the welfare state, see Gough.

[17] Lurie suggests that Alice is a "personification of England itself" (10).

Dorothy is not only a rejecting and withholding mother who cannot or will not gratify her daughter's needs. She is also an overbearing, devouring mother who inhibits the development of autonomy in her daughter. Readers may well be exasperated—as Dorothy is—by Alice's utter lack of autonomy. But the exasperation might be mitigated by the mother's unwillingness or inability to let the daughter go. Dorothy's shortcomings, like Alice's, have a public and political, as well as a "private," psychological resonance.

The national family romance in Christina Stead's *The Man Who Loved Children,* as I argue in Chapter 1, is a battle of the sexes in which the father and mother represent different—Australian and American—national cultures and diverse traditions within each national culture. The national family romance in *The Good Terrorist* is a Thatcherite allegory. In this generational saga, the children are smothered by a maternal welfare state that does not permit them to develop initiative and consequently makes them unable to compete in the marketplace. As Stuart Hall observes, "The discourse of the 'spendthrift state,' recklessly giving away wealth the nation has not earned . . . and thereby undermining the self-reliance of ordinary people . . . produces as its discursive opposite, the 'welfare scrounger,' living off society, never doing a day's work."[18]

Lessing moderates any judgment a reader might render against Dorothy, however. Dorothy, long since divorced from her husband, Cedric, loses the flat where Alice grew up. For several years, Alice and Jasper had lived there, sponging off Dorothy and using their dole to support the CCU, until she eventually kicked them out because she couldn't pay the rent. From Dorothy's perspective, Alice—like Ben, the title character of *The Fifth Child*—is a selfish monster who sucks the life out of a long-suffering, oppressed mother.[19] Dorothy is angry because Alice does not use the university education that she herself, working class in origin, never had. She says that she wanted the best for Alice (404–9). That she cannot realize her hopes for her daughter—or realize her own hopes through her daughter?—suggests, again, the predicament of the mother in a society hostile to women and their aspirations.[20]

The association of Dorothy with the postwar welfare state is destabi-

---

[18] S. Hall, "Popular-Democratic vs. Authoritarian Populism," 144–45. On the welfare state as target of the radical Right, see also Gough 154.

[19] Whether the mother or the child is the exploiter may be a function of vantage point. Gardiner *(Rhys, Stead, Lessing),* Hirsch *(Mother/Daughter Plot),* and Sprengnether *(Spectral Mother)* discuss the maternal position as a new perspective for women writers.

[20] See *Under My Skin* on mothers—specifically Lessing's own mother, once the object of Lessing's rage—as products of systemic social hostility.

lized by other identifications that work at cross-purposes to it and to each other. Dorothy is fused, in Alice's thoughts and feelings and those of her comrades, with the figure of Margaret Thatcher, the personification of British power and castrating, punitive motherhood. The "Iron Mom," as Michael Biddiss puts it (8), is the target for a demonstration that consists entirely of "shouting and screaming at Maggie Thatcher" (284). By assimilating Thatcher to Dorothy as the object of Alice's rage, Lessing short-circuits anger at Thatcherism—that is, at the policies that can be said to have caused, or exacerbated, the situation the novel describes.

The identification of Dorothy with Thatcher is as unstable as that of Dorothy with the swinging sixties. Dorothy also suggests the author herself.[21] Like Lessing, Dorothy was once a leftist; she now repudiates her earlier left-wing politics (409–12). Dorothy's values—the values of liberal socialist humanism tinged with a mild feminism—offer an alternative to Thatcherism, on the one hand, and an obsolete, discredited leftism—like the Communism that Anna leaves behind in *The Golden Notebook*—on the other. Dorothy's values resemble those of Lessing, or at least the Lessing who sees in the feminine an alternative to a decadent social order and a Left in disarray.[22] The fact that Dorothy evokes such radically contradictory figures and political formations as Doris Lessing, Margaret Thatcher, and the swinging 1960s London scene might be a manifestation of the novel's rejection or subversion of conventional political categories such as right and left. But it is also a sign of ideological incoherence, a symptom of the crisis of representation that Stuart Hall identifies in the popular and political discourse of the time.

The Good Terrorist ends abruptly with a bomb plot botched by the CCU. Alice loses her nerve and, unbeknownst to the rest of the group, phones in the bomb threat. She survives the explosion, and the very end of the novel finds her awaiting a meeting with Soviet-backed terrorists from the house next door and with a British intelligence agent. Alice's passivity and emotional dependence make her vulnerable to exploitation by real, uppercase, Communists or by the British state. One could read Alice's situation and Alice herself as the product of Althusserian overdetermination: the decline of British power after empire; the collapse of the British economy; the demise of the working

---

[21] Lurie (10) and Scanlan (195) note the resemblance between Dorothy and Lessing.

[22] A version of this Lessing appears in Jane Somers, the pseudonymous author of and main character in Lessing's two rather conventionally feminine novels, *The Diary of a Good Neighbour* (1983) and *If the Old Could* (1984). See Gardiner, *Rhys, Stead, Lessing*, 116–17, and Hite 102.

class as an actor on the political stage and hence of orthodox Marxist class analysis as an interpretive framework; and the infantile psychosexual constellation and inadequate object relations induced in women by patriarchal constructions of the mother-daughter relationship and reinforced by patriarchal politics left, right, and center. Or, as I have been doing, one could read Alice's situation as a set of ideological contradictions that produce narrative incoherence. Like *The Golden Notebook*, *The Good Terrorist* suggests that relations of gender, as well as those of race and class, must be rearranged, reformed, revolutionized. Yet this insight is radically and repeatedly undermined by the slippage of the satire on Thatcherism into Thatcherite shibboleths.

The Enemy Within; or, England's Hideous Progeny

And now, once again, I bid my hideous progeny go forth and prosper.
I have an affection for it, for it was the offspring of my happy days, when
death and grief were but words, which found no true echo in my heart.
—Mary Shelley, 1831 introduction to *Frankenstein*

In *The Fifth Child*, England is once again represented as a house that simultaneously stands for the nation—it is "gloomy and detestable, like England" (13)—and stands in opposition to a morally bankrupt national culture. Here, the house-as-England genre is grafted onto a gothic science fiction tale: *Howards End* meets *Frankenstein*. The house in *The Fifth Child* is the home of a proper English family, but like the squat in *The Good Terrorist*, it is also a scene of tensions and competing and shifting alliances. The novel elaborates a critique of gender that simultaneously reproduces and subverts Thatcherite discourses on gender and family. Thus, the ideological and narrative incoherence of *The Good Terrorist* is intensified in *The Fifth Child*.

The Fifth Child chronicles the family life of Harriet and David Lovatt. Throughout the late 1960s, 1970s, and into the 1980s, Harriet and David see their family as a bulwark against moral corruption: their notion of family closely parallels the Thatcherite conception of the family as the site of moral renewal.[23] The Lovatts try to resist the ordinary challenges posed by a debased national culture and the extraordinary challenge posed by their monstrous fifth child. In describing the shifting fortunes of the Lovatt family, *The Fifth Child* raises questions about

[23] See Gamble, "Thatcherism and Conservative Politics," 121.

the grounds of morality in an immoral age. The chief narrative agent of this interrogation is the character of Harriet.

David and Harriet, an old-fashioned couple, marry soon after they meet. Four children are born in six years, perhaps too many too soon even for the Lovatts, but contraception and abortion, which was legalized in Britain in 1967, are not in their game plan. Harriet is exhausted, and the salary David earns as an architect cannot quite support them, but they manage with the financial assistance of David's wealthy father, James, and the domestic assistance—that is, the unpaid, unproductive labor—of Harriet's mother, Dorothy. In this generational national story, the Lovatts' fragile domestic idyll depends on the capital accumulated by their parents, who represent the British middle and upper-middle classes. James's wealth derives from shipbuilding, once an industry crucial to Britain's imperial power but now, in the present moment from which the novel is retrospectively narrated, the source of yachts for a leisure class that has grown increasingly wealthy in the Thatcher years.

The Lovatts cope, until Harriet becomes pregnant with their fifth child. From the very beginning, this pregnancy differs from the others. Harriet is "frantic, exhausted . . . peevish" and fears that the fetus kicking in her womb is poisoning her (32). When a son is born, he is huge, monstrous, subhuman, yet of superhuman strength. This child, Ben, soon takes up all Harriet's energies. In just the first two or three years of his life, he nurses so violently that he bruises her breasts; he kills a dog with his bare hands; he threatens his next-older brother, Paul; and he climbs to an open window and is about to jump out when Harriet rescues him. She soon bars the windows to his room, turning it into a kind of prison.

Eventually, David's mother, Molly, and stepfather, Frederick, Oxbridge types who represent the moral nullity of the traditional cultural elite, persuade David that Ben must be institutionalized. At first Harriet demurs: *"He's our child,"* she says, but David replies, "He certainly isn't mine" (74). Harriet acquiesces, but soon visits Ben in a holding pen where "freaks" and "monsters," products of genetic mutations (81), are drugged, starved, warehoused, and expected to expire. When she sees him unconscious, straitjacketed, and lying in his own excrement, she brings him home. He is now the feral child he only seemed to be before, but she controls him by threatening to return him to the institution. The novel suggests that British society, for which the Lovatt family is a microcosm, cannot be maintained by liberal values such as tolerance and civility or by traditionally feminine values of nurturance but rather through violence or the threat of violence; the survival of tolerance requires that the vicious impulses of Ben and others like him are purged or brought under control.

After Ben is brought back, the family disintegrates. Soon, this "invader of their ordinariness" (58) displaces the "real" children and makes the Lovatt home so unpleasant that members of the family no longer gather there for holidays. The older children go to boarding school; Harriet neglects the next youngest, the hypersensitive Paul, who suffers badly. David works long hours because he can't stand to be at home, and Harriet is more or less left alone with Ben. Unable to care for him herself, she engages an unemployed, alienated, motorcycle-driving tough to do so. Ben attends a school where he learns virtually nothing and gets into all kinds of trouble. At the end of the novel, he takes up with a gang of delinquents, who go off to unnamed places to engage in riot and rape and then return to occupy Harriet's house. Under their dominion, what was once the quintessence of England becomes a travesty of postcolonial, postmodern, transnational commodity culture, represented in the array of multinational fast foods they consume.

The focus of this highly schematic plot is the title character, Ben. Like Alice in *The Good Terrorist*, Ben is the principal site of ideological contradictions that fracture the narrative. But unlike Alice, who is ambiguously sympathetic, Ben draws the reader's sympathy only fleetingly, if at all. He threatens what little remains of bourgeois civility. Yet Lessing forbids readers to interpret him as a social type or to read the novel as social commentary or moral fable. Rather, she claims that Ben is absolute evil and that *The Fifth Child* is a "horror story."[24] The novel itself suggests that Ben's monstrosity is inexplicable or at least that it is not susceptible to traditional—psychological, sociological, historical—modes of analysis. His kicking in the womb cannot be the result of bad parenting, and the ravenous appetite and unchecked aggression that distinguish him from the other children are similarly unmediated by prior experience. But at the same time, the novel describes Ben through conventions of characterization that underwrite both English social novels and the interpretive protocols—the very protocols that the author forbids us to use—by means of which we understand them.

Throughout, Ben is imagined as a kind of absolute alterity. He is not a "performative subject" of national or any other kind of identity. Rather, he is the ultimate "pedagogical object," constituted by the novel's narrative of nationality—its association of the family or the

[24] Rothstein, "Doris Lessing and Her 'Fifth Child,'" C19; Sinkler, "Goblins and Bad Girls."

house with England—as ineluctably other or different.[25] Ben plays havoc with the categories of analysis and signifying systems (class, race, gender, history) through which we read English novels and decode the cultural text of contemporary England itself. But, ironically, because he is purely an object of conjecture, like a screen on which people—other characters, the narrator, readers—project their own thoughts and feelings, he becomes a figure in the sociolects of everyone from his parents to the custodians of English culture and society: doctors, police, social workers, and school officials. The tangle of self- and mutually contradictory explanations leads to an interpretive gridlock, like that in the denouement of the Mashopi episode of *The Golden Notebook*. The only credible interpretation of Ben is that he cannot be explained at all or that he is an eruption of unmediated evil or ineffable otherness.

Yet, paradoxically, it is precisely this ineffable otherness that connects him to a significant social narrative of the period. When Harriet is pregnant, she thinks of the fetus as a "savage thing inside her" (41) and feels herself invaded by an alien, an outsider, an enemy. The figure of the alien invader is a crucial component of exclusionary notions of national identity advanced by Enoch Powell and other proponents of the "new racism." In the late 1960s and 1970s, the "dark stranger" that Chris Waters traces in the race relations discourse of the postwar period is replaced by the figure of the "enemy within," and "crime" displaces "immigration" as a signifier of race.[26] Restrictions set in place by the 1962 Commonwealth Immigrants Bill and subsequent legislation resulted in a decrease in immigration from Asia, Africa, and the Caribbean, but many New Commonwealth immigrants remained in England, along with their children and grandchildren. The figure of the "enemy within" is a discursive strategy that enabled Powell to exclude blacks—immigrants and their children who settled in England—from his version of a national community in which Britishness is identified with whiteness.[27]

In the national narrative that unfolds in *The Fifth Child*, the alien invader, a version of the enemy within, is Ben—that is, the discursive construction of Ben's difference reproduces the discursive construction

---

[25] On the performative and the pedagogical, see Bhabha, "DissemiNation," 145–46.

[26] Waters, " 'Dark Strangers' "; Solomos 62–63; Gilroy, *There Ain't No Black*, 45. Powell delivered his "enemies within" speech during the 1970 election campaign (A. M. Smith 163).

[27] See also Goulbourne, *Ethnicity and Nationalism*, 1. Gilroy explains that "the new racism" makes "the limits of 'race' . . . coincide . . . precisely with national frontiers" (*There Ain't No Black*, 46).

of racial difference common to Powellite "new racism" and Thatcherite ideology. In the England of *The Fifth Child*, Ben plays a part analogous to that ascribed to blacks by Powell. As an alien invader, he embodies a threat like the one that Thatcher brings to the attention of the nation in the speech, made during the run-up to the 1979 election, in which she warns that England is in danger of being "swamped by people with a different culture," enemies who have no ties to and no respect for British cultural traditions.[28] Ben not only colonizes the body of the mother—the mother country, the body politic that Harriet represents in this version of the national fable—but also displaces the "real" children who belong in ways that he never can. As an enemy within who attacks the culture of postimperial Britain, Ben also suggests a return of the colonial repressed, akin to the voices who announce on posters in England in the 1970s, "We are here because you were there."

Lessing's version of alterity differs from Powell's in one important way. For Powell, racial difference is cultural but nonetheless absolute, whereas Ben's otherness is a product of genetic, not cultural, inscription. Among the words used to describe Ben are "Neanderthal," "goblin," "dwarf," "troll," "changeling," and "throwback"; the word *kind* is used to signify his biologized otherness.[29] Yet despite the characterization of Ben as a genetic throwback, the novel echoes the Thatcher-Powell sense that the "enemy" is a creature whose utter difference from the English (or the British) cannot be bridged. In this, Ben constitutes a departure from the members of the CCU, who still make use of a recognizably English vocabulary of class, even though it no longer has any descriptive or explanatory power. Ben's "tribe" (121), the flotsam of Thatcher's England, consists of skinheads, punks, Asians, and consumers of multinational popular culture; the message of the novel is that, like Ben, they do not belong.

There is in *The Fifth Child* no place for cultural hybrids, or hybrid cultures; rather, the novel features a rhetoric of "us" besieged by a menacing "him" or "them." Yet at the same moment at which Lessing was writing the novel, cultural hybridity was being examined in theoretical studies by Bhabha, Gilroy, and others, and hybrid cultures, celebrated in both imaginative and theoretical works. In *Sammy and Rosie Get Laid*, a mixed group of Afro-Caribbean and white singers serenade the mainly black squatters with a reggae-inflected rendition of the Temptations' Motown hit "My Girl": this performance exemplifies both

---

[28] Quoted in A. M. Smith 179–80.
[29] See, for example, in Lessing, *The Fifth Child*, 53, 49, 56, 59, 106. See Chapter 8 for a discussion of the different usage of the word *kind* in Gordimer's *My Son's Story*.

Gilroy's notion of a diasporic culture of the "black Atlantic" and Bhabha's idea of "dissemination." In Loach's *Riff Raff*, construction workers are hired to renovate a house in London. The workers, illegals from all over the British Isles, initially quarrel with one another, with factions formed predictably on the basis of region and race. But eventually, as the men work together and suffer and protest against exploitation by their employers, they develop cohesion and solidarity. After one of the men—a black man—is killed when he falls off a roof that has not been secured, two of the others—whites from Glasgow and Bristol—torch the site. In this apocalyptic ending, the purging of the old looks toward a new, multiracial Britain. Despite the bleak economic picture, with thousands out of work, *Riff Raff* shows us class solidarity and affective ties achieved across differences of race and culture. Loach's utopian vision of brotherhood, even though tenuous, is a bracing corrective to *The Fifth Child*'s portrait of an England under siege by an alien horde.

The novel's rejection of what is seen as alien is not monolithic. Harriet, unlike the others, accepts or at least acknowledges the "enemy": in this respect, she is the vehicle of a gender critique consistent with that in Lessing's earlier work. Harriet not only bears witness to social corruption and cultural decadence, she also sets herself apart, insisting that nurturance is both an obligation and a positive value. Harriet assumes responsibility for Ben even though she is repulsed by him. After she retrieves him from the institution, she civilizes him, and when the other family members disperse, she remains in the house with him. Yet the novel calls into question Harriet's capacity to enforce her morality.

Harriet is held responsible for Ben and for the damage he does: the displacement of her "real" children; the destruction of her family and her home; and the decline, or demise, of the England that home and family represent. A mother's care, the novel suggests quite unsentimentally, cannot preserve the family—or the nation—against its enemies. A mother's care might destroy the very order it is supposed to preserve. In making a place for Ben, Harriet harbors the enemy within, protecting the savage who will destroy a civilization that has been built up over hundreds of years.

The tensions and contradictions that fracture *The Fifth Child* are more than a symptom of the crisis of representation that Stuart Hall identifies. They also ask us to consider the racial history distorted or suppressed in so many accounts of English national identity, Lessing's included. The gender critique that links Harriet to the protagonists of Jane Austen, Charlotte Brontë, and George Eliot underwrites the novel's exclusionary concept of national identity. As an immigrant from the settler colony in Rhodesia and an exile, like Stead, from provincial sexual mores and morality, Lessing was able to find or make a place in a postwar England hostile to the aspirations of white women like herself. England was less welcoming to immigrants of color, men and women alike. Like *In Pursuit of the English* and *The Golden Notebook*, which reach back to the 1940s and 1950s, *The Good Terrorist* and *The Fifth Child*, which describe the contemporary scene and look toward the future, invite us to ask whether national identities such as the one that Lessing established through a long and productive career must always be consolidated by exclusion or whether, as we imagine new national communities, we can begin to invent identities that embrace instead of repressing difference.

Part III
Nadine Gordimer:
Literature and Politics in South Africa

6

European Genealogies and South African Identity in *Burger's Daughter*

Nadine Gordimer, born in South Africa in 1923, published most of her work during the era of apartheid, which extended from 1948, when the National Party took power, through the early 1990s. Unremitting in her opposition to racism and to the apartheid laws and extralegal repression that codified, consolidated, and intensified the already existing color bar, Gordimer nevertheless chose to remain in South Africa at a time when many whites were leaving. The meaning of her decision to stay and be or become a white African, or a white South African, changes over her long and prolific career. Many of her novels explore the ramifications of this decision, as they respond imaginatively to a question that she poses as the title of a 1959 essay, "Where Do Whites Fit In?"[1] Gordimer suggests that whites who want to belong to a multiracial society might make a place for themselves by improvising or by regarding themselves as immigrants in a new country (32, 34). The improvisation that she proposes in 1959 is more difficult to conceive in the late 1970s, when Black Consciousness had become the dominant ideology of the liberation movement and put the role of whites in the liberation struggle very much in question. But *Burger's Daughter* (1979) is just such an improvisation.[2]

Gordimer reflects on national identity, and specifically on the role of culture in producing and reproducing a nation, in an essay titled "Lit-

---

[1] See Stephen Clingman's introductory note to the essay in Gordimer, *The Essential Gesture*, 31. Apartheid laws eventually caused the demise of the vibrant, multiracial culture Gordimer found in Johannesburg in the 1950s.

[2] Clingman reads *Burger's Daughter* as a response to Black Consciousness and an exploration of a possible "role for whites in the context of Soweto and after" (*Novels of Nadine Gordimer*, 7, 170). See also Gordimer, "Letter from Johannesburg, 1976" and "Living in the Interregnum" (1982).

erature and Politics in South Africa" that was published in 1974, while she was working on *Burger's Daughter*. She says:

> The dilemma of the writer in a multi-racial society, where the law effectively prevents any real identification of the writer with his society as a whole, so that ultimately he can identify only with his colour, distorts this mean [between selfhood and otherness] irreparably. And cultural identity is the ground on which the exploration of self in the imaginative writer makes a *national literature*. (226; emphasis added) ·

Gordimer suggests that apartheid deforms, even forecloses, the imagination of community that, as Benedict Anderson argues, constitutes a nation *as* an imagined community. Yet *Burger's Daughter* attempts to imagine a nonracial South African nation over and against the barriers that apartheid sets on doing so.[3]

The novel represents South Africa from the perspective of its title character, Rosa Burger, a young white woman opposed to apartheid. Throughout, Rosa is both an actor or potential actor in the politics of the nation and an angle of vision through which a nation and its conditions of possibility or impossibility are framed.[4] The strategy of imagining South African nationality from the point of view of a white protagonist is determined in part by the exigencies of apartheid. But only in part, for the situation of Rosa Burger also underwrites the novel's exploration of the ways that whites might participate in a South African national community at a moment when the Black Consciousness movement has redefined the role of whites in the liberation struggle and in the emergent political order.

Rosa is identified, in the novel's title, as someone's daughter. Her parents, Lionel and Cathy Burger, are Afrikaners, prominent Communists, and leaders in the struggle against apartheid in the 1940s, 1950s, and through the 1960s. When Rosa's parents die, her legacy is their commitment to justice. But the role that they and others like them—Communists, white Communists—played in the struggle is not available to her. Rosa must stake her own claim to her inheritance, come to terms with the history that her parents incarnate, and find her place in a changing South Africa.

Rosa's trajectory takes her back into memories of the past, carries her into exile in Europe, and returns her to a South Africa in upheaval, at

---

[3] The tenets of nonracialism are set out in the 1955 Freedom Charter of the Congress of Peoples: "South Africa belongs to all who live in it, black and white, and . . . no Government can justly claim authority unless it is based on the will of the people" (quoted in Lodge and Nasson et al., *All, Here, and Now*, 331).

[4] On Rosa as a national subject, see White, "Politics and the Individual," 209.

the moment when the Soweto students' school boycott has literally turned the nation upside down.[5] (The boycott originated as a protest against instruction in Afrikaans; it escalated into a much larger revolt led by students and later joined by their parents and others.) In moving from the present, in which the politics of nonracialism seems to have reached an impasse, to the past, in which South Africa appears— at least to Rosa—in the guise of "Lionel's country," to a future projected in an optative mode, *Burger's Daughter* asks what role whites such as Rosa might play in a history that remains to be written and whether or how whites (European in origin) can identify and be identified as (South) Africans. It offers a provisional model for such an identification in its own translation of such British and European political and cultural traditions as the novel of ideas and Communism into hybrid South African idioms.[6] In attempting to transform European genealogies into South African cultural identity, *Burger's Daughter* presents itself as a work of South African literature. But this performative project is inflected by European antecedents that call into question the achievement of South African identity by *Burger's Daughter* and Burger's daughter alike.[7]

Imagined Community: Representing the Nonracial Nation

The nonracial South African nation as set out in the 1955 Freedom Charter does not exist in the moment in which *Burger's Daughter* is written and which it describes. But it is portrayed in the novel in several different ways: as a disarticulated, disaggregated collectivity;[8] as a set of recollections; and as a desire for a future that has not yet come into being. In its narration of a national story, the novel stakes out for its protagonist—and, by implication, for the white South African readers for whom she stands—a place in a community that exists in the novel's here and now as absence, memory, or utopian desire.

[5] Gordimer said that Soweto "overtook" her while she was writing the novel ("Interview," 182). On the Soweto students' revolt, see Lodge, *Black Politics in South Africa*, chap. 13. On *Burger's Daughter* as a record of the revolt, see Clingman, "Literature and History," 107, 110.

[6] On Gordimer's notion of South African literature as "intercultural" hybrid, see Head, *Nadine Gordimer*, 17.

[7] Wagner regards Gordimer as "enmeshed" in "colonialist paradigms" (*Rereading Nadine Gordimer*, 6). Jonathan White sees her writing as part of the antiapartheid struggle (219). Head finds "a productive tension" in the conflict between Gordimer's European literary heritage and African experience (6).

[8] *Burger's Daughter* literalizes Bhabha's metaphor of "dissemination" as a scattering of national fragments.

The first scene depicts the nonracial nation as a community exiled in and exiled from the apartheid state.[9] When Rosa's mother, Cathy, is jailed, Rosa goes to the prison with a group bringing parcels to those detained inside. The nonracial nation includes the group standing outside the prison and those "on the other side of the thick-studded door" (14). Rosa has a hot-water bottle, ostensibly to comfort her mother, but actually to smuggle into the prison the message that her father has not been arrested. Family matters and a language of personal life were used by opponents of apartheid in South Africa as a code for political discourse.[10] But Gordimer's transcoding practice opens up that of the antiapartheid movement. In the Communist Party and the African National Congress (ANC), the personal was used to signify the political; in the novel, there is no privileged political signified made manifest in a personal signifier implicitly debased by comparison. Rather, the personal is played off against the political; there is no master code that takes precedence over the others.[11]

As Rosa puts it, *"When they saw me outside the prison, what did they see? I shall never know. It's all concocted. I saw—see—that profile in a hand-held mirror directed towards another mirror"* (13–14). Rosa alludes here to the different ways that she appears—is "concocted" or reflected—in the different discourses that make up the cultural text of contemporary South Africa: those of the mass media, the Communist "faithful," government surveillance reports, the gossip of her schoolmates, the language of her own bodily sensations, and so forth.[12] The figure of a set of reflections without an authoritative "original" also suggests a strategy for imagining the nation itself. This figure undermines the hierarchy of signifying practices whereby certain representations are privileged, others are devalued, and still others are repressed

[9] Cf. Nelson Mandela's description of the community that existed in jail among the defendants in the Treason Trial (*Long Walk to Freedom*, 175).

[10] "The family" was the code name for the South African Communist Party when it was underground. Only family matters could be discussed during prison visits, so the family was used as a code for other, political matters. See Clingman, *Novels of Nadine Gordimer*, 175; Mandela 351; Mashinini, *Strikes Have Followed Me*, 66.

[11] Martin notes that the novel "resist[s] any illusion of direct access to the 'real' " ("Narrative, History, Ideology," 11). On the opposition between the personal and the political, see Winnett, "Making Metaphors"; Roberts, "Nadine Gordimer's 'Family of Women' "; Meese, "Political Is the Personal"; and Radhakrishnan, "Negotiating Subject Positions."

[12] Gordimer returns to the figure of the mirror in her account of the genesis of *Burger's Daughter*. She says that the the writer resembles "Primo Levi's metamir, . . . a 'metaphysical mirror, [which] does not obey the law of optics but reproduces your image *as it is seen by the person who stands before you.' "* Gordimer was part of a scene outside a prison like the one that begins the novel—"I was the metamir standing before them"—and created in *Burger's Daughter* "alternate lives" for real personages (*Writing and Being*, 5–8).

or occluded altogether. And, reflecting all South Africans alike, it enables the circumventing of the prohibitions of apartheid. It gives us a nation as it is collectively imagined by subjects occupying different positions. But, at the same time, the figure of a set of mirror images raises the question of whether what is reflected—the nation itself—exists at all. This question haunts both Burger's daughter and *Burger's Daughter.*

The nonracial nation is portrayed as a scattered and transitory community—fragments assembled and unified for a brief moment—in an episode in which Lionel Burger addresses the court after he has been tried and convicted of treason. In this speech, he reaffirms his opposition to apartheid and explains that he has worked to end racial discrimination and bring about a just order in South Africa. Lionel's speech reproduces the words of the chief model for his character, the Communist Party leader Bram Fischer, a lawyer whose father and grandfather were prominent Afrikaner political figures.[13] By giving Fischer's words to a fictional character, Gordimer evades the prohibition on quoting him.[14] At the same time, the novel reenacts the performative project of Fischer/Burger in the dock. It attempts to actualize a community which is founded on "the national liberation of the African people" (26) and which potentially embraces everyone in the courtroom, proponents and opponents of apartheid alike. Blacks and whites are physically separated in the courtroom of the apartheid state, but the reaction of Lionel's supporters to his speech prefigures a national community that transcends racial difference and subverts white domination. In the call-and-response initiated by blacks and subsequently joined by whites, the novel suggests that whites might participate in the nonracial national community by joining—responding to—the call for liberation initiated by blacks.[15]

The reaction of Lionel's supporters looks toward the future, but an image of a nonracial nation also inhabits Rosa's memories of the past. Throughout the novel, Rosa recalls the house where she grew up.[16] There, black and white lived together in a closeness fostered by Lionel's nurturing presence. Lionel's house was a site of opposition to

---

[13] In research notes for *Burger's Daughter,* Gordimer meticulously traces the Communist Party's involvement in antiracist, later antiapartheid activity and places Lionel in this history. Gordimer Collection, Lilly Library, box 6, folders 2, 6, 7, and 8. On Fischer, see Gordimer's 1966 article, "Why Did Bram Fischer Choose Jail?"

[14] Clingman, *Novels of Nadine Gordimer,* 186, 188; Gordimer, *Writing and Being,* 7.

[15] On the idea that South African whites must follow the leadership of blacks, see Gordimer, "Living in the Interregnum," and Chapter 7, this volume.

[16] On the house as a key site for Gordimer's analysis of social space, see Barnard, "Leaving the House of the White Race," *Apartheid, Literature, and the Politics of Place,* chap. 2.

the existing racial hierarchy and therefore at least potentially a micro-cosm or prefiguration of a nonracial South Africa. But despite the ef-forts of Lionel and his colleagues, the order in which a white minority holds power over a black majority remained intact, not only in the na-tion at large but also in Lionel's house.

Rosa is brutally reminded of this late one night in London after at-tending a meeting of supporters of the liberation movement. She re-ceives a phone call from a young African who had lived for several years of his childhood in the Burgers' house. Nicknamed Baasie, Afrikaans for "little boss" (baas), as a boy, he now tells Rosa his real name, Zwelinzima, which means "suffering land."[17] Bitter, angry, and unaware that Rosa smuggled a pass and forged identity papers to his father, a liberation fighter who subsequently died in jail, Zwelinzima denounces her: "Whatever you whites touch, it's a take-over" (321). She decides soon afterward to return to South Africa: like the whites who respond to the call of the blacks in the courtroom, Rosa responds to Zwelinzima's call by taking action.

Rosa's memories of Lionel's house, as we encounter them in the novel, are prompted by events that unfold after his death. On one occa-sion, Marisa Kgosana, the wife of a jailed leader of the liberation move-ment, invites Rosa to the home of her cousin Fats Mxenge, a boxing promoter. There, Rosa finds both a social gathering and a heated ideo-logical debate. The participants in the debate include Duma Dhladhla, a young exponent of Black Consciousness;[18] James Nyaluza, a black Communist; Orde Greer, a white journalist who wants to help the lib-eration struggle; and Fats himself, representing a nascent black middle class accused by James and Duma of colluding with the white authori-ties for the sake of their own economic advancement. Rosa remains on the sidelines. We see the conversation through her reflections on the terms on which she might enter the discussion, but she remains silent.

The lively political discussion and the generous hospitality of Fats and his wife remind Rosa of her parents and the house where she grew up. Her recollections juxtapose past and present, black and white; in this ensemble of hybrid cultural forms, no one element has authority over the others. Rosa assimilates the "boerewors" (sausages) of her childhood to the "mealie-pap in gravy" eaten by the children at Fats's place and associates "black sociability" with the Afrikaner traditions of

---

[17] On Baasie and Rosa as brother and sister, see Greenstein, "Miranda's Story," and Newman, Nadine Gordimer, who read their relationship through that of Caliban and Mi-randa in The Tempest.

[18] Clingman explains that Duma Dhladhla speaks the words of Steve Biko, who could not be quoted (Novels of Nadine Gordimer, 186 and 245 n. 26).

Lionel's family (166).[19] Rosa remembers the house as a locus of social relations that had no model or that grafted diverse, even incongruous models onto each other. The house was a product of a specifically South African history and an exemplar of a uniquely South African assemblage of political ideologies and practices, that of the Communist Party (Communism) as it developed in South Africa. Yet the novel also asks whether transplanted European political traditions can take root in South Africa as an authentic or indigenous growth.

Gordimer herself worries this question in her research materials for the novel.[20] In her notes on her sources, she scrutinizes the transformation of a European ideology and movement, (Soviet-affiliated) Communism, into a South African political institution. As she documents it, this transformation was effected through the efforts of black South African Communists and through connections between the Communist Party and the ANC and other organizations such as the South Africa Indian Congress (SAIC) and the Coloured People's Congress (CPC). Following her sources, she comments frequently on whether a political ideology and interpretive framework imported from Europe can either explain or bring about meaningful change in South Africa. Yet, in thinking through the character of Lionel, she repeatedly notes that affiliation with the Communist Party was the most—possibly the only—effective way for whites to oppose the racist order in the era that extends from the 1920s through the 1950s or 1960s.

In the novel itself, Rosa's positioning with respect to the Communist faithful is similar to that of Gordimer in the research notes.[21] Rosa is critical of the orthodoxy of the faithful, but at the same time, she believes that South African Communists, black and white, developed authentic and enduring connections across racial difference. But Rosa cannot engage herself in political activity. She is estranged from the politics of the faithful that Lionel exemplifies and, in quite a different way, from the liberation politics of the Black Consciousness movement. She resists the efforts of the faithful to put her in her parents' place or to treat her life as an extension of theirs. Here, her predicament is that of the protagonist of the bildungsroman, who must find her or his way by emancipating herself or himself from parental claims. But her situation is complicated—like that of Virginia Woolf's Lily Briscoe—because she must free herself of parental influence while also mourning parental

---

[19] Bruce King regards the novel's treatment of rural Afrikaner communities as nostalgic ("Introduction," 11).

[20] Gordimer Collection, box 6, folder 2, p. 28.

[21] Jonathan White argues that Gordimer writes from a position like that of Lionel (219).

loss. Unlike Lily, Rosa mourns the death of parents whom she regards as heroes, even while acknowledging their inadequacy as parents.

As Rosa puts it, she has "lost connection" (172). She can neither come to terms with the past nor let go of it; she can neither situate herself in the present political scene nor look toward the future. Rosa's state of mind is that of someone in the early stages of mourning: in this respect, *Burger's Daughter* might be read as an elegy for Lionel and for the politics he exemplifies, a politics whose moment has passed.[22] But while Rosa is initially reluctant to involve herself in political struggle, the novel does not endorse individual fulfillment over social and political responsibility.[23] The novel's spokesman for the priority of the individual is a character who plays the part of a narrative straw man.

Only Connect

The connection whose loss Rosa laments is emphasized in the dialogical narrative structure of *Burger's Daughter* itself. Much of the novel consists of Rosa's first-person narration. Her account is supplemented by an omniscient third-person narration that is itself composed of many contending narrative voices that, taken together, represent the language-world of South Africa.[24] Rosa's own narrative is also dialogically constructed. In each of the three parts of the novel, she addresses a silent interlocutor, using both the second person, "you," and the first person, "I."

In the first part of the novel, Rosa is addressing a young man named Conrad with whom she becomes involved after her father's death. Conrad is Rosa's opponent in debate, a skeptical listener, and the object of her retrospective reflections. As an imagined interlocutor, he underwrites Rosa's attempt to come to terms with her parents' deaths and her exploration of her own identity, especially as these bear on her place in the contemporary political scene. Gordimer's Conrad, a deracinated member of the English-speaking middle class, recalls his

[22] On Lionel as a representative of an earlier epoch, see Daymond, *"Burger's Daughter: A Novel's Reliance on History,"* 160.

[23] On the conflict between private life and social responsibility as the theme of the novel, see Gordimer's contribution to *What Happened to "Burger's Daughter,"* 17.

[24] See Clingman, *Novels of Nadine Gordimer,* 190 and 250 n. 41. Bakhtin defines a "language-world" as one in which languages "intersect with each other . . . [are] juxtaposed to one another, mutually supplement one another, contradict one another and [are] interrelated dialogically," as in what he terms "heteroglossia" ("Discourse in the Novel," 291–92). Burton argues that heteroglossia in *Burger's Daughter* is partial, because the novel does not include African languages ("Exile, Identity, and the Dialogic").

namesake, Joseph Conrad, the deracinated Polish aristocrat and British novelist of empire.[25]

The word "connection" evokes E. M. Forster, another British novelist of empire and one whom Gordimer acknowledges as an influence.[26] The epigraph to *Howards End*, "Only Connect," asserts as an imperative the necessity of connection—specifically, connection between classes—in Edwardian England. *A Passage to India* explores the possibility of friendship between a white, European colonizer and a member of a colonized group. Like the Schlegel sisters in *Howards End* and Cyril Fielding in *A Passage to India*, Rosa Burger seeks connections apparently foreclosed in a political order named for the antithesis of connection, apartheid. *Burger's Daughter* refashions Forster's examination of connection across class and gender and friendship between colonizer and colonized—that is, across racial difference—as an inquiry into the possibility of connection, or friendship, between blacks and whites in apartheid South Africa.

Rosa's contention with Conrad restages a debate similar to that between Forsterian and Conradian versions of the British novel of empire: between a desire for connection and a sense that connection cannot be achieved. *Burger's Daughter* reframes this debate in a postcolonial, or potentially postcolonial, idiom and relocates it in a South African context. The contest is complicated by the fact that throughout, the voices of Rosa and Conrad are themselves dialogically constituted. The voice of each character is infiltrated by the language of the other so that not only the boundaries between "I" and "you" but also the positions that "I" and "you" stake out are unstable, permeable, fluid.[27]

The Forsterian imperative of connection occupies a privileged position in Rosa's debate with Conrad. Rosa, after all, is the narrator and protagonist; Conrad is a silent interlocutor. Yet despite the silencing of Conrad and the subordination of Conrad and his beliefs to Rosa and hers, the novel suggests that the connection that Rosa seeks is tenuous and can scarcely be achieved—or imagined—in the world that she inhabits. Conrad conceives of freedom as the absence of encumbering

[25] Greenstein regards him as a "debilitated version of his namesake" ("Miranda's Story," 234).

[26] See Gordimer, "Notes of an Expropriator" (1964). Some thirty years later, Gordimer noted the influence of Forster in an address to high school students at the Unterberg Poetry Center, 92nd Street YMHA, New York, 7 November 1994. On Forster's influence on Gordimer, see Haarhof, "Two Cheers for Socialism," 59.

[27] Cf. Bakhtin: "The word . . . is half someone else's. It becomes 'one's own' only when the speaker . . . appropriates the word, adapting it to his own semantic and expressive intention" ("Discourse in the Novel," 293). On Gordimer and Bakhtin, see my "Problems of Gordimer's Poetics."

ties of family, class, and culture, as the negative freedom of bourgeois liberal ideology. For Rosa, historical events have the same valence as personal crises: "At twelve years old what happened at Sharpeville was as immediate to me as what was happening in my own body" (115).

Throughout the novel, Conrad is skeptical about authenticity, intentionality, and agency. He speaks for the priority of the personal and equates the vicissitudes of pleasure and desire—individual subjectivity—with existence itself: "Fantasies. Obsessions. They're mine. They're the form in which the question of my own existence is being put to me" (47). Rosa rejects Conrad's notion that politics (or any collective action) is necessarily an expression of inauthenticity. Instead, she invokes the conscription and mobilization of desire in larger structures and political formations, such as the nation itself. She mentions the "satisfactions" and "pleasures" in "outsmarting the police" (65) and suggests that the assumption of multiple identities, a concomitant of clandestine activity, enabled those in the movement to circumvent the restrictions inherent in Conrad's all- encompassing "I."[28]

Rosa's involvement with Conrad coincides with her experience of personal loss and political alienation; it occurs at a moment when the position of whites in the struggle against apartheid is very much in question. His insistence that political events are inauthentic might well be attractive to someone in a state of mourning, withdrawal, and disengagement. But for Rosa, disengagement is a phase in a longer process, not an end in itself as it is for Conrad.[29] Eventually, she rediscovers political commitment on her own terms.

Gordimer's Conrad particularly recalls the character of Martin Decoud in *Nostromo*. Decoud "recognized no other virtue than intelligence and . . . erected passions into duties" (413). His skepticism cannot sustain him when he is left alone on an island with stolen silver, and he rows out to sea, shoots himself, then jumps overboard, leaving behind traces of blood discovered later. Like Decoud, Gordimer's Conrad is lost at sea. But unlike Decoud, he disappears without leaving a trace; we never learn whether he survived. Conrad's uncertain destiny and the finality with which he is set adrift signal the novel's emphatic repudiation of the position he represents but suggest, as well, its se-

---

[28] Rosa's notion of the mobilization of desire in multiple orders of knowledge and power resembles that of Michel Foucault in *The History of Sexuality*, vol. 1, published at virtually the same moment as the novel.

[29] In a notebook that Gordimer kept while she was working on the novel, she described the Conrad episode as a regressive escape from responsibility. Gordimer Collection, box 6, folder 8.

ductive power. Rosa, too, rejects Conrad's skepticism, egoism, solip-
sism, and alienation, yet she cannot achieve or sustain the connection
so important to Lionel Burger, E. M. Forster, and Nadine Gordimer.

The Curse of Pathos

Some time after Lionel Burger dies in prison, Rosa decides to leave
South Africa. Her decision is a complicated and attenuated response to
two events she witnesses. First, she sees a white man, a tramp, dead on
a park bench; some time later, she comes upon a drunken black man
brutally beating a donkey. Taken together, these two events recall the
horse-beating episode in Dostoevsky's *Crime and Punishment* and a
similar incident in Olive Schreiner's *The Story of an African Farm*.[30] In
appropriating the work of a Russian, male precursor and a white,
English-speaking, South African female one, Gordimer refashions the
European and colonial genealogy of *Burger's Daughter*, translating it
into South African identity. But the translation is effected in a conditional mode that calls it into question.

The horse-beating episode in *Crime and Punishment* is actually a
dream. Raskolnikov dreams that he is a child (part 1, chapter 5). He
watches in horror as a drunken peasant, spurred on by a crowd of jeer-
ing onlookers, beats his horse to death. This dream vividly dramatizes
Raskolnikov's psychic conflicts and the poverty, drunkenness, and
brutality that pervade his world, a world that he is apparently powerless to alter. Rosa, too, observes a brutal scene. Like Raskolnikov, she
does not act to change what she sees, but her inaction differs significantly from his.

The rewriting of Raskolnikov's dream in *Burger's Daughter* foregrounds race as a determinant of identity in South Africa; at the same
time, it rejects essentialist or totalizing conceptions of race and represents race as it is constituted in the historically specific circumstances
of apartheid.[31] *Burger's Daughter* divides Dostoevsky's drunken, brutal
peasant into two figures, one white, the other black. The man who dies
on a park bench is white; to Rosa, his death is a mystery, an event that

[30] Gordimer based this episode on an incident that occurred while she was writing the
novel ("South Africa's Nadine Gordimer," 97). *Crime and Punishment* shapes the ways
that readers of European fiction grasp such incidents. Cf. Bakhtin: "Any concrete discourse (utterance) finds the object at which it was directed already . . . overlain with
qualifications, . . . or, on the contrary, by the 'light' of alien words that have already been
spoken about it" ("Discourse in the Novel," 276).

[31] On the historical construction of race in South Africa, see McClintock and Nixon,
"No Names Apart."

is not susceptible to explanation or interpretation.[32] It forces her to confront the limits of the materialist analysis that she inherits from her parents. This legacy enjoins on her the moral responsibility of ending suffering and injustice: apartheid. But it does not enable her to come to terms with loss.

Rosa's assertion that the death of the tramp is "mystery itself" (79)—contingency, or mortality in the abstract—is played off against her political understanding of the donkey-beating scene. The man who beats his donkey in *Burger's Daughter* is black. Along with Rosa, we see his brutality as an image of apartheid, a product of the political and racial economy of South Africa. The very site of the donkey beating—a road between Johannesburg and a nameless, unmapped "place" inhabited illegally by blacks—is a metonym for South Africa in the 1970s.[33] To most whites, the nameless place does not exist because the cartography of apartheid renders it invisible. That Rosa is driving on this road at all distinguishes her from most other white South Africans. Rosa has attended a political meeting, a quixotic effort by white feminists who wish to unite South African women across differences of race and an effort about which Rosa is skeptical. After the meeting, Rosa drives one black woman home and is on her way to a clandestine visit to another black woman, her friend Marisa Kgosana, the banned political activist. On the road, she comes upon the man beating a donkey.

Although Rosa witnesses brutality and suffering, she does not intervene, believing that to do so would be to misuse the power and privilege she happens to have because she is white:

> I could have yelled before I even got out, . . . and then there I would have been standing, inescapable, fury and right, might, before them, the frightened woman and child and the drunk, brutal man, with my knowledge of how to deliver them over to the police, to have him prosecuted as he deserved and should be, to take away from him the poor suffering possession he maltreated. I could formulate everything they were, as the act I had witnessed. . . . I could have put a stop to it, the misery . . . those people, peasants, . . . would have been afraid of me. . . . No one would have taken up a stone. I was safe from the whip. I could have stood between them and suffering—the suffering of the donkey. . . . I don't know at what point to intercede makes sense for me. . . . I drove on because the horrible drunk was black, poor and brutalized. If somebody's going to be brought to account, I am accountable for him, to him, as he is for the donkey. Yet the suffering—while I saw it it was the sum of suffering to me. I didn't do anything. I let him beat the donkey. The man was a black. So a kind of vanity counted for more than feeling; I couldn't bear to see myself—her—

---

[32] Meese observes that the tramp's death "eludes discursive captivity" (259).
[33] See Read, "Politics of Place in *Burger's Daughter*."

Rosa Burger—as one of those whites who can care more for animals than people. (209–10)

In describing this scene, Rosa uses concrete terms ("drunk," "brutal"); a language of morality ("suffering"); a language of race ("black"); and a language of class ("peasants"). All these discourses are versions of novelistic pathos, as Bakhtin describes it:[34]

> a surrogate for some other genre that is no longer available to a given time or a given social force . . . The discourse of . . . the prophet without a mission, the politician without political power, the believer without a church and so forth—everywhere, the discourse of pathos is connected with orientations and positions that are unavailable to the author as authentic expression for the seriousness and determination of his purpose, but which he must, *all the same,* conditionally reproduce by using his own discourse.[35]

The rhetoric of counterfactuals "conditionally reproduce[s]" what is unavailable to Rosa or to other whites similarly situated, an unequivocal declaration of moral purpose or political belief.[36]

Like the boy in Raskolnikov's dream, Rosa witnesses a brutal scene that epitomizes the world she inhabits; like him, she does not act.[37] The boy in Raskolnikov's dream is confused, even unhinged; unlike him, Rosa *chooses* not to act. But the scope of her choice is severely limited, as is evident if we compare this scene with an incident it recalls in *The Story of an African Farm* (1883).[38] Schreiner's Waldo Farber, alone and poor, works as a driver on a wagon train. When Waldo's master whips, then stabs and kills one of the oxen, Waldo attacks him. Because Waldo can no longer remain with the team, he walks away, penniless (part 2, chapter 11).

This episode dramatizes the limits of self-reliance (Waldo) and the exploitation of the working class (Farber), but it does so by occluding race. Waldo not only sympathizes with but also stands (in) for the suffering of South African blacks in the late nineteenth century.[39] His iden-

[34] I thank Jane Marcus for bringing this to my attention.

[35] Bakhtin, "Discourse in the Novel," 394–95.

[36] Winnett notes that "Rosa knows that telling this story calls into question her authority to tell all stories" (143).

[37] Meese sees Rosa's inaction as a failure (260).

[38] I thank Alan Scott, a student at Purchase College, for pointing out the echo. Clingman sees *The Conservationist* (1975), the novel immediately preceding *Burger's Daughter,* as Gordimer's "reply" to *The Story of an African Farm* (*Novels of Nadine Gordimer,* 5, 135–36, 243 n. 4). Gordimer noted in 1980 that in Schreiner's "wronged sense of self as a woman . . . she shared the most persistent characteristic of her fellow colonials (discounting the priorities of the real entities around her) while believing she was protesting against racism" ("Afterword," 226).

[39] DuPlessis, *Writing beyond the Ending,* 21 and 203 n. 5.

tification with the ox makes him a surrogate for the exploited Africans that the ox also represents. The rewriting of this scene in *Burger's Daughter* lays bare the colonial construction of race in *The Story of an African Farm*. It also suggests that Schreiner, in the 1880s, had ways of expressing opposition to racial injustice that are "unavailable," as Bakhtin puts it, to antiracist, English-speaking, South African whites in the 1970s.

Rosa's situation is different from Waldo's. She is not in danger, and the man she sees beating his animal is a black "peasant," not a white boss. Yet Waldo's expression of moral outrage—the obverse of the passivity of the boy in Raskolnikov's dream—is not possible for Rosa, who will not assume authority. As a result, she risks not acting at all and thus acquiescing in the suffering that Waldo protests against, however ineffectively. Her moral actions—the words in which she bears witness—unfold entirely within her own thoughts or in a silent dialogue with the novel's readers that cannot affect the situation she describes. Rosa's refusal to intercede leads to a narrative and political dead end, one that she attempts to escape by "defecting" from South Africa (210, 264).

If the rewriting of Dostoevsky's peasant as two characters, one black, the other white, and the exposure of Schreiner's occlusion of race emphasize the significance of race as a determinant of South African identity, *Burger's Daughter* also underscores the importance of gender. Rosa observes the man who beats his donkey with his wife and child who look on, afraid that he might turn his violence on them. This scene suggests that women and men are differently affected by apartheid and that sexual oppression intensifies the effects of racial exploitation. The horse in Raskolnikov's dream is female, or feminized;[40] the feminization of the beast figures woman as victim and specifically as inert or subjugated nature. Both *The Story of an African Farm* and *Burger's Daughter*, in contrast, obliterate the sex of the beast of burden, while drawing attention to its suffering. They destabilize a crucial element of patriarchal constructions of gender, the association of woman and (bestial) nature. But unlike *The Story of an African Farm*, which emphasizes gender by eliding race, *Burger's Daughter* focuses on both race and sex without dissolving either into the other. In other words, it offers a paradigm of identity that encompasses multiple determinants of difference (positionality). Yet it cannot realize this paradigm in the

---

[40] The Coulson translation also gives *nag* and *mare*. For a reading of the gender inscription in this scene in Dostoevsky, see Straus, *Dostoevsky and the Woman Question*, chap. 1.

world it describes and inhabits. Thus, like Rosa's silent speech, *Burger's Daughter* itself exemplifies the discourse of pathos.

Patience on a Monument

In *Burger's Daughter*, Gordimer not only puts forth her own models of cultural appropriation and translation but also rejects a radically different way of transforming European traditions into South African idioms, that of the Verligte ("enlightened") Afrikaners who couple cultural sophistication with racism. The chief representative in the novel for the model it rejects is a character named Brandt Vermeulen. An Afrikaner with connections in the government, Vermeulen helps Rosa obtain the passport that the state would surely deny to Lionel Burger's daughter. The novel rejects his version of modernity and "enlightenment" and repudiates his concept of South African identity.

Vermeulen sees no conflict between cultural sophistication and commitment to the racist order in South Africa. In his view, Plato, Shakespeare, modern art, and the so-called sexual revolution belong to the same package as apartheid and the Broederbond, a secret organization composed of the Afrikaner elite. Vermeulen speaks for the homelands policy designed to settle (the state would say "resettle") blacks in "homelands," spurious "nations" that have no existence except in the official rhetoric of the South African government.[41]

Vermeulen displays his cultural sophistication by alluding to Shakespeare. (He cautions Rosa that to get her passport she will have to be "Patience on a monument" [*Twelfth Night*, act 2, scene 4, line 113].) "Shakespeare," as Shula Marks and Stanley Trapido point out, often signifies the *cultural* hegemony of English in South Africa.[42] By quoting Shakespeare and speaking English, Vermeulen declares his cultural literacy, associates himself with the hegemonic culture, and purports to distinguish himself from the old-fashioned, narrow-minded, culturally backward Afrikaners who run the government. Yet he supports the apartheid regime. Vermeulen's allusion to Shakespeare exemplifies the ways that culture—even when or especially when it is apparently sev-

[41] The "homelands" were recognized as nations only by South Africa and one another (Omond, *Apartheid Handbook*, 97). The Nationalist Party's Bantustan policy created so-called national homelands, using a "language of *nationalities* rather than that of *color*." By 1981, the official discourse of the Nationalist regime had, "as far as possible, been purged of open references to race" (McClintock and Nixon 343–44).

[42] Marks and Trapido, "Politics of Race, Class, and Nationalism," 12. In *My Son's Story*, Gordimer offers a different perspective on Shakespeare as a cultural icon and signifier of cultural hegemony. See Chapter 8, this volume.

ered from politics—maintains, legitimates, and reproduces political hegemony. *Burger's Daughter* undermines the distinction, crucially important to Vermeulen and men like him, between politics and culture; it shows how the very notion of an autonomous cultural or aesthetic realm colludes in the South African political order.[43]

In the treatment of Brandt Vermeulen, *Burger's Daughter* not only registers the contemporary political and cultural climate but also prefigures its own reception history.[44] This history is recorded in a pamphlet entitled *What Happened to "Burger's Daughter" or How South African Censorship Works*. *Burger's Daughter* was published in England and immediately embargoed and banned in South Africa. Within a few weeks, the director of publications appealed the decision of his own committee to ban the novel. A "committee of literary experts" advised that the novel be unbanned (1–3). The Publications Committee saw the novel as an attack on the Republic of South Africa. But the committee of experts thought that it had literary merit and should be considered as "a *literary work of art*" (37; emphasis added). An expert on security matters concurred with the literary specialists that the novel should be unbanned; he thought it was unlikely to cause trouble (38). Unlike the Publications Committee, the literary and security experts use exclusively *literary* criteria of evaluation; consequently, they evacuate the political content of the novel. These experts describe *Burger's Daughter* as a text that is so difficult that it could not harm ordinary readers who would be unlikely to understand it. By deeming the novel acceptable as a work of art—high art consigned to an autonomous aesthetic realm—the experts effectively divorce it from worldly actuality, defuse its power, and depoliticize it.

Gordimer rejects the authority of the censorship system. She substitutes her own standards, representing *Burger's Daughter* as both literary and "worldly," in Edward W. Said's sense of that word: "enmeshed in circumstance, time, place, and society . . . in the world, and hence worldly" ("The World, the Text, and the Critic," 35). Gordimer describes her text as a political novel and as a novel of ideas. She explains that a political novel "explicates the effects of politics on human lives and, un-

---

[43] Cf. "Literature and Politics in South Africa," in which Gordimer insists that South African literature depends on politics for its very existence and history (205).

[44] The early reception history of the novel coincides with what Rosemary Jolly identifies as a "period of so-called reform (from 1980 on) that followed the phase of extreme censorship in South Africa." During this period, the Publications Appeal Board introduced " 'mitigating' factors including consideration of 'the likely reader,' 'literary value,' 'research and academic value,' 'historical or period value,' 'satire,' 'limited distribution' and 'price of publication' " that made possible the unbanning of some significant texts ("Rehearsals of Liberation," 18 and 27 n. 2).

like a political tract, does not propagate an ideology" and that a "novel of ideas seeks to explore concepts of the meaning of life and its social ordering—the ideas men live by" (*What Happened to "Burger's Daughter,"* 19). Like Stead and Lessing, Gordimer rescripts a traditional European and traditionally masculine genre, the novel of ideas, so that it renders the situation of a female protagonist on the margins of empire.

Gordimer's rejection of the censorship system recalls Rosa's resistance in the novel itself to Brandt Vermeulen. Rosa takes his measure, but as in the donkey-beating episode, she is silent or, more precise, she addresses only Conrad and the novel's readers. Her silent words express thoughts that might put her in jeopardy if spoken aloud in the apartheid state. The novel ends, in fact, with a censor's erasure of her words. But she exposes as shams Vermeulen's ersatz "dialogue" and the Vorster initiative, the bogus "dialogue of people and nations" (*Burger's Daughter*, 194). That the exposure is silent epitomizes the provisional character of Rosa's intervention in the novel's version of a national debate.

Thinking Back through Our Mothers

> For we think back through our mothers if we are women.
> —Virginia Woolf, *A Room of One's Own*

When Rosa leaves South Africa, she goes to the south of France to visit her father's first wife, Katya. She seeks Katya out because, she explains, "I wanted to know how to defect from [Lionel]" (264). Under Katya's tutelage, Rosa is introduced to the pleasures of art, experiences a sexual awakening, and finds an idealized, symbolic mother.[45] But her sojourn with Katya is an interlude; eventually, she returns to South Africa, the place that she identifies as "Lionel's country" (210). The recuperation of the maternal, the novel suggests, like the denial and disengagement that inaugurate the process of mourning, is a phase in a process whereby whites like Rosa might assume their identity as South Africans.

Katya is Rosa's narratee in the second part of the novel. Like Conrad, Katya speaks for the priority of personal—sexual and aesthetic—fulfillment over political responsibility. But Conrad cannot comprehend Lionel's commitment to justice or Rosa's allegiance to her parents' po-

---

[45] On Katya as a symbolic mother who "re-parents" Rosa, see Read 129 and Cooke, *Novels of Nadine Gordimer*, 81.

litical goals; Katya, however, accepts Rosa unconditionally, and although she resisted and then escaped the discipline of the Communist Party, she honors Lionel as a great man. Katya's vision of Lionel is amplified in Rosa's notion of her father's sublime "sweet lucidity" (349).[46]

Katya is in many ways the antithesis of Rosa's own mother, Cathy Jansen Burger. Cathy is a political activist, organizer of a union for African workers. For her, as for Lionel, the claims of justice (morality, politics) take precedence.[47] Cathy is a version of the mother who is always already allied with the rule of the father—here, with revolutionary politics in South Africa. Her work as a labor organizer is distinct from yet part of the larger national struggle that Lionel exemplifies.[48] Cathy's unflinching political commitment has equivocal effects on her daughter. In the novel's first scene, Rosa uses the hot-water bottle she carries not to relieve the "leaden, dragging, wringing pain . . . the peculiar fierce concentration of the body's forces in the menstruation of early puberty" (15), but as a vehicle for a message for her mother and others inside the prison. Cathy is a shadowy figure as a mother: she dies of multiple sclerosis before her daughter reaches adulthood.

Katya is Cathy's opposite number or double. Her name, Katya, echoes Cathy's, and she harks back to the idealized mother of fantasy or family romance, the mother that the female subject of classical psychoanalytic theory has never known or, having known, has forgotten.[49] Katya fosters aspects of Rosa that have been neglected; she introduces her to modern art and French cuisine and creates for her an oasis of sheer feminine companionship. As Rosa says, "I've never talked with anyone as I do with you, incontinently, femininely" (262). Rosa's relationship with Katya unfolds in a domain "outside" the law of the father, a space like the " 'elsewhere' of female pleasure" theorized by Luce Irigaray ("The Power of Discourse," 77). But the portrayal of Katya represents this elsewhere as potentially regressive, a return to a pre-oedipal then before the political now. The novel therefore launches a critique of the poetics and politics of maternal recuperation canonized in both Anglo-American and French feminist theory.

The idealized mother of fantasy, the nurturing mother that Rosa has never known, the sisterly mother that she longs for, and an exile from South Africa, Katya is associated with Europe, specifically France. Her

[46] In a notebook she kept while writing the novel, Gordimer identifies Lionel, along with the Soweto schoolchildren, as "sublime." Gordimer Collection, box 6, folder 8.

[47] Cooke sees Cathy as "oblivious" to Rosa's needs (74).

[48] Gordimer distinguishes the political strategies of Lionel and Cathy in her research materials. Gordimer Collection, box 6, folder 2, pp. 40, 43, 87, 131.

[49] See Freud, "Femininity," 130, and Freud, "Female Sexuality," 253–54.

given name—the name she was known by before she married Lionel
Burger, became the mistress of a man named Ugo Bagnelli, and in-
structed Rosa to call her Katya—is Colette Swan.[50] This name recalls
the quintessential mothers of twentieth-century French literature,
those of Colette and of Proust's Swann. Like the naming of the character called Conrad and of Rosa herself—she is named for her grandmother Marie Burger and for Rosa Luxemburg (72–73); *Die Burger* is
also the name of the leading Afrikaans newspaper in Cape Town—the
naming of Katya raises questions about the relationship of *Burger's
Daughter* and Burger's daughter to European literary and political genealogies. The maternal roles that Katya enacts in the novel, the bodily
and aesthetic pleasures she nurtures, and the gynocentric literature in
which these are portrayed are associated with Europe as a site of exile
from South Africa and as the center of the colonial or neocolonial
order that Lionel, Cathy, and Rosa work to overthrow.[51] What Katya
evokes—the desire for the mother, sensuous experience, European culture—may be tangential, subordinate to other concerns, irrelevant, or
otherwise unable to be accommodated in the nonracial South African
nation in which Rosa is attempting to find her own place.

In the balancing of the claims of its European and South African affiliations, *Burger's Daughter* takes shape as a national family romance.
Like *The Man Who Loves Children*, it extends to questions of national
identity the "interrogation of origins" that for Marianne Hirsch defines
the genre of the family romance (*Mother/Daughter Plot*, 9). Rosa Burger
is engendered as a national subject as the daughter of Katya, the
mother who lives "outside" the father's domain; Cathy, the mother
who occupies a public sphere traditionally associated with paternal, or
patriarchal, prerogatives; and Lionel, the martyred father whose example threatens to overshadow his daughter as it has overshadowed his
wives. Rosa's return to "Lionel's country" suggests that her relationship with Katya—as it figures a pre-oedipal constellation or the seduc-
tions of Europe, exile, or aesthetic pleasure—is a detour from the quest
for justice in South Africa.

In *Burger's Daughter*, France is not only the site of a maternal locus
suppressed or invisible in South Africa but also the place where Rosa

[50] On the naming of Colette Swan, see Liscio, *"Burger's Daughter:* Lighting a Torch in
the Heart of Darkness."
[51] Cf. Frantz Fanon's identification of the European metropole, the "mother country,"
as a "bloodthirsty and implacable stepmother," and his characterization of colonialism
as a "mother who unceasingly restrains her fundamentally perverse offspring from managing to commit suicide and from giving free rein to its evil instincts" (*Wretched of the
Earth,* 145, 211).

experiences a sexual awakening. Rosa falls in love with a married French academic named Bernard Chabalier, who is studying the "influence of the *pied noir* on French culture" (273). The post- or neocolonial situation that shapes Rosa's life is for him an intellectual exercise. Rosa's affair is an attempt "to live within the ambit of a person not a country" (302), but for Chabalier, as the echo of chivalry in his name suggests, adultery is a romantic adventure.

Eventually, prompted by the phone call from the man she knew as Baasie, Rosa returns to a South Africa turned upside down by the Soweto children's school boycott and its aftermath. She resumes working as a physical therapist and rejoins—or joins—the struggle. As she explains:

> No one can defect.
>   I don't know the ideology:
>   It's about suffering.
>   How to end suffering.
>   And it ends in suffering. Yes, it's strange to live in a country where there are still heroes. Like anyone else, I do what I can. I am teaching them to walk again, at Baragwanath Hospital. They put one foot before the other. (332)

In the wake of Soweto, Rosa is one of thousands, mainly black, who are arrested when the government intensifies its repression. The end of the novel finds her in prison, in the place of her parents. But Rosa also differentiates herself from them, making a commitment on her own terms: "I don't know the ideology," she says. Like her mother before her, she belongs to an incarcerated interracial sisterhood. But she is more closely identified with her father. Her cell resembles the one that he occupied, and the police captain who interrogates her reminds her "that he had known her father well" (353).

At the end of the novel, then, Rosa turns or returns to her father; the turn is underscored by the fact that he is the narratee of part 3. In the turn toward the father, *Burger's Daughter* rewrites a narrative of female development prominently recorded in British, American, and European novels and theorized in Anglo-American feminist criticism. This narrative identifies development with a sexual awakening that recovers a lost or absent mother or with a quest, a struggle to voice and realize aspirations, that emancipates the protagonist from filial bonds.[52] Here, again, the figure of the mother exercises a seductive and trou-

---

[52.] See DuPlessis, *Writing beyond the Ending*, and Abel, Hirsch, and Langland, Introduction, 11–12.

bling power. Unlike Conrad, the representative of radical skepticism, and Chabalier, who dabbles in politics and romance, Katya is not dispatched from the novel. Rather, she has the last word, or at least the penultimate one. The novel ends with the omniscient narrator's report of a prison censor's deletion of part of a letter that Rosa writes to Katya. In this letter, Rosa puts herself—literally—in her father's place, describing "something Lionel Burger once mentioned" (361).

The fate of Rosa's words epitomizes her situation as a subject of a South African nation in transition. Having discovered what it means to be Burger's daughter, Rosa takes up her role as her father's successor. But the struggle for justice is now led by blacks (in fact, by black children), and South Africa cannot be identified as Lionel's country. The nonracial nation that Lionel and the faithful worked to bring into being exists, at the moment the novel describes, in diaspora or confinement. It lives in banned organizations that cannot be named; in those like Marisa Kgosana and Rosa, in prison or in exile; in the future; as a memory. Rosa belongs to the national community imagined here, but she is not and cannot be the principal subject of a narrative written as absence, in a past tense as memory, in a future or conditional tense as desire.

If the national story is ruptured, fragmented, and deformed, it nevertheless exists not only as it is being written but also as it is being read. Katya's attempt to make out the words deleted from Rosa's letter points to a role that readers, too, might play in overriding the censors and rewriting absence as presence. But Katya's limitations as a reader are patent. The ending that gives us the erasure of Rosa's words from Katya's perspective represents an eruption of the maternal constellation and of Europe (France), or the Eurocolonial order, for which it is a figure. Unaware of the existence of Zwelinzima, Katya replicates in her reading of Rosa's letter the discursive strategies whereby Europeans legitimated the colonial enterprise by rendering its objects and victims invisible. The ending of the novel, then, does not resolve but rather reframes the question of whether European antecedents will be recursively reproduced in neocolonial repetition or whether they can be transplanted and translated into South African identity.

7

Decolonizing the Novel:
A Sport of Nature
as Postcolonial Picaresque

There are a few who maintain that they positively have no colour sense whatsoever; but they are, biologically speaking, sports, or they have overcome traditional weakness, or they are, perhaps, from the noblest of motives, deceiving themselves.

There seems to be only one thing that can, to any noticeable extent, override this profound feeling (call it instinct or call it acquired prejudice) which physically divides white from black: and that is the force of sex. A white man who would not touch a male Kaffir will take to himself the Kaffir's sister, and make her the vehicle for perpetuating his being, and give his own children the blood he abhors.

—Sarah Gertrude Millin, *The South Africans*

In the years after Soweto, the crisis of apartheid intensified. According to historian Leonard Thompson, "Black resistance soon became more formidable than before. . . . A protest culture pervaded the black population of South Africa." The 1980s also saw a return to a politics of nonracialism and, consequently, increased participation by whites in antiapartheid activity.[1] In 1983, the United Democratic Front (UDF), a black-led, nonracial coalition of labor unions, community and church groups, and women's, youth, and student organizations, was formed. The UDF became the leading antiapartheid organization, coordinating the internal opposition to apartheid and the resistance to the limited reforms with which the government tried to strengthen its authority. During the mid-1980s, there was an intensification of legal and illegal

[1] Thompson, *History of South Africa*, 228; on nonracialism in this period, see Frederikse, *Unbreakable Thread*, chap. 21.

resistance activities, including strikes, boycotts, sabotage, and attacks on police.[2] In 1985, in response to the heightened activity, the government declared a limited state of emergency in many parts of the nation. Martial law was declared, and thousands were arrested and detained. In June 1986, as Nadine Gordimer was completing revisions on a novel tentatively titled "Hillela—A Sport," a nationwide state of emergency was declared. Thousands were detained, and military rule was imposed in the townships.[3]

A Sport of Nature (1987) is a response to a state of emergency at once literal and figurative. In this chapter, I approach the novel by looking first at two essays that delineate the political and cultural climate in which it was produced and anticipate its concerns. A Sport of Nature also answers the quotation from Sarah Gertrude Millin that appears as the epigraph to this chapter.[4] The South Africans catalogues the characteristics of the different groups that make up the black, white, and colored population of South Africa. For Millin, the idea of segregation makes possible a conception of South African identity that encompasses racial difference, but it affirms the racial hierarchy in which white is superior, black is inferior. A Sport of Nature deconstructs Millin's discourse. In the career of its title character and protagonist, the novel imagines an articulation of sex and race that simultaneously acknowledges and transcends difference. In this articulation, it seeks a model for a nonracial South Africa.

The Late Interregnum

"Living in the Interregnum" (1982) and "The Essential Gesture" (1985) explore the position of whites, especially those whites opposed to apartheid, in the world they describe and point to ways that whites might participate in a postapartheid order toward which they beckon. Like "The Small Personal Voice," in which Doris Lessing addresses the cultural crisis of the late 1950s by proposing agendas later realized in The Golden Notebook, these essays define the discursive terrain in which

[2] Lodge and Nasson et al., All, Here, and Now, 31–55; Thompson, History of South Africa, 228–29.

[3] Lodge and Nasson et al., All, Here, and Now, 87–90; Gordimer Collection, box 14, folder 25.

[4] Millin was a white, English-speaking, Jewish writer primarily known for her novels. The South Africans (1926) is a documentary account of the different racial groups in South Africa in which Millin treats race and especially racial mixing as a "problem." Millin later became a virulently racist apologist for apartheid.

A Sport of Nature takes shape and prefigure its postmodern, postcolonial textual strategies.[5]

Gordimer defines the present moment as an interregnum "not only between two social orders but also between two identities, one known and discarded, the other unknown and undetermined" ("Living in the Interregnum," 269–70). What she describes politicizes Jean-François Lyotard's conception of the "postmodern condition."[6] The postmodern, as Lyotard defines it, involves "incredulity" toward the metanarratives of enlightenment and emancipation that constitute modernity itself (xxiv). Because these narratives have not been replaced by new ones with comparable power to organize experience, Lyotard argues, postmodern artists and writers "are working without rules in order to formulate the rules of what *will have been done*" (81; Lyotard's emphasis). Lyotard's juxtaposition of the present and future perfect tenses represents the postmodern condition as a chronotope of liminality.[7] Gordimer similarly identifies the moment in which she writes as a hovering between a present in the process of unfolding—a "being without structures" ("Living in the Interregnum," 269)—and a future that will have happened. She seeks a standpoint adequate to what "will have been done" in a crisis that outstrips writers' ability to describe it and in an "undetermined" future that cannot quite be envisaged.

Gordimer focuses on the "segment" of South African society to which she belongs, the minority within the white minority who oppose apartheid and its regime. This group, like Lyotard's postmodern artists and writers, is "working without rules in order to formulate the rules of what will have been done"; it is reinventing itself in response to demands that are just now being or will soon have been made by the black majority. Gordimer allies her work as a writer with this project of reinvention. In asserting that the white writer must "declare himself as answerable to the order struggling to be born," Gordimer reaccentuates the imperatives of Bishop Desmond Tutu and the poet Mongane Wally Serote, who say that blacks must lead and whites must follow,

[5] On continuities between "Living in the Interregnum" and *A Sport of Nature*, see Clingman, *"Sport of Nature,"* 173. On the interplay of modern and postmodern, colonial and postcolonial, see King, "Introduction," 8, and Wagner, *Rereading Nadine Gordimer*, 6.

[6] Lyotard, *Postmodern Condition*. Cf. Fredric Jameson on the postmodern as "little more than a transitional period between two stages of capitalism, in which the earlier forms of the economic are in the process of being restructured on a global scale, including the older forms of labor and its traditional organizational institutions and concepts" (*Postmodernism*, 417).

[7] Turner defines a liminal state as one in which "the possibility exists of standing aside not only from one's own social position but from all social positions and of formulating a potentially unlimited series of alternative social arrangements" (*Dramas, Fields, and Metaphors*, 13–14).

blacks must talk and whites must listen (278, 266–67). To declare one-self "answerable" is to respond (listen, follow) but, at the same time, to be actively engaged. The stance of answerability supersedes the pos-ture of dissidence—"defiant negativity"—that, as Neil Lazarus argues, has traditionally defined the role of oppositional white writers in South Africa and is reflected in Gordimer's self-identification as a member of a "dissident" minority.[8] In the notion of answerability, Gordimer marks out a place for white writers like herself in the nation that she defines as a posited—imagined—community. Addressing whites about a racial history and colonial legacy that must be repudi-ated even if they cannot be abolished and invoking the perspective of those who were there before the Europeans arrived, Gordimer effects a "putative opening onto . . . forms of psychic, social, and cultural other-ness" that, Fredric Jameson asserts, associates the postmodern with "political third worldism" and that Andreas Huyssen aligns with a postmodernism of resistance.[9]

In "The Essential Gesture," Gordimer again takes up the theme of responsibility. She suggests that white writers, although "alienated from . . . the historical and existential situation of whites," are responsi-ble—answerable—to a nonracial polity. This responsibility takes the form of an address to whites: "The white writer's task as 'cultural worker' is to raise the consciousness of white people, who, unlike him-self, have not woken up." [10] The identification of the writer as a cultural worker and the white writer's task as raising the consciousness of whites calls into question both the idea of the writer as dissident and the modernist notion of the writer as a creator.[11]

Gordimer consigns the modern, or modernism, to a time and place distinct from the one that she herself occupies: specifically, to the West in the late nineteenth and twentieth centuries. She insists that the high modernist project that "seeks to transform the world by style" (296) is historically and geographically specific. She does not speculate about what might follow the modernism she treats as a historical phenome-non. But her association of the modern with the European is sugges-tive, and it is illuminated by contemporary critical taxonomies that link the postmodern and the postcolonial. Jameson identifies mod-

[8] Lazarus, "Modernism and Modernity," 147.

[9] Jameson, *Postmodernism*, 389; Huyssen, *After the Great Divide*, 188, 220.

[10] Gordimer "Essential Gesture," 293; Gordimer reflects on her relationship to readers, especially black readers, in South Africa in "The Gap between the Writer and the Reader."

[11] Wagner criticizes Gordimer for continuing to "claim superior insight and vision for the writer" and for defending "the right of society to impose responsibility on writers" (30–31).

ernism with the period of imperialism and postmodernism with "late" or multinational capitalism (*Postmodernism*, xix). Anthony Appiah suggests that "the *post* in postcolonial, like the *post* in postmodern is the *post* of the space-clearing gesture" (149). He traces the convergences and antagonisms of these two "posts" in the writings of a "comprador intelligentsia," among whom he includes Gordimer herself (149, 155).

A Sport of Nature is a product of the moment—the late interregnum, the state of emergency—that the two essays define and of the postmodern, postcolonial discursive strategies that they describe. These strategies underwrite the novel's examination of the role of whites in a black-led, nonracial movement and in the nonracial nation imagined in a utopian future tense. But the utopian moment of *A Sport of Nature* is subordinate to the ironic tone that dominates its narrative surface. The tension between them raises questions about whether or how a poetics of critique can be transmuted into a politics of affirmation.

Decentering the (White, Female) Subject

A Sport of Nature confronts the exigencies of the mid-1980s.[12] Like *Burger's Daughter*, it explores the role of whites in the struggle against apartheid and in the coming order presaged by that struggle, but it asks not whether but how—in what capacity, under what conditions—whites might take part. Gordimer addresses the imperatives of Tutu and Serote speculatively, by imagining white characters who can follow or listen and by placing them in the liberation struggle and in relation to a new order glimpsed in the last scene.

As in *Burger's Daughter*, the main character of *A Sport of Nature*, Hillela Capran, is a white woman who grows up in southern Africa in the era of apartheid. Like Rosa, Hillela is situated in the history the novel recounts. The "personal" milestones that punctuate her life are set against well-known public events that make up a "chronology of South African development . . . from the 1950s . . . to the 1980s."[13] The articulation of public and private plots is significantly different in *A Sport of Nature* from that in *Burger's Daughter*, however. In the earlier novel, public and private converge in Rosa's decision to return to South Africa. The foregrounding of this convergence in the novel's turning point makes for a narrative economy in which whites occupy a privileged position and Africans are marginalized or occluded, as

[12] See Clingman, "*Sport of Nature*," 186.
[13] Ibid., 175.

Zwelinzima angrily reminds Rosa. As in *Burger's Daughter*, in *A Sport of Nature* Gordimer tracks the protagonist's involvement in liberation politics, but here she distances us from Hillela's consciousness by representing her as the object of an ironic, omniscient, retrospectively rendered narration.[14] In de-emphasizing Hillela's thoughts and feelings, *A Sport of Nature* destabilizes the colonial discursive organization that focuses on the concerns and preoccupations of whites.

Throughout the novel, Hillela is portrayed not as subjectivity—consciousness or self-consciousness—but from the outside as an object of attention, conjecture, surveillance, as a cinematic vantage point. The decentering of Hillela's subjectivity enacts a version of the "space-clearing gesture" that, Appiah argues (149), links the postmodern and the postcolonial.[15] In the opening scene, Hillela is described by an unidentified narrator as a perspective, like a camera eye, on a scene that passes by as she watches from a train window: "Somewhere along the journey the girl shed one name and emerged under the other. As she chewed gum and let slide by the conveyer belt of balancing rocks, the wayside halts where black children waved, the grazing buck sloping away to the horizon in a blast of fear set in motion by the passing train, she threw Kim up to the rack with her school panama and took on Hillela" (3). Here and throughout the novel, identity is a function of name and costume as well as race and gender: Kim is a boy's name at the turn of the twentieth century when Rudyard Kipling writes, but by the mid-1950s, when this episode takes place, it is a name for girls, specifically for Christian girls.[16] We rarely get close to Hillela. Rather, we watch her from a certain distance as she moves from one place to another, one set of parents (or surrogate parents) to another, and one man to another, and we encounter the world she traverses from her vantage point as it is refracted through the novel's ironic narration.

Hillela is abandoned in early childhood when her mother, Ruthie, goes to Mozambique to live with a Portuguese lover. Her father, Len, sends her to boarding school, and she spends her school vacations with Ruthie's sisters, Olga and Pauline. Along with or alongside Hil-

---

[14] Susan Winnett ("Making Metaphors," 151) and Richard Peck ("What's a Poor White to Do?" 162–63) are among the few critics who do not regard the distance from which Hillela is portrayed as a flaw in the novel.

[15] Cf. Jameson: "The disappearance of the individual subject, along with its formal consequence, the increasing unavailability of the personal style, engenders the well-nigh universal practice today of what may be called *pastiche*" (*Postmodernism*, 15–16).

[16] Gordimer changed the name of the protagonist late in the composing process. See the 28 October 1986 letter to Jill Sutcliffe at Jonathan Cape, Gordimer Collection, box 14, folder 25. The name Kim also alludes to Kimberley, site of South African diamond mines and a repressive racial and economic hierarchy (Thompson 118–19).

lela, we scrutinize the photographs of Ruthie and read the unsent love letters—they catalogue the sexual pleasures for which Ruthie leaves husband and daughter—that constitute Hillela's maternal legacy. With Hillela, we take note of the upper-middle-class milieu of the stylish, antique-collecting Olga and the liberal circle of the passionate but self-righteous Pauline and her gentle husband, Joe, a lawyer who defends opponents of apartheid. Later, we accompany Hillela to Tanzania, where she lands in a community of South African exiles in the mid-1960s; Ghana, where she falls in love with and marries Whaila Kgomani, an ANC leader who is soon assassinated by South African security forces, in the late 1960s; Eastern Europe in the early 1970s; the United States in the mid-1970s; and, eventually, an unidentified West African country whose head of state, known as the General, becomes her second husband.

Hillela's experience makes up the plot of *A Sport of Nature*, but it affords an inconsistent, shifting, unstable vision of the novel's represented world. The objects, events, and persons that Hillela encounters or observes seem to be caught almost at random: overheard, not heard; seen, but not noticed. As a young girl at Pauline's house, Hillela hears a tape of Nelson Mandela addressing the All-In African Conference, held in Pietermaritzburg in March 1961, but she does not pay attention to what he is saying.[17] She has a tangential, contingent relationship to a politics which she does not (yet) understand, a liberation struggle she has not (yet) joined. Thus, she represents those whites who, as Gordimer puts it in "The Essential Gesture," have not woken up (293).

Hillela meets *The Brothers Karamazov* at a similar remove. She first discovers Dostoevsky's novel when her cousin Sasha, the son of Pauline and Joe, is reading it, and she "reads" it along with him over his shoulder. Later, she finds it in the library of a deracinated German living in Tanzania and, still later, in the conversation of a disaffected intellectual, a former Communist, in an unnamed Eastern European country. Throughout *A Sport of Nature, The Brothers Karamazov* signifies the classical, European political novel and the (European) politics and family plot the genre represents. It also suggests a posture of dissidence exemplified by Fyodor Dostoevsky, Milan Kundera, and Georg Lukács, among others. Gordimer identifies *Burger's Daughter* as a political novel, but the treatment of *The Brothers Karamazov* in *A Sport of Nature* suggests that the classical European political novel, like the work

---

[17] At this conference, Mandela, recently unbanned, announced plans for a strike, the last day of which would coincide with the proclamation of a South African republic on 31 May. Mandela disappeared soon after the conference (Lodge, *Black Politics in South Africa*, 232).

of symbolists, dadaists, avant-gardists, and modernists, cannot convey the writer's "essential gesture" in contemporary South Africa ("Essential Gesture," 296). Yet this residual genre, seen here as an item in a cultural archive, has not been replaced by others with a comparable power to organize experience.

As *A Sport of Nature* revises the classical, European political novel, it also decolonizes the novel of sensibility, a dominant form of the British or Anglophone woman's novel.[18] Postcolonial feminist writers—novelists, critics, and theorists—have examined the role of the Anglophone novel of sensibility in sustaining, legitimating, and reproducing colonial and imperial orders of power and knowledge.[19] In decentering the subjectivity of its white, female protagonist, *A Sport of Nature* dismantles the conflation of women's agency and white women's consciousness that looms large in the British woman's novel of sensibility and joins the project of postcolonial critique.

The rupture of linear chronology in *A Sport of Nature* also advances the novel's decolonizing project. Seen chronologically, Hillela's life consists of a series of losses, of which the first is her abandonment by Ruthie and perhaps the most important is the death of Whaila. Throughout, the sequence of events is interrupted by proleptic images of a future that has not yet happened and by flashbacks that revisit and reconstruct the past. Hillela's life is given shape and meaning by her conversion to the liberation struggle, but the conversion occurs, as it were, offstage. It is given not as it unfolds but in retrospect. The retrospective mode is like a narrative equivalent of Lyotard's future perfect tense: it represents a subject—Hillela—engaged in a world that is (or will have been) always already constituted. This structure de-emphasizes Hillela's conversion and, by implication, that of other whites for whom she stands. The distancing effect is magnified by the irony that dominates the narrative.

Irony governs the narration of virtually every episode in the novel; one of the very few exceptions is the description of Hillela's sexual desire for Whaila:

---

[18] On the novel of sensibility and its close kin, the domestic novel, see Jehlen, "Archimedes," and Armstrong, *Desire and Domestic Fiction*. Armstrong places the emphasis in these genres on women's "qualities of mind" in a larger political and cultural history.

[19] See, especially, Spivak, "Three Women's Texts"; David, *Rule Britannia*; Ferguson, *Subject to Others*; Meyer, *Imperialism at Home*; Donaldson, *Decolonizing Feminisms*; and Said's discussion of *Mansfield Park* in *Culture and Imperialism*. Similarly, novels such as Jean Rhys's *Wide Sargasso Sea* and Caryl Phillips's *Cambridge* take up what *Jane Eyre* and *Mansfield Park* suppress or relegate to the attic or the background: Bertha Mason, slavery, and colonial political economies.

Lying beside him, looking at pale hands, thighs, belly: seeing herself as unfinished, left off, somewhere. She examines his body minutely and without shame, and he wakes to see her at it, and smiles without telling her why: she is the first not to pretend the different colours and textures of their being is not an awesome fascination. How can it be otherwise? The laws that have determined the course of life for them are made of skin and hair, the relative thickness and thinness of lips and the relative height of the bridge of the nose. That is all; that is everything. The Lilliesleaf houseparty[20] is in prison for life because of it. [The political exiles] with whom she ate pap and cabbage are in Algeria and the Soviet Union learning how to man guns and make bombs because of it. He is outlawed and plotting because of it. Christianity against other gods, the indigenous against the foreign invader, the masses against the ruling class—where he and she come from all these become interpretative meanings of the differences seen, touched and felt, of skin and hair. (177)[21]

Hillela is a desiring subject who actively seeks the object of her desire, but the marriage in which her desire is realized is an idyllic interlude in an ironic, episodic narrative. This marriage is not the end of her erotic career or the denouement of the novel's public plot, which ends with the celebration of the liberated South African nation, but a moment—a moment cut short by Whaila's death—that influences her in ways that are not spelled out in the text.

A Sport of Nature explores the relationship between sexual love and "another kind of love" that has to be "risked" (250).[22] The novel does not probe Hillela's beliefs and motivations, but it implies that her desire for Whaila leads her—in ways left unexplored—to liberation politics. The relationship of Hillela and Whaila might be seen as a version of romance, a mystification of a woman's love for an idealized, powerful man. But it is just as plausible to regard transracial erotic desire as a prefiguration of an emancipated order in which race does and does not make a difference or to see the love of a white woman for a black man as a sign of her attachment to the nation that he symbolizes: "Whaila's country" are the novel's last words. Here, and again in My Son's Story, love between a white woman and a black man offers an affirmation,

[20] A group of ANC leaders staying at Lilliesleaf Farm in Rivonia, outside Johannesburg, were arrested in a government raid in July 1963. They became the defendants in what was known as the Rivonia Trial.

[21] Gordimer comments on the eroticization of the racial body in "Off the Page," 304. On the connection between the body and the body politic, see Ettin, Betrayals of the Body Politic.

[22] Gordimer reflects on this question in a notebook she kept while writing the novel. Gordimer Collection, box 14, folder 25.

however equivocal, transitory, and vulnerable to the violence of the apartheid state, of utopian possibility.[23]

The relationship of Hillela and Whaila raises questions about whether desire (eros) might influence whites to listen and follow, yet it emphatically leaves unsettled the question of whether sexual love is a substitute for, a symbol of, or a source of social justice or the ethical position identified with Hillela's namesake, Rabbi Hillel.[24] In any case, the idyll is brief, and the marriage is violently ended when Whaila is brutally assassinated. What remains is a memory that kindles hope—a utopian image—but utopian affirmation is relegated in the latter part of the novel to a subplot of which Sasha is the protagonist, while the story of Hillela is resumed in the mode of intertextual critique and picaresque irony.

Decolonizing *Kim*

"Are there any more like you in India?" said Father Victor.
"Or are you by way of being a *lusus naturae?*"
—Rudyard Kipling, *Kim*

If, in the opening scene of *A Sport of Nature*, Gordimer "throws up to the rack" the British and European literary traditions that constitute her literary genealogy—especially the Anglophone, feminine novel of sensibility and the classical, European political novel—she also opens up a space in which the novel takes shape, under the sign of *Kim*, the name Hillela sheds with her hat. Gordimer refashions Kim's treatment of spying and surveillance, undermines the authority of its narrator, and dismantles its colonial articulation of race and gender. In rewriting Rudyard Kipling's imperial picaresque in *A Sport of Nature*, Gordimer deploys the anticolonial hermeneutic of Aimé Césaire's *Discourse on Colonialism* and Frantz Fanon's *The Wretched of the Earth* and the antipatriarchal textual politics of many women's novels. The novel's irony is directed at whites who, blinded by colonial (racist) misconceptions, misinterpret Africa and Africans; at men who misread Hillela as a free

---

[23] Nancy Topping Bazin ("Sex, Politics, and Silent Black Women," 38) notes the occlusion of black women in this narrative. Ian Glenn, writing before the publication of *My Son's Story*, remarks that black women are "a crucial lacuna in Gordimer's work" ("Hodiernal Hillela," 77–78).

[24] See Clingman, *"Sport of Nature,"* 182, on Hillela's echo of Hillel's "ethical paradox": "If I am not for myself, who will be? If I am for myself only, what am I? And if not now, when?"

spirit, femme fatale, eternal feminine; and at women who collude in men's misreadings and the masculinist values they inscribe.

Gordimer revises both Kipling's treatment of spying as a "great game" and the plot that conscripts Kim as an imperial agent—at once master and subject—of the British secret service. The violence that sustains the imperial order in *Kim*'s India is occluded by the novel's sense of fun.[25] In *A Sport of Nature*, however, the violence of the apartheid order is palpable in the shootings, bombings, imprisonment, and torture that punctuate the narrative. Like Kim and picaresque protagonists generally, Hillela offers us a vantage point on the world she travels through. But while Kipling details the instruction Kim is given in the arts of espionage and his adventures as a British agent, we must speculate about whether Hillela actually does intelligence work for the ANC, because we never see her at it.

In rescripting Kipling's treatment of spying as a great game, *A Sport of Nature* calls into question the authority of his narrator and the idea of narrative authority in general. Kipling's narrator recounts Kim's career in a confident voice that makes the narrative appear to be as unproblematic as the empire it represents.[26] In *A Sport of Nature*, however, the competing perspectives of numerous characters and the conflicting political formations of the apartheid state and its changing opposition give rise to contradictory accounts of many of the novel's events.

Hillela is edited out of some accounts of Whaila's life, and after his death, she edits her own story to highlight her political conversion:

> The girl is mother to the woman, of course; she has been acknowledged. In fact, the woman has generally chosen to begin her existence there, when asked about her early life: —I was very young, working at an embassy in Accra when I met Whaila at a reception given by the late Kwame Nkrumah.—
> Well, it's not impossible. (170)

In echoing Wordsworth—"The child is father to the man," Wordsworth says, in the epigraph to the "Intimations Ode"—and Dickens in *David Copperfield*, *A Sport of Nature* points to the disingenuousness of Hillela's self-fashioning.[27] In beginning with her marriage, Hillela erases her childhood and her family, the parents who abandoned her

---

[25] On pleasure in *Kim*, see Said, *Culture and Imperialism*, 136.

[26] Said identifies Kipling's narrator with the all-seeing, all-knowing Colonel Creighton (ibid., 151–56).

[27] *David Copperfield* chooses "to begin my life with the beginning of my life," but *David Copperfield* suggests that all such beginnings exclude something else. See also Said, "The Novel as Beginning Intention" (*Beginnings*, chap. 3).

and the aunts and uncles who brought her up. But this beginning, erasure and all, might also suggest that the political commitment that starts in desire is a second birth. The idea of political commitment itself is undermined by the interjection of an unidentified voice that says, "Well, it's not impossible." But this voice has neither more nor less authority than others in the novel.

In much the same way as *A Sport of Nature* destabilizes *Kim*'s imperial monologue, it also dismantles Kipling's construction of race. In the early part of the novel, Kim playfully assumes and discards a series of different racial (ethnic) identities, using race as a kind of disguise, but eventually he is brought within the imperial ambit and takes up his place as a British subject.[28] Like *Kim, A Sport of Nature* unsettles race as a category of identity, but it does not reach closure through the kind of racial sorting that *Kim* enacts. Rather, *A Sport of Nature* presents *race* as an assemblage of contradictory or incongruous political, economic, cultural, and ethnic attributes. In some instances, race is a signifier of political allegiance or economic position (class): the notion of race as a political category recalls Fanon's argument against a naïvely racial or nationalist conception of anticolonial struggle.[29] Such whites as Bram Fischer, the principal model for Lionel Burger, are said to have given up being white; in contrast, blacks who collaborate with the apartheid regime are seen by other blacks as not "their own" (186, 322). Race also designates ethnicity, but this designation is relative, a matter of perspective. The daughter of Hillela and Whaila is at once "our color" and black like her father (177–79). In short, *A Sport of Nature* treats race as a category of ascribed, significant difference and a category in which difference appears insignificant.[30]

Finally, *A Sport of Nature* unravels Kipling's colonial articulation of race and gender and rewrites the national family romance elaborated in *Kim*. Kim is constituted as a British subject through his relationships with a series of symbolic mothers and fathers. At first glance, it appears that some of the fathers—Creighton and Lurgan, Father Victor and Mr. Bennett—are British, and others are "Indian": that is, Bengali, Pathan, Punjabi, Muslim, Hindu, Buddhist, and so forth.[31] But even the Indian fathers are identified with the Raj and hence with Britain. The

[28] On the treatment of race in *Kim*, see JanMohamed, "Economy of Manichean Allegory," 97–100.

[29] Fanon mentions "certain settlers [who] . . . go so far as to condemn the colonial war [,] . . . go over to the enemy, become Negroes or Arabs, and accept suffering, torture, and death" (*Wretched of the Earth*, 145).

[30] See Gates, "Introduction."

[31] JanMohamed divides Kim's fathers into English and Indian (99).

Pathan horse dealer Mahbub Ali and the Bengali Babu Hurree Chunder Mookherjee work for the secret service, while the Teshoo Lama subsidizes Kim's imperial education.

Kim's surrogate mothers include the prostitute Huneefa, the woman of Shamlegh, the Kulu woman who nurses him back to health when he falls ill, and the Mother Earth at whose breast he is revived. All are identified with India, which becomes, in effect, his mother; taken together, these women represent "Mother India" itself. The plenitude of nurturing mothers is one aspect of *Kim*'s imperial strategy of domesticating—feminizing, pacifying, or, in Said's terms, Orientalizing—India. Oedipal-patriarchal and colonial narratives (gender and race) reinforce each other, as Kim consolidates his (British, male) identity by acquiring mothers, fathers, language, and culture.

A Sport of Nature unbalances the colonial equilibrium achieved in *Kim*. Like Kim, Hillela negotiates her identity through relationships with a series of symbolic parents who substitute for the ones who abandon her. Her mothers are identified not with the colonized other but with the culture of colonialism, but the national affiliations of her fathers vary.[32] In different ways, Olga, Ruthie, and Pauline belong to the dying, Eurocolonial order: Olga represents a kind of high-colonial good taste; Pauline illustrates an obsolescent political style, one that might be called late-colonial dissidence; and Ruthie exemplifies rebellion against colonial sexual mores. Hillela's father, Len, who consigns her to the care of Olga and Pauline, is a traveling salesman left behind by the sweep of history in southern Africa, while her uncle Joe represents the same colonial liberalism as his wife. Other father figures become Hillela's lovers and, sometimes, mentors who foster her involvement in liberation politics. As an object of masculine desire and feminine, especially maternal rivalry, Hillela exposes the hypocrisy of colonial sexual codes. In this, she is the protagonist of a postmodern, postcolonial picaresque.

The Postcolonial Picaresque

A distinctive feature of the feminine picaresque is the sexual character of the protagonist's adventures.[33] Whether the picara actually

---

[32] John Cooke notes the identification of mother with colonial culture in Gordimer's novels (*Novels of Nadine Gordimer*, 46). Cf. Fanon's characterization of the "mother country" as a "bloodthirsty and implacable stepmother" (*Wretched of the Earth*, 145).

[33] On the sexual character of the picara, see Monteser, *Picaresque Element*, 4. On *A Sport of Nature* as a picaresque, see Gordimer's interview with Anthony Sampson, quoted in Clingman, "*Sport of Nature*," 174; and Brink, "Mutants of the Picaresque," 270.

trades on her sexuality or whether she is simply rumored to do so, she affronts the hypocritical sexual morality that exemplifies the disintegration of the society on whose margins she moves. Like the classical picara, Hillela appears to be an opportunist who uses sex as a strategy for survival. But sex, in South Africa, is inscribed in the racial taxonomy of apartheid, and at least some of Hillela's sexual transgressions are offenses against "laws of skin and hair." These transgressions represent her as the protagonist of a postcolonial picaresque that is postmodern in its engagement with the problematic of otherness.[34]

In one of the earliest episodes in the novel, Hillela is expelled from a Salisbury boarding school because she goes out with a colored boy whom she meets in a movie theater. (She does not recognize when she meets him that he is colored.) This episode prefigures Hillela's later career. The same picaresque conjunction of innocence and transgression is found in her involvements with men either married, black, or otherwise inappropriate and with her cousin Sasha. This conjunction asks us to consider whether she is a freak of nature or whether she anticipates a new economy of sex and race.

Hillela's sexuality is her mode of inscription into postcolonial African politics. She has numerous lovers and two black African husbands. In Hillela's marriage to Whaila, transracial desire figures or prefigures a utopian order, but her marriage to the General, rendered in the cool idiom that dominates the narrative, is portrayed as a mutually convenient political arrangement. In both marriages, Hillela's self-realization appears to be identified with her husband's political program. Actually, all of Hillela's sexual involvements after Whaila, including her second marriage, seem to be intended to advance the program of the ANC.

Throughout, the ironic narration distances readers from the emancipatory potential of Hillela's desire, but the novel evidently prefers Hillela's unorthodox sexual career to that of her mother. Ruthie runs away from a banal, lower-middle-class colonial existence. Her trajectory suggests that sexuality is an arena in which political contradictions are contested and displaced but illustrates, too, the limits of a purely sexual politics. Ruthie falls short of the example of two namesakes, the biblical Ruth, prototype of marital fidelity, and Ruth First, an exiled, white South African Communist who was assassinated in Maputo by a South African letter bomb. Like Ruthie, Hillela escapes the claustrophobic family (families) in which she grows up. But unlike Ruthie, Hillela is not circumscribed by family pathology.

Hillela is also contrasted with Sasha, from whom she is distin-

---

[34] Jameson, *Postmodernism*, 389; Huyssen 219.

guished by differences of gender and genre. As a man, Sasha must decide whether to serve in the South African army or become a conscientious objector, but Hillela never has to confront the issue of military service. Differences in temperament and family situation may be as important as gender, however, for Hillela is not bound by the family constraints against which Sasha chafes; she does not appear to agonize over any ethical question, and he agonizes over all such questions. As teenagers, Hillela and Sasha also have a love affair that comes close to transgressing the taboo against incest and, like all Hillela's erotic encounters, offends the prevailing sexual morality. This affair is abruptly ended when Pauline discovers Hillela and Sasha in bed together and sends Hillela away.

Hillela and Sasha belong to different generic traditions. She is a typical picaresque protagonist, but he belongs in the classical political novel. Sasha resembles the Dostoevskyan hero that Bakhtin classifies as a man of ideas.[35] This affiliation is signaled by his absorption in *The Brothers Karamazov*. Sasha is imprisoned for his part in the liberation struggle. In the letters that he writes Hillela from jail (they are intercepted, so she never receives them), he describes his changing political involvement and invokes classics of prison literature, including the writings of Ruth First, Breyten Breytenbach, and Jeremy Cronin, white South Africans imprisoned for their opposition to apartheid. Sasha's story and its generic prototypes, prison writings and the classical political novel, are subordinated in *A Sport of Nature* to the picaresque, ironic treatment of Hillela. But these residual genres retain a certain expressive power.[36]

Hillela and Sasha represent not only different generic traditions but also complementary relationships to postcolonial African politics in general and the South African liberation movement in particular. Sasha inherits his fierce political passion from both his parents and especially his mother. As he explains in his letters (300–302, 314–23), he is initially a participant in protest movements led by whites like his parents. Forced by the Black Consciousness movement of the 1970s to reassess his position and that of whites generally, he subsequently becomes an organizer for a black trade union that eventually affiliates with the UDF. In one of the novel's most poignant ironies, he speaks for a utopian future he will see only from a distance, addressing his thoughts to Pauline: "Don't you see? It's all got to come down, mother.

---

[35] Bakhtin, *Problems of Dostoevsky's Poetics*, 78.
[36] This power was evident in Gordimer's reading from one of Sasha's letters at Poets' House in New York in April 1987.

Without utopia—the idea of utopia—there's a failure of the imagination—and that's a failure to know how to go on living. It will take another kind of being to stay on, here. A new white person. Not us. The
chance is a wild chance—like falling in love" (187). But he experiences
his mother as a constraining, even suffocating presence, except when
he is in prison and she works with the detainees' parents group. After
his release from prison, he bombs a police station and eventually goes
into exile, remaining outside South Africa.

Unlike Sasha, Hillela returns to South Africa. In the last scene of the
novel, she attends the celebration of a liberated South Africa as the
wife of the General, now head of the Organization of African Unity.
This ending suggests that "spontaneous mutations" are capable of
adapting to and might even anticipate the demands of the postcolonial
future. Hillela is unencumbered by the burdens of family, class, and
culture that have weighed Sasha down; she is in South Africa, but he
remains in exile. If the ending tempts us to see Hillela as the "new
white person" that Sasha envisages, it also cautions us not to idealize
Hillela as Sasha does. She does not belong to South Africa but rather
visits "Whaila's country" (341) as the wife of an honored guest. She is
not in but on the margins of the new order that the last scene presents.

Utopian Pastiche

In juxtaposing Sasha's passion with Hillela's detachment and politicizing Hillela's sexuality by making it her mode of connection to an
African future that Sasha observes from the distance of exile in Europe,
A Sport of Nature elaborates a poetics of pastiche and bricolage. This
poetics corresponds to the improvisations of postcolonial African politics, hybrids that graft indigenous and European political traditions.[37]

The General and Sasha are the novel's chief advocates of the politics
of improvisation. The General describes himself as a "Catholic Nationalist Marxist—African made," a "new combination" (266). Although
Sasha is a white South African, not a black West African, he describes a
similar ensemble in one of his letters from prison: "I say there is un-
beatable purpose expressed in the horrible mishmash of Marxism,
Castroism, Gandhism, Fanonism, Hyde Park tub-thumping (colonial
heritage), Gawd-on-our-sideism (missionary heritage), Black Consciousness jargon, Sandinistism, Christian liberation theology with

---

[37] On the hybrid character of contemporary African culture and politics, see Appiah,
"Postcolonial and the Postmodern," 155.

which we formulate" (315). Sasha's mishmash suggests the heteroglot coalition of the UDF. As Tom Lodge and his coauthors explain, "The UDF sought initially to be as all-embracing as possible, cheerfully accommodating Islamic preachers, township capitalists, a variety of Christian notables, Marxists, socialists, Gandhists, liberals, and African nationalists."[38] The heterogeneous politics of both the General and Sasha are answers to racist pretexts: for Sasha, the major who interrogates him; for the General, colonial oppression and neocolonial exploitation. Both Sasha and the General, that is, describe new forms of resistance. These forms exemplify what Françoise Lionnet identifies as métissage, a transcultural interweaving of diverse traditions and discourses.[39]

The improvisatory practice of métissage is also represented in the novel in State House, the presidential residence where Hillela lives with the General when he once again becomes head of state after defeating the military rulers who deposed him and governed his country with the help of the United States. In State House, formerly Government House in the imperial era, métissage coexists with elements of a kitsch identified with neocolonial political and cultural economies and with the aesthetic commodification that Jameson defines as the cultural logic of late, or multinational, capitalism.[40] The General wants to install air conditioning and brick up old walls in State House, but Hillela demurs. She favors both European architecture and a stylistic assemblage that represents the hybrid cultures of contemporary Africa, an aesthetic equivalent of the politics that the General designates as a "new combination." The General's affection for the "idiom of the Hilton and the Intercontinental"—neocolonial kitsch—and Hillela's affinity, acquired under the tutelage of her elegant Aunt Olga, for the "stylistic graces and charms of the past" (305) are both objects of the novel's irony. In juxtaposing kitsch with métissage and holding them in tension, the novel elaborates a pastiche like Sasha's "horrible mishmash," his politics of revolutionary bricolage.

A Sport of Nature is a generic hybrid, a narrative sport of nature. It grafts Hillela and Sasha, the picaresque and the classical political novel, the affirmative and critical moments of postmodernism, revolutionary utopianism and political pragmatism, indigenous and borrowed political and cultural traditions, métissage and kitsch. Along with Sasha, it holds out the hope of the "wild chance." But in the end-

[38] Lodge and Nasson et al., *All, Here, and Now*, 52.
[39] See Lionnet, *Postcolonial Representations*, 6, 16, 18.
[40] Jameson, *Postmodernism*, 4–5.

ing that situates Hillela on the margins of and Sasha in exile from the nation it identifies as Whaila's country, it raises questions about its own status: it asks how the whites that Hillela and Sasha represent can help bring into being and participate in the utopian future it envisages and whether the writings of English-speaking whites can transmute postmodern, postcolonial practices of cultural critique into an indigenous South African growth.

8

Beyond Identity:
The Poetics of Nonracialism
and the Politics of Cultural Translation
in *My Son's Story*

My Son's Story was published in 1990, the same year that Nelson Mandela was released from prison. During the period when it was being written, the late 1980s, the contradictions that betokened the crisis of apartheid intensified.[1] Beginning in 1985, secret negotiations began between Nelson Mandela, who remained in prison, and the National Party government.[2] These negotiations continued for several years, until and even after Mandela's release in February 1990. The national state of emergency declared in June 1986 continued through the end of 1990, but with less force after early 1989, when F. W. de Klerk succeeded P. W. Botha as head of the National Party and then as president.

The late 1980s saw strikes, boycotts, and national campaigns by the UDF in 1986 (against the state of emergency) and in 1987 (to unban the ANC). The ANC stepped up guerrilla activities beginning in October 1988, with attacks on police and government buildings, railroad lines, and, in 1989, a South African Defence Force radar station. Beginning in January 1989, resistance and rebellion intensified, with a hunger strike among prisoners and an ANC call for a "Year of Mass Action for Peoples' Power." At the same time, the ANC, in exile in Lusaka, Zambia, held a series of meetings that produced the 1988 "Constitutional Guidelines for a Democratic South Africa." These guidelines reaffirm the ANC's commitment to the politics of nonracialism, as set out in the 1955 Freedom Charter. They "promote the growth of a *single national identity* and loyalty binding on all South Africans," while recognizing the "linguistic and cultural diversity of the people."[3]

During this period, official government repression abated some-

---

[1] Gordimer gives February 1987–February 1990 as the dates of composition. Gordimer Collection, box 11, folder 5.

[2] See Sparks, *Tomorrow Is Another Country*, and Mandela, *Long Walk to Freedom*, 445–87.

[3] Quoted in Lodge and Nasson et al., *All, Here, and Now*, 354; emphasis added.

what. The UDF, banned in February 1988, was unbanned early in 1990, along with other organizations, most important, the ANC. But throughout and even after the lifting of the state of emergency, members of South Africa's black majority and others involved in the liberation struggle and in antiapartheid activities more generally were censored, detained, and subjected to violence sanctioned or perpetrated by the government.[4] The state, or parts of its security apparatus, condoned, tacitly permitted, and sponsored assassinations in black townships and elsewhere by right-wing terrorists and vigilantes. Despite the mounting toll of dead and wounded and years of antagonism and mutual distrust between the National Party government and the liberation movement, the secret negotiations continued, resulting in the release in 1989 of a number of important political prisoners—many of whom, like Mandela, had been in jail since the early 1960s—and, in 1990, of Mandela himself.[5]

Like *Burger's Daughter* and *A Sport of Nature*, *My Son's Story* examines the recent past; unlike its predecessors, it does not reach back to the 1940s but rather begins in the almost present of the late 1970s.[6] A more significant departure is its narrative focus. The title characters in both *Burger's Daughter* and *A Sport of Nature* are white women opposed to apartheid; the main characters of *My Son's Story* are a colored family: father, mother, daughter, and son. Members of South Africa's colored population do not form one group; they are descendants of unions between Europeans and Khoisan (hunter gatherers), of Malay slaves brought to southern Africa by the Dutch, and of Indonesian Muslims sent to the Cape as political prisoners or indentured servants.[7] In *My Son's Story*, Gordimer exploits the various and changing meanings of "colored." The ancestry of the novel's protagonists is not specified; in the way that they come to see themselves as black, Gordimer registers the increasing identification of at least some of South Africa's colored population with the nation's black majority.[8]

---

[4] Gordimer's research materials for the novel include newspaper accounts of violent attacks on the homes of a colored family and an Indian family living in white suburbs in Johannesburg. Gordimer Collection, box 11, folders 5 and 6.

[5] This account of the political climate in which *My Son's Story* was written is taken from Sparks; Lodge and Nasson et al. 87–115; and Mandela 445–544.

[6] Gordimer's chronology dates its events between 1978 and 1989. Gordimer Collection, box 11, folder 6.

[7] Goldin, *Making Race*, 9; Marks and Trapido, "Politics of Race, Class, and Nationalism," 27. Goldin explains that "colored" is preferred to "mixed race" because, except in the ideology of apartheid, all races are mixed (xxv–xxvi).

[8] Dominic Head notes Gordimer's "attempt to 'cover all colours and no colour' by eschewing racial categorization" (*Nadine Gordimer*, 151). Kathrin Wagner speculates that Gordimer saw "the 'new African[s]'" as a fusion of European and African traditions

My Son's Story destabilizes racial classifications in another way as well. The story of the protagonists—we do not learn the family surname—is told by the son and by an unidentified, third-person narrator. In impersonating the son, Gordimer audaciously circumvents a prohibition on writing across a real and imagined racial divide; she writes across differences of gender and generation too.[9] The first-person narrative is intercut with an omniscient narration in which race, gender, and other determinants of identity are not specified. The juxtaposition of two narratives, one marked, the other unmarked by race, gender, and generation, underwrites a poetics of nonracialism analogous to the nonracial politics of the ANC. *My Son's Story* attempts to construct—to "perform," in Homi Bhabha's sense—a nonracial South African identity: an identity that is not defined by ethnic or racial distinctions but respects racial difference. But the performative construction of a nonracial South African identity remains vulnerable to pedagogical imperatives that call it into question.

The main characters of *My Son's Story* raise the same kinds of questions about the relationship of South African politics and European cultural traditions as *Burger's Daughter* and *A Sport of Nature*. The father is an English teacher named Sonny; he names his son Will, after his beloved Shakespeare. Sonny joins and later becomes a leader in the liberation movement. In Sonny's career and Will's, the novel asks whether or how the European traditions that Shakespeare represents can be salvaged, recycled, and put to use in the making of a new political order. The mother, Aila, and the daughter, Baby, suggest different economies of politics and culture. In portraying all four members of the family, *My Son's Story* attempts to inscribe itself in and bring into being a nonracial South African nation, but the novel also reminds us that the utopian moment that it longingly anticipates has not yet arrived.

The Ghosts of Hamlet

My Son's Story begins when Will discovers Sonny walking out of a movie theater with a white woman. Much of the novel is taken up with

---

(*Rereading Nadine Gordimer*, 218). On the recent history of South Africa's colored population, which belies the novel's treatment of race, see Finnegan, "The Election Mandela Lost," and Wells, " 'Coloreds' Struggle to Find Their Place in a Free South Africa."

[9] Rob Nixon sees the transracial narrative as an instance either of "racial arrogance" or of "utopian refusal" ("Sons and Lovers").

Will's oedipal conflicts.[10] He rages at his father and pities his mother, whom he regards as a victim of his father's betrayal. Will's rage and pity fuel his ambition to become a writer, an ambition that produces the first-person narrative that he identifies as "my first book—that I can never publish" (277).[11] The family story is inflected by the politics of race and nation in South Africa. When Sonny joins the liberation struggle, the life of the family is turned upside down. He loses his teaching position and becomes a full-time organizer; eventually he is jailed, tried, and convicted. After his release from prison, he resumes political work and begins a passionate affair with a white woman, a human rights observer named Hannah Plowman.

Sonny is with Hannah when Will "discovers" him at the movie theater. Will, absorbed in his own conflicts, does not notice the unhappiness of his sister, Baby. She tries to kill herself but soon afterward joins the liberation movement and eventually goes into exile with the ANC in Lusaka. Apparently unnoticed by either Sonny or Will, Aila, too, becomes a revolutionary. When she is arrested on suspicion of terrorism, her husband and her son both assume, wrongly, that she has been framed. While Sonny's star in the movement has been declining, perhaps because of his involvement with Hannah, Aila becomes a leader in the underground.[12] During her trial, she flees the country to avoid compromising others. The end of the novel finds Hannah working for the United Nations, Baby in Lusaka, Sonny resuming political work in South Africa, Aila traveling around the world on behalf of the ANC, and Will becoming a writer.

As befits a novel in which one of the main characters names another one after William Shakespeare, there are numerous allusions to Shakespeare in *My Son's Story*. The novel's epigraph—"You had a Father, let your son say so"—is taken from Sonnet 13. Sonny, who confronts a loss of potency and power, recalls Lear and Prospero. Sonny and Hannah take their secret password from *As You Like It*.[13] The Shakespeare text

[10] On the novel's oedipal dynamics, see Weinhouse, "Paternal Gift."

[11] Head notes that Will is alluding to South African censorship that reflects the influence of racial discrimination on literary production (159–60).

[12] See Gordimer's outline for the novel in Gordimer Collection, box 11, folder 5, p. 12. See also Greenstein, "*My Son's Story*," 197.

[13] The password, "Sermons in stones," comes from the famous speech given by the exiled Duke: "Sweet are the uses of adversity, / Which, like the toad, ugly and venomous, / Wears yet a precious jewel in his head; / And this our life, exempt from public haunt, / Finds tongues in trees, books in the running brooks, / Sermons in stones, and good in everything: I would not change it." (2.1 12–18). A notebook Gordimer kept while writing the novel contains numerous quotations from plays and sonnets. Gordimer Collection, box 15, folder 87.

most prominently recalled in Will's narrative, a story about the making of a writer, a family romance, a genealogy of masculine subjectivity, an "exposure of the rot in the State" (113), is *Hamlet*.[14]

My Son's Story revises—in Mikhail Bakhtin's terms, "novelizes"— the son's story that occupies center stage in *Hamlet*.[15] By juxtaposing Will's narrative with those of his mother, father, and sister, Gordimer treats it as one among an array of possible accounts of the events described in the novel. In making it the story of a colored South African in the 1980s, Gordimer implies that the story told in such works as *Hamlet* is not the exclusive property of traditional—European, upper-class—cultural elites. The example of Sonny, who loves literature in general and Shakespeare and Kafka in particular, suggests the appropriation by emergent groups of a traditional (British, European) canon and the concomitant democratization of the hegemonic cultural histories—his-stories?—it canonizes. And Will's story reaccentuates the preoccupations of Hamlet (*Hamlet*)—specifically the conjunction of oedipal angst, cultural production, and the construction of identity as interiority—as these are codified and recorded in the play and in the later history of its reception.[16]

Will's narrative reimagines Hamlet's punning remark, "I am too much in the sun" (act 1, scene 2, line 67). Will identifies with and resents the father who taught him to read and who proudly declares, "My son's going to be a writer" (*My Son's Story*, 36). His self-involvement is treated as one among several possible vicissitudes of desire, but one with a privileged place in histories of cultural production, transmission, and reception. Baby offers a point of contrast. Yet Will's self-absorbed reflections are the genesis of his vocation as a writer; his fantasies and his curiosity provoke his imagination and issue in the story he eventually writes.

In Will's snooping and compulsion to interpret, the novel points to a schism between acts and their significance, a gap between words and their meanings. This gap, the object of Will's meditations, is also one of the central concerns of *Hamlet* and Hamlet alike. Hamlet repeatedly draws attention to the relationship of act, action, and acting with whatever might underlie them—thoughts, feelings, motives. Arguably, it is

[14.] On *Hamlet* as the "paradigmatic pre-text" for the novel, see Greenstein, "*My Son's Story*," 199.

[15] Bakhtin, "Epic and Novel," 7, 39. Ettin says the title designates a "story written in the capacity of a son" (*Betrayals of the Body Politic*, 137); Wagner says it refers to the stories of the mother, father, and son (219).

[16] See Jacqueline Rose, "Sexuality in the Reading of Shakespeare," on the reception of *Hamlet* as a product of subjectivity coded and constructed as masculine.

his worrying of this relationship, especially in the soliloquies, that has made him a (the?) paradigmatic figure of European, bourgeois, masculine subjectivity (identity) construed as interiority: consciousness or the eruption of traces of unconscious conflicts in conscious processes such as speech and action.[17] The association of identity and interiority, among other features of the bourgeois ideology of individualism, makes possible the construction of the subject as author. This construction conflates Hamlet and his creator, William Shakespeare, and accordingly represents *Hamlet* as a generic precursor of the *kunstlerroman*, the genre to which Will's narrative of himself as a writer in the making belongs.[18]

Summing up his relationship to the story he has been telling, Will begins by quoting *Hamlet*:

> *I have that within that passeth show.*
> I've imagined, out of their deception, the frustration of my absence, the pain of knowing them too well, what others would be doing, saying and feeling in the gaps between my witness. . . . I was excluded from [politics], it didn't suit them for me to have any function within it, but I'm going to be the one to record, someday, what he and my mother / Aila and Baby and the others did, what it really was like to live a life determined by the struggle to be free, as desert dwellers' days are determined by the struggle against thirst and those of dwellers amid snow and ice by the struggle against the numbing of cold. That's what struggle really is, not a platform slogan repeated like a TV jingle. (276)

This summing up suggests that Will's story is one among many possible histories of the events he has recounted. It simultaneously foregrounds his narrative and brackets it as a son's story, one in which the other characters play minor parts. At the same time, it sets this story in the context of a larger political narrative that he himself intends to write, a tale in which the main roles are taken by other members of his family.

Cover Stories: The Politics of Maternal Parables

If we shift our attention from Will to Aila, we get a different perspective on the events that he describes. Gordimer presents Aila largely

---

[17] Two exemplary treatments of Hamlet's interiority, both originally published in 1919, are Jones, *Hamlet and Oedipus,* and Eliot, "Hamlet and His Problems." Cf. Horkheimer and Adorno: "Since . . . *Hamlet,* the unity of the personality has been seen through as a pretense" (156).

[18] See Greenstein, *"My Son's Story,"* 204.

from the outside, not as the interiority that defines Sonny, Will, and, to a lesser extent, Hannah. We see Aila—as we see Hillela in *A Sport of Nature*—through the lens of a narrative irony that refracts her thoughts and feelings as the conceptions or misconceptions, the conjectures or projections, of others. But irony here has a different valence than in the earlier novel. In representing Aila as a product of misprision, while maintaining a certain distance from her, *My Son's Story* acknowledges differences of race (and sex and class) yet refrains from the interpretive colonization that, as Chandra Talpade Mohanty argues, too often characterizes the discursive construction of "third world women." [19] The novel's treatment of Aila suggests nonexploitative ways of reading and writing across racial difference: cross-cultural, transracial signifying practices that figure or prefigure a nonracial order. [20]

Interpretive colonization is thematized in the way Aila is seen by others in the novel. We meet her as the object of Sonny's gaze, as an opportunity for interpretation, as a screen on which others project their own assumptions. But we readers recognize perforce that what they see tells us more about them than about her. Sonny regards Aila as an exemplar of self-presence, a vessel of transparent meaning, a paradigm of literalness; he believes that she is incapable of duplicity. Consequently, he mistakes her silence about his love affair as a sign of her ignorance of it. And when she visits him in prison, he believes that she cannot use discussion of family matters, the only topic of conversation permitted by the authorities, as a code for communication about political subjects or information about public issues (48). [21] Will colludes in seeing Aila as Sonny does; he, too, misperceives her silence as a sign of her innocence or ignorance. Aila seizes the opportunity afforded by Sonny's absences and lapses of attention, Will's self-absorption, and Baby's exile and joins the struggle herself.

Throughout the novel, the omniscient narrator draws attention to the errors of perception and interpretation that distort the way that Aila is seen by others: her brothers "mistook her gentleness for disdain; perhaps [Sonny] mistook it, too" (7). But the narrator emphatically does not interpret Aila's thoughts and actions, use a rhetoric of assertion or a logic of explanation, or engage in the hermeneutic appro-

---

[19] Mohanty, "Under Western Eyes," 52.

[20] The novel parallels or anticipates recent work in comparative feminist criticism. See, for example, Françoise Lionnet on the "interweaving" of diverse texts and traditions (*Postcolonial Representations*, 15) and Susan Sniader Lanser's idea of "comparative specificity," which embraces both difference and similarity ("Compared to What?" 296).

[21] On "family matters" as a prison code, see Mashinini, *Strikes Have Followed Me*, 66; Mandela 351 and 454; and Chapter 6, this volume, p.114, and n. 10.

priation that constitutes Sonny's knowledge and Aila's brothers' mistaken ideas. Instead, the narrator relies on strategies of negation, indirection, and figuration. The narrator affirms what is *not* known— "*No-one knows* the reserves that remain even in the most profound understanding between a man and a woman"—and describes Aila's gentleness by contradicting Sonny's notion that it was "what it appeared to be instead of the strength of will it softly gloved" (7). In presenting Aila this way, the narrator posits her subjectivity but does not make it manifest in the text. The novel maintains a respectful distance toward Aila but does not code her silence as "mystery," a crucial trope in colonial and patriarchal repertoires. Nor does the novel engage in the "othering" that variously constructs "the third world woman" as feminized colony and colonized femininity.[22]

The narrator's interpretive reticence contrasts with the eagerness of Sonny, among others, to claim Aila or to speak for her. Sonny sees Aila as an object of his desire, "a lovely body with all its features there for him: the dark nipples like grapes in his mouth, the smooth belly with its tiny well of navel, her entry satiny within as the material of the nightgown her mother had provided for her bridal 'bottom drawer' " (8). The erotic prose, with its blazon of body parts, seems to present Aila as an object to be possessed—colonized. (Shakespeare satirizes this kind of erotic discourse in Sonnet 130, which begins, "My mistress's eyes are nothing like the sun.") But the narrator's irony disrupts Sonny's colonizing gaze.

Aila is more than an occasion for a critique of the politics and poetics of sex and race. She is also an agent, a secret agent, in the political world that *My Son's Story* represents, South Africa and its liberation movement in the late 1980s.[23] Aila is a *secret* agent in part because her actions are invisible or illegible. Her apparent propriety, femininity, and fidelity to marital and maternal obligations open up a space in which she becomes a political operative, an "accomplice of Umkhonto weSizwe" (251). (Umkhonto weSizwe, the army wing of the ANC, was intensifying its guerrilla campaign in the period the novel describes.)[24] Aila visits her daughter in Lusaka; like Rosa Burger, who leaves South Africa by acting like "Patience on a monument," Aila obtains a passport by showing "she was not involved; a stay-at-home wife" (147). When Aila returns to South Africa, she abandons her ladylike deco-

---

[22] On Aila's silence and reserve, see Ettin 77 and Greenstein, *"My Son's Story,"* 205. Cf. Busia, "Silencing Sycorax," on the silent, or silenced, colonized woman.

[23] Bhabha associates Aila with a politics of performativity ("Introduction: Locations of Culture," 14–15).

[24] See Lodge and Nasson et al. 173–84.

rum. Her son, wrapped up in himself, and her husband, wrapped up in his love affair, do not notice, and the police catch on only later.

Although Aila is generally seen from the vantage points of Sonny, Will, and the state surveillance apparatus, she does speak for herself on one occasion. When she is arrested, the police find grenades hidden in her darning basket and charge her with conspiracy to engage in terrorism.[25] When Sonny asks, "What made you do it?" (239), Aila responds "like someone telling a story":

—Baby and he take the child with them everywhere, you know. And he's still so little. Meetings, parties—he's up at parties until one in the morning. The first time, I was really shocked, I told them it was wrong, poor little thing. I mean, you and I . . . when we went out while the children were small, someone came to sit in with them, they were at home in their own beds by eight o'clock to get a good night's rest. But one time when I arrived—I don't remember whether that was the fourth visit or the third—they told me that they took the little one with them to a party one night and when they came home they found the house had been bombed. You remember that second South African raid over the border, Baby sent a message after the bombing of a safe house, reassuring us it wasn't where they were living? Well, she did that because she didn't want you—us—to worry; and when she told me, she made me promise not to tell you. But it *was* the house where they'd been living. If they'd left the child at home with a sitter that night—with someone like me. . . —(240–41; ellipses in original)

Aila does not answer Sonny's question, and she draws no explicit moral or meaning from her story. Rather, she offers an exemplary narrative with the force of a parable. In Aila's account, motherhood—maternal feeling and maternal practice—is a point of departure for political awakening (conversion).[26] Maternity is also an alibi, a ruse that conceals or disguises the meaning of Aila's actions. When Aila refuses to let Will testify at her trial, everyone assumes that she is protecting him, until she skips bail and flees the country.

In Aila's narrative, and in her actions as well, motherhood plays a different part from the ones assigned it in various versions of patriar-

---

[25] Gordimer's research materials for the novel include a clipping dated March 1989 and headed "Soweto mother on terrorism charges." Gordimer Collection, box 11, folder 5.

[26] In Aila's story, the moment of conversion is not specified. Cf. Gordimer, *A Sport of Nature*, in which Hillela's political conversion occurs offstage, and Lessing, *The Golden Notebook*, which gives two accounts of Anna's conversion to Communism. All depart from such classical accounts of conversion as St. Augustine's *Confessions* and *The Autobiography of Malcolm X*.

chal ideology—as in *Hamlet*, say, or the South African security apparatus—or in Anglo-American psychoanalytic feminist theory.[27] Aila's
story differs from the sons' stories—or the fathers'—inscribed in patriarchal cultural texts. It differs, too, from the daughters' stories that
have largely preoccupied women's writing in English, as Marianne
Hirsch observes, and dominated Gordimer's own oeuvre.[28] Baby, the
daughter of Aila and Sonny, is a relatively minor character in *My Son's
Story*, yet she plays a central role in Aila's narrative, which barely mentions Sonny and omits Will altogether. Exiled in Lusaka, Baby is important as the mother of Aila's grandchild and as the occasion and
inspiration for Aila's political awakening.

Aila's elliptical tale insistently yokes together maternity and the politics of national liberation. In this conjunction, it recalls the *testimonio* of
Rigoberta Menchú, the Guatemalan (Quiché Indian) woman who won
the Nobel Peace Prize in 1992, and the autobiography of Emma
Mashinini, founder and general secretary of the Commercial, Catering,
and Allied Workers Union in South Africa. Rigoberta Menchú speaks as
a woman who gives up the desire to be a mother because of the urgent
necessity of resistance and struggle.[29] In observing that "we have hidden our identity because we needed to resist" (170), Menchú posits but
does not specify the "hidden identity" of the Quiché; she links the strategy of concealment to resistance. Aila's maternal cover story similarly
disguises histories of agency and subversion that remain unspecified.
Mashinini, who was imprisoned, held in solitary confinement, and tortured by the apartheid regime, writes explicitly as a mother. To convey
what she endured when she was tortured, a topic about which she is
otherwise reticent, she says that she forgot her daughter's name.[30]

The textual ruptures that fissure Aila's story have political implications as well. In presenting Aila, a colored woman, as the subject of a
narrative punctuated by lacunae and ellipses, the narrator at once
speaks for—represents—her and draws attention to the material conditions in which such acts of representation occur.[31] Contextualizing

---

[27] See Greenstein, "*My Son's Story*," 205. American feminist object-relations theory
stresses the relational character of female identity but often foregrounds the daughter's
point of view.

[28] Hirsch, introduction to *Mother/Daughter Plot*, passim; Chevigny, "Daughters Writing"; Cooke, *Novels of Nadine Gordimer*, 44. Hirsch's reading of the myth of Demeter as a
prototype of maternal narrative (5) illuminates Aila's story about Baby, exiled from her
native land.

[29] Menchú, *I, Rigoberta Menchú*, 223–25.

[30] Mashinini, *Strikes Have Followed Me*, 86.

[31] On the politics of representation, see Alcoff, "The Problem of Speaking for Others."
On cross-racial representation, see Marks, *Not Either an Experimental Doll*, which sutures

Aila's story in an interchange with Sonny, an interlocutor who does not understand what he hears, the novel points to a strategy for circumventing the impasses of essentialism or identity politics—the notion that only I or others "just like" me can speak for myself—and the ethnocentricity and inequalities of power too frequently reproduced in cross-cultural reading and writing.[32]

If Aila's story links her to South African autobiographers such as Emma Mashinini, it also participates in the novel's revision of *Hamlet*. Aila's narrative inscribes the position of a mother who not only haunts the imagination of her son but also speaks for herself, however briefly and cryptically.[33] The reimagining of Hamlet's mother through Aila's parable allows us to glimpse an alternative to the patriarchal cultural hegemony transmitted as property from fathers to sons and to the maternal phantasm—the mother as seen by the daughter—found in many American feminist appropriations of object relations theory, in much Anglophone (British and American) women's writing, and in Gordimer's earlier novels. Yet the truncated shape of Aila's account of her political awakening, the inability of others to decipher it, and the reiterated emphasis in the novel on her silence suggest that her full story has not yet been told.

Eros and Difference: The Uses of Adversity

In a 1988 interview, Gordimer observes that "the two greatest drives in people's lives, the two most important things, are sex and politics." She goes on to note "a particular connection between sexuality, sensuality and politics inside South Africa. Because, after all, what is apartheid all about? It's about black skin, and it's about woolly hair instead of straight, long blond hair, and black skin instead of white skin. The whole legal structure is based on the physical, so that the body becomes something supremely important" ("Off the Page," 304). In this

---

together the stories of women divided by race, class, and culture. On reticence as a cross-cultural reading strategy, see Sommer, "Textual Conquests," 259–61.

[32] Cf. Lionnet: "If 'difference' . . . makes culture visible to observers, then the emphasis on difference has the merit of underscoring specificities that would be muted and ignored otherwise. But an overemphasis on dissimilarities is likely to lead from racial and biographical determinism into an essentialist impasse" (14).

[33] Feminist criticism of Shakespeare amply documents male commentators' reproduction of the patriarchal assumptions implicit in the plays' portrayal of mothers. See Heilbrun, "*Character of Hamlet's Mother*"; Rose; and Adelman, *Suffocating Mothers*. In "Stabat Mater," Kristeva elaborates an alternative model of maternal discourse, that of the mother as split subject.

formulation, apartheid is a "legal structure" in which the "physical" is always already political, and the body, defined by the body politic. "Race" is subsumed under "politics"; racial characteristics—black skin, white skin; straight hair, woolly hair—are given, but only as part of a system, a "legal structure," of ascribed differences. In *My Son's Story*, these ascribed differences are the foundation of prohibitions that incite as well as regulate desire. Thus, the novel racializes Michel Foucault's notion of sexuality as "an especially dense transfer point for relations of power" (*History of Sexuality*, 1:103). At the same time, *My Son's Story* treats sexual desire across the color bar as a matter-of-fact feature of life in South Africa.

The relationship of Sonny and Hannah exemplifies the erotics of race described in Gordimer's interview. Their passion, like that of Hillela and Whaila in *A Sport of Nature*, transgresses the laws that forbid interracial sex in the years when each comes to sexual maturity. (The Immorality Act was repealed by P. W. Botha in 1985.) In this respect race, or the racialized sexual body, is "supremely important." Yet, to the lovers themselves, race sometimes seems insignificant. What matters to them is shared politics, mutual delight in literature, pleasure. The reciprocity of this relationship destabilizes colonial constructions of race and gender whereby a (the) white woman symbolizes or stands as the object of a (the) black man's desire. The fact that race is at once important and insignificant makes their love affair a prefiguration—at least potentially—of the nonracial order that both are working to bring into being.

Sonny, the son of an upholsterer, is an English teacher. He yearns to "improve himself," yet he cannot join the "cultural circles" in the mining town where he lives or enter the municipal library (12, 16), site of Gordimer's own education, as she explains in her Nobel Lecture.[34] Sonny's exclusion, an exclusion based on race, distinguishes him from his author, yet like her, he lays claim to literary culture (the canon). Sonny's claim is enacted in reading that translates such differently canonical figures as Shakespeare and Kafka. In Sonny's reading of their works, Gordimer asks whether cultural texts and traditions once regarded as an elite preserve can be diffused and democratized:[35]

[34] Gordimer, "From the Nobel Lecture," 20; cf. Gordimer, "Off the Page," 301. Sonny's exclusion from the library amplifies two famous instances of the thwarting of cultural aspiration in British literature: the class-based exclusion of Hardy's Jude Fawley from Christminster and the exclusion of Woolf's female narrator in *A Room of One's Own* from an Oxbridge library that admits "only fellows," that is, men.

[35] Gordimer takes a darker view of the possibility that culture might be democratized in "The Gap between the Writer and the Reader."

Kafka named what he had no names for. The town whose walls were wandered around by the Saturday people was the Castle; the library whose doors he stood before were the gates of the law at which K. sat, year after year, always to be told he must wait for entry. The sin for which the schoolteacher's kind were banished to a prescribed area, proscribed in everything they did, procreating, being born, dying, at work or at play, was the sin Joseph K. was summoned to answer for to an immanent power, not knowing what the charge was, knowing only that if that power said he was guilty of something, then he had decreed so. . . . Although Kafka explained the context of the schoolteacher's life better than Shakespeare, Sonny did not go so far as to believe, with Kafka, that the power in which people are held powerless exists only in their own submission. (17)

Gilles Deleuze and Felix Guattari examine Kafka as a Prague Jew who wrote in German; they treat his work as an exemplary instance of a minor literature, "that which a minority constructs within a major language." In a minor literature, as Deleuze and Guattari define it, "everything is political" and "everything takes on a collective value."[36] Sonny's appropriation of Kafka illustrates the collective, political dimension of minor literature. Sonny attempts to relocate Kafka in contemporary South Africa, to translate Kafka into his own idiom, to refashion Kafka's writings as a text that can name, explain, and perhaps thereby slightly mitigate the oppression and injustice he experiences. In crafting a South African Kafka, a cultural hybrid, Sonny parrots a cultural language that does not quite capture South African experience. He also levels Kafka, assimilates too easily what in Kafka is intractable, unassimilable, untranslatable.[37]

The man of culture becomes a man of politics when, inspired by his students, he joins them in solidarity with the Soweto school boycott. Sonny's political trajectory makes him a representative figure among the colored middle class in the 1980s. The historian Ian Goldin explains: "The attempt by the students to overcome the divisions between African and Coloured youth was matched by their determination to overcome the generation gap which in 1976 had strained the black communities. The involvement of teachers and parents in the students' cause added weight to the boycott campaign whilst simultaneously

[36] Deleuze and Guattari, *Kafka*, 16, 17.
[37] I thank Bella Brodzki for helping me to work through Sonny's relationship with Kafka. "All these parables really set out to say merely that the incomprehensible is incomprehensible, and we know that already. But the cares we have to struggle with every day: that is a different matter" (Kafka, "On Parables").

politicising the older generation."[38] Sonny's political commitment is complemented by his relationship with Hannah, a relationship in which, in turn, political danger intensifies erotic pleasure.[39]

The sexual involvement of Sonny and Hannah begins in companion-ability and shared political beliefs—they are friends and comrades before they are lovers—and thrives on difference. Their relationship is not encompassed by the colonial narrative in which a white woman's whiteness makes her desirable to a black man, who is entrapped, victimized, by his desire. In *My Son's Story*, this narrative, a colonial commonplace, is filtered through the lens of Will's jealousy and resentment. It appears as a sign of the psychosexual conflicts of the son who is simultaneously privileged and disenfranchised in patriarchal culture and who sees his father's adulterous desire as a symptom of the racial oppression that denies black men the power held by white men: "She is blonde, my father's woman. Of course. What else would she be? How else would he be caught, this man who has travelled so far from all the humble traps of our kind"(13).

Will later acknowledges that this vision of Hannah is a distillation of his own rage, but at first, he sees her as a "composite" (15)—a pastiche—of white liberal stereotypes. In this "composite," a teenage fantasy, the son's desire is identified with and at the same time repudiates the father's. (The composite parodically recalls Sonny's catalogue of Aila's erotic attributes; it also travesties Shakespeare's enumeration, in Sonnet 130, of the "imperfections" of the dark lady, the mistress whose "eyes are nothing like the sun.") Will's pastiche is played off against Hannah's own political history. Her "dossier" begins with her missionary grandfather, describes her decision to remain in South Africa when others in her family leave, and spells out the commitment that impels her work for human rights. Hannah's lifelong commitment to "struggle against evil" (88) becomes a point of departure for the political work she does later on.

In setting the history of Hannah alongside the history of Sonny, the novel undermines the construction—a construction reproduced in Will's jealous pastiche—of the white woman as seducer or unwitting victim of the black man's desire. It also destabilizes a corollary construction, prominent in colonial discourse from *The Tempest* onward, of the

[38] Goldin, *Making Race*, 209; see also Frederikse, *Unbreakable Thread*, chap. 19. Between April 1980 and June 1981, one hundred thousand students in colored and African schools and five college campuses boycotted classes (Lodge et al. 36).

[39] In a handwritten outline for the novel, Gordimer reflects on clandestinity. Gordimer Collection, box 11, folder 5.

black man's desire for the white woman as a version of rape. Sonny, clearly, is no Caliban; in fact, he more closely recalls Prospero. Like Prospero, he is devoted to his books, he is an overprotective father reluctant to let go of his adolescent daughter, and he is the cause of a shipwreck, albeit an emotional one. Nor should Hannah be read as a version of Miranda. In the relationship of Sonny and Hannah, *My Son's Story* envisions an alternative to the colonial family romance that structures *The Tempest* and that continues to draw the attention of feminist critics who treat Miranda as the prototypical daughter in colonial patriarchy and of postcolonial theorists who explore the position of Caliban.[40]

Beyond Identity: The Poetics of Nonracialism

My Son's Story dismantles the representation of the black woman as the colonized feminine/feminized colony of colonizing white masculinity and the representation of the white woman as object/victim of the black man's desire. At the same time, it questions the idea of race as a determinant of identity.

The examination of race encompasses an array of strategies. First, the novel represents race in contemporary South Africa as a discursive product of apartheid, a category of analysis implicated in the maintenance and reproduction of the regime. Next, it destabilizes the binary oppositions that structure racial difference. In telling the story of a colored family, Gordimer evokes the history of South Africa's diverse colored population. In this history, as Goldin argues, colored identity is contested and periodically reconstituted in struggles involving South Africa's white rulers, the African majority, and colored communities themselves.[41] Finally, through its affiliation with the nonracialist politics of the UDF and ANC, the novel opposes the construction and reconstruction of race by the apartheid state. This reconstruction continued, in the 1980s, even after the repeal of many of the most repressive statutes.

The novel's exploration of race is conducted, in part, through a meditation on one of the key words in *Hamlet, kind.*[42] Throughout *My Son's*

---

[40] On Miranda, see Donaldson, chap. 1, "The Miranda Complex," in *Decolonizing Feminisms*; Greenstein, "Miranda's Story"; and Newman, chap. 4, "Prospero's Complex," in *Nadine Gordimer*. On Caliban, see Nixon, "Caribbean and African Appropriations of *The Tempest*"; Houston Baker, "Caliban's Triple Play"; Fernandez-Retamar, "Caliban"; and Lamming, "Caliban Orders History."

[41] See Goldin, *Making Race* and "Reconstitution of Coloured Identity."

[42] On Doris Lessing's use of the word *kind* to mean biologized racial alterity in *The Fifth Child*, see Chapter 5, this volume.

Story, kind is both a signifier of race or ethnicity and a signifier of morality or ethos (culture, cultural value). In drawing on two sets of meanings of *kind*, Gordimer fashions a discursive strategy, a poetics, analogous to the politics of nonracialism. She accommodates but does not reify racial difference, treating race as a significant determinant of identity but repudiating the racial categories of apartheid.

The changing meanings of the word *kind* in the period the novel describes register changes in the constructions of colored identity that Goldin documents, and especially the self-identification of members of the colored community, particularly students and youth, as black.[43] These changes punctuate the lives of Sonny and his family, much as the lives of Rosa Burger and Hillela Capran are marked by public events in the history of the apartheid era in South Africa. Here, again, Sonny appears to be a representative figure.[44] As a young man during the 1950s, he identifies himself and his "kind" as colored, a racial category reconstituted, as Goldin explains, by laws such as the Group Areas Act, which restricted residence in certain areas to whites. The Group Areas Act was carried out through the forced removals of masses of colored people from areas such as Cape Town's District Six and Johannesburg's Sophiatown.[45] The identification of the colored population as colored forecloses solidarity with Asians and Africans, despite the oppression of all these groups by the white minority and their exclusion from the privileges of whites, as Sonny himself eventually realizes. Later, the erosion of the "distinction between black and real black, between himself and them" (25), makes possible Sonny's political vocation and his work in the liberation movement. It is ironically underscored when angry whites hold up a placard that reads, "OUR HOME WHITE GO TO YOUR LOCATION COMMUNISTS + BLACKS = END OF OUR CIVILISATION GET OUT KEEP SA WHITE" (272). Eventually, Sonny rejects apartheid's definition of race; political practice supersedes race (color) as an influence on "kind"—identity, community—especially when blacks begin to serve in the police or become clients of the state.

[43] Goldin, *Making Race*, 157, 186.

[44] Sonny's name recalls a leader of the (colored) Labour Party, Sonny Leon. But he moves in a direction opposite from Leon's. In the early 1970s, Leon identified with Black Consciousness, but in 1980, he accepted nomination to the President's Council composed of twenty whites, ten coloreds, and five Indians; blacks were excluded (Goldin, *Making Race*, 157, 210).

[45] Goldin, *Making Race*, 134. On the redefinition of "coloured ethnicity" through such laws as the Population Registration Act, the Prohibition of Mixed Marriages Act, the Immortality Amendment Act, the Group Areas Act, and the Separate Representation of Voters Act, see Marks and Trapido, "The Politics of Race, Class, and Nationalism," 30. Don Mattera *(Sophiatown)* vividly describes the demolition of and violent removal of colored people from Sophiatown.

Yet residual meanings linger, as in Will's observation that Aila is arrested by "a white officer and the others *our kind*" (205).

The performative concept of race elaborated in the meditation on
kind and in Sonny's political career is reinforced by the novel's deconstruction of racial categories. Sonny's own "kind" (colored) is a discursive product of South African racism that disrupts even as it is
inscribed in apartheid's taxonomies.[46] Through the 1890s, the term
"colored" designates all non-Europeans; by the middle of the first
decade of the twentieth century, "colored" designates a third group,
neither Bantu nor white. In the 1950s, as the National Party is attempting to consolidate its power by settling the system of racial classification, the ideologues of apartheid cannot explain what "colored"
means.[47]

Ostensibly regulated through prohibitions on interracial sexual relations that may have already occurred—these prohibitions have been
rescinded by the time the novel takes place but leave behind a legacy
of taboos—the very existence of colored people and of the category
"colored" exposes apartheid as a system of classification violently imposed after the fact. But the experiences of Sonny, Aila, and their
"kind" remind us that, until the achievement of a nonracial order, race
cannot be insignificant. At the same time, the existence of a colored
population, defined by race and by the impossibility of absolute racial
sorting, prefigures the nonracial nation that Sonny, Aila, and Baby
struggle and Will wishes to bring into being.

Liberating the Body Politic

Burger's Daughter, A Sport of Nature, and *My Son's Story* all imagine a
nonracial, liberated South Africa. In *Burger's Daughter,* the nonracial
nation is ironically prefigured in the interracial sisterhood with whom
Rosa is incarcerated. *A Sport of Nature* ends with the inaugural celebration of the new nation, "Whaila's country," which Hillela attends as the
wife of the General and Sasha observes from the distance of exile in
Europe. *My Son's Story* shares with *A Sport of Nature* a utopian vision of
the new order toward which it beckons, but as in *Burger's Daughter,* the
nonracial nation is still subject to the power and violence of the white
minority and its apartheid regime. In *My Son's Story,* the nonracial na-

---

[46] On the discourse of apartheid, see Derrida, "Racism's Last Word," and McClintock
and Nixon, "No Names Apart." Mattera catalogues the obsessions of a "pigmentocracy"
that proliferate in the numerous subdivisions of colored (22).
[47] Goldin, *Making Race,* 9, and Goldin, "Reconstitution of Coloured Identity," 168.

tion is envisioned in two episodes that represent it as fragments scattered in South Africa and in an elsewhere that is not-yet, not-here.

The first of these episodes describes a funeral in Alexandra for young blacks killed by the police. Whites, Hannah among them, come to the funeral from Johannesburg. Some of the whites are fearful of blacks who had "stoned white drivers on the main road, who had taken control of this place out of the hands of white authority, who refused to pay for the right to exist in the decaying ruins of the war of attrition against their presence too close across the veld" (108), but their fears prove unfounded. Here, the whites are subject to the control of the blacks who surround them; the inversion of dominance and control by the white minority is seen as a precondition of a liberated, nonracial future.[48]

The nation prefigured in this episode is represented, to borrow from Iris Marion Young, as "openness to unassimilated otherness."[49] Throughout this scene, blacks and whites mingle but remain separate. Initially, the whites are confined in combis (vans) and surrounded by blacks, but then physical barriers break down. For a brief moment, the individuals merge into a collective body, yet their differences are not obliterated. Whites, customarily "distanced from each other in everything but sexual or parental intimacy," experience a physical closeness to which blacks are accustomed because they are literally crowded together and unable to "keep the outline of space" (110).

To bring about the nonracial future, the novel suggests, whites will have to experience the world as blacks have done:

> But now in the graveyard the people from the combis were dispersed from one another and the spatial aura they instinctively kept, and pressed into a single, vast, stirring being with the people of the township. The nun was close against the breast of a man. A black child with his little naked penis waggling under a shirt clung to the leg of a professor. A woman's French perfume and the sweat of a drunk merged as if one breath came from them. And yet it was not alarming for the whites; in fact, an old fear of closeness, of the odours and heat of other flesh, was gone. One ultimate body of bodies was inhaling and exhaling in the single diastole and systole, and above was the freedom of the great open afternoon sky. (110)

[48] The inversion of the apartheid order here recalls the demands of Tutu and Serote that whites must learn to follow and listen (Gordimer, "Living in the Interregnum," 266–67).

[49] Young, "Ideal of Community," 319. On the utopian dimension of this scene, see Head 156–57 and Barnard, *Apartheid, Literature, and the Politics of Place;* Wagner dismisses it as banal (223).

Racial and sexual differences are not fully specified in the pairs people from combis/people from the townships, nun/man, woman/drunk, and black child/professor. All make up a "single, vast, stirring being," a body politic that embraces difference. The utopian vision anticipates the nation of the future—a liberated body politic—but it remains vulnerable to the violence of the apartheid state: the police fire on the crowd as it disperses, killing at least one young man.

If the Soweto funeral represents the nonracial future as a not-yet, the ANC, exiled in Lusaka and elsewhere and underground in South Africa, represents it as a not-here or a not-exactly-here. To the white liberals who travel to Lusaka to meet the leaders of the liberation movement, "the *feared* future seemed to exist, already, there, outside the country" (267). But Sonny, Aila, Baby, Will, and their kind—an imagined community that might draw in the novel's readers—look forward to the "unitary, non-racial, democratic country" (114) that Sonny invokes in his eulogy for the slain youths.

At the very end of the novel, Sonny goes to Lusaka to meet with the leadership. While he is gone, his house is burned down by whites. The house and all its contents are destroyed in the fire. The burning of the house is an index of the violence of apartheid, violence condoned even when not enacted by the state. But the fire may also be a prelude to a new order, one that will replace the fathers' houses and the sons' and daughters' stories that have traditionally sheltered both culture and politics.

My Son's Story only sketches the characteristics of the emergent order. But the figurative strategies of the novel, and especially those associated with Aila, invite us to imagine a future that could not, in 1990, be specified. When Sonny asks Aila, "What made you do it?" she responds with a story that he finds difficult to follow. Aila's maternal parable cannot be translated into the conventional political language that Sonny, at once father and son, has made his own. Similarly, the narrator describes Aila in figures of speech that cannot be literalized.

Although Sonny is the self-proclaimed lover of Kafka, Aila speaks in the manner of Kafka's parables. Throughout, Aila's untranslatability is juxtaposed with Sonny's appropriation and transformation of European, patriarchal cultural traditions and with his ability to be translated and hence understood by all who hear him. I am not arguing here that Sonny assures the continuing importance of the canon in the postcolonial future. Nor am I proposing that Aila represents (figures or prefigures) the emergent order. To do so against the grain of the novel's cautionary rhetoric would be to make "woman" a symbol of "nation" and to engage in an act of interpretive colonization like those the novel discredits. Rather, I would suggest that the nation that did not exist when the novel was written and is still in the process of being created must accommodate both Sonny and Aila and articulate Sonny's (and Will's) refunctioning of culture with Aila's gnomic discourse.

My Son's Story does look toward what is not yet known, and it therefore operates analogically or, as Aila's story does, parabolically. In this sense, Aila's maternal discourse, the parable that cannot be decoded by the hermeneutic of the dominant culture, stands (in) for the nonracial nation that is coming into being. The conflagration that ends the novel brings destruction, but it also presages an order that, like Aila's maternal linguistic practice, remains not only to be read but also to be written.

Conclusion:
Writing beyond the Margins

In the first scene of *Burger's Daughter*, Rosa Burger stands in front of a prison where her mother is being held. Looking around at the group assembled to visit those inside the prison and wondering how she is viewed by them and by others, Rosa muses, *"When they saw me outside the prison, what did they see?* I shall never know. It's all concocted. I saw—see—that profile in a hand-held mirror directed towards another mirror" (13–14). Toward the end of the novel, prompted by an angry phone call from Zwelinzima, Rosa returns from her European exile to a nation turned upside down by the Soweto revolt. As she explains, "No one can defect. . . . Like anyone else I do what I can" (332). In the narrative that unfolds between these two episodes, Rosa assumes her place as a (white) South African, citizen of a nonracial nation imagined in an optative mood. Rosa elaborates two fundamental, competing notions of national identity: that it is "concocted," a fictive product of our own and others' perceptions and that it is negotiated through our actions, through the moral and political choices we make.

The Golden Notebook also offers two different ways of conceiving national identity. At the beginning of the novel, alluding to the global political situation, Britain's recent explosion of an atomic bomb, and her own psychological state, Anna Wulf remarks that "everything is cracking up" (9). Toward the end, before giving Anna the sentence that begins *The Golden Notebook*, Saul Green announces, "There are the two women you are, Anna" (547), and Molly Jacobs declares, with a certain irony, that she and Anna will "be integrated with British life" (568). In presenting Anna as a subject of a nation poised at a crucial moment in its postwar history, the novel dissects both "British life" and the character doubly doubled as Anna-Molly and Anna-Saul.[1] The fracturing of narrative form, the juxtaposing of a "conventional novel" and "notebooks" that simultaneously amplify and disrupt it, presents identity as a set of unevenly overlapping templates held in an unstable ensemble. But if *The Golden Notebook* anatomizes Anna's identity and undermines her political agency—and the idea of political agency in general— Anna's acknowledgment, however ambivalent, of membership in a national community also affirms the identity the novel deconstructs. In other words, it shows us the inexorability of national affiliation.

All the novels discussed in this book oscillate between these two complementary, conflicting conceptions of identity: as a concocted fictive construct and as a negotiated, improvised way of being in the world of nations. At the same time, the novels model for us the processes and practices that they describe; the novels themselves improvise, invent, fashion, and refashion national identities that they also scrutinize. Writing primarily about gender, Judith Butler defines performativity as the "dramatic and contingent construction of meaning."[2] Butler's dramatic contingency is for Homi Bhabha a "repetitious, recursive strategy," a "narrative act [that] interpellates a growing circle of national subjects."[3] In Bhabha's sense and Butler's, the novels of Stead, Lessing, and Gordimer perform nationality, inventing it out of available materials. Adapting actual historical circumstances, expressing the desire to belong to a community or to resist such belonging, rewriting cultural texts, often critically, these writers explore heterogeneous national identities produced by complex processes of political commitment and cultural transmission and translation. Their novels negotiate identity while circumventing the impasses of identity politics.

Most of the novels discussed in this book belong to a hybrid genre that grafts the political novel or novel of ideas and the family romance. In *The Family Romance of the French Revolution*, the historian Lynn Hunt argues that the family is "material for thinking politically ... not ... as some kind of modal social experience, but ... as an imaginative construct of power relations." In Hunt's compelling analysis, the family romance is a "kind of prepolitical category for organizing experience."[4] In *The Mother/Daughter Plot*, the literary critic Marianne Hirsch asserts that the genre of the family romance offers an "interrogation of origins ... which embeds the engenderment of narrative

---

[1] On doubling in *The Golden Notebook*, see Sprague, *Rereading Doris Lessing*, chap. 4.
[2] Butler, *Gender Trouble*, 139.
[3] Bhabha, "DissemiNation," 145.
[4] Hunt, *Family Romance of the French Revolution*, 196.

within the experience of family." Amplifying this conception of the family romance in a later essay, Hirsch notes that the "fantasy of the family is a fantasy of relationship" and suggests that a critical perspective focused on the genre of the family romance is capable of articulating issues such as race, class, and empire with concerns about family, identity, and authority.[5] The family romance conceptualized in the work of these psychoanalytically oriented feminist scholars and critics not only shows us how gender inflects our understanding of experience but also emphasizes the crucial importance, as Joan W. Scott puts it, of gender as a category of historical analysis ("Gender").

The experience of nationality has traditionally been explored in the novel of ideas or in the encyclopedic political novel, like those Benedict Anderson has in mind when he suggests that the novel offers the "technical means" for representing nationness.[6] According to Bakhtin, the protagonist of the classical political novel is an ideologue, a "man" of ideas.[7] As Gordimer defines the genre, a political novel "explicates the effects of politics on human lives and, unlike a political tract, does not propagate an ideology"; a "novel of ideas seeks to explore concepts of the meaning of life and its social ordering—the ideas men live by."[8] Lessing and Stead, too, find in the novel of ideas a way of conveying what Stead calls the "multiplicity" of today.[9]

The hybrid produced by the crossing of the family romance with the novel of ideas is a genre that I have been calling the national family romance. This genre narrates the ways that sexual politics, including the politics of the family, intersects with the politics of race, class, and nationality: it shows us how gender cuts across, shapes, and is in turn shaped by national location. Politicizing what Anna Wulf calls the "little novel about the emotions" (42), a genre devalued because of its association with feminine concerns, it also foregrounds gender issues suppressed in the classical (male) political novel.

In the national family romances narrated in these novels, the "fantasy of relationship" plays off maternal and paternal claims, balancing, often precariously, allegiances to mother and father. The treatment of Henny in *The Man Who Loved Children*, Katya in *Burger's Daughter*, Harriet in *The Fifth Child*, and Dorothy in *The Good Terrorist* insists that the claims of mother, or of the maternal constellation, often repressed in traditional notions of politics, must be acknowledged in

[5] Hirsch, *Mother/Daughter Plot*, 9, and Hirsch, "Jane's Family Romances," 165, 167.
[6] B. Anderson, *Imagined Communities*, 30.
[7] Bakhtin, *Problems of Dostoevsky's Poetics*, 79.
[8] *What Happened to "Burger's Daughter,"* 19.
[9] Stead, "Uses of the Many-Charactered Novel."

the formation of national communities like those the novels imagine. The very different examples of Lionel Burger and Sam Pollit illustrate the exigencies of literary and political paternity. Lionel Burger's legacy to Rosa is a commitment to justice or, as Rosa puts it, to doing what one can; Sam Pollit suggests the pressure of oppressive patriarchal authority that must be struggled against even though or especially because it cannot be escaped.

In the situation of the daughter-protagonists, these novels frame imaginative answers to Gordimer's question about where whites fit into the national—political and cultural—orders they portray. Hillela Capran, a guest on the margins of a liberated South Africa, and Teresa Hawkins, in exile from family and nation of origin, suggest that white women may not fit in easily or indeed at all. In the psychological regression of Alice Mellings in *The Good Terrorist*—and, with her, of England itself—Lessing insists that gender constraints, among them what Hirsch calls the "mother/daughter plot," cannot simply be dispensed with. However heroic Louisa Pollit's departure on a walk around the world might seem, her zigzagging between the "natural outlawry"(244) of a mother associated with Australia and a father identified as Uncle Sam illustrates the difficulty of opting out of national affiliation, however unsettled. Indeed, these novels underscore the limits of the project of invention and improvisation imagined vividly in Doris's pursuit of an Englishness constituted by exclusion, in Rosa Burger's return to a South Africa in which her role is uncertain, and in Teresa Hawkins's placement between men.

But the family romance is not the whole story these novels tell. Rather, they set family paradigms in a wider context. In *A Sport of Nature* Gordimer contrasts Sasha, weighed down by ties to family, class, and culture, and Hillela, who flees from such ties whether she feels them or not; thus the novel attempts ways of imagining identity beyond conventional categories, such as family. In *My Son's Story*, too, Gordimer reaches beyond the confines of family by bracketing Will's oedipal obsessions as a son's story and reconceiving both family relations and political conversion from Aila's perspective, a maternal position not fully realized in the narrative. In audaciously presenting itself as transracial writing and cross-cultural reading, *My Son's Story* looks toward and helps bring into being a nonracial South Africa. At the same time, it hints at forms of imagining and notions of identity barely glimpsed in Aila's maternal parable.

Gordimer continues to think beyond the constraints of family plots in *None to Accompany Me*, published in 1994, the year that Nelson Mandela was elected president of South Africa in the first democratically held elections in the nation's history. The protagonist of this novel, Vera Stark, is an aging lawyer. Uncompromising, for most of her life, in the pursuit of sexual fulfillment and political justice, Vera works for a legal foundation that represents "squatters" attempting to regain lands stolen from them and their ancestors by the white minority. Later, she joins a commission designing a constitution for the transition to democracy. At the same time, she is shedding the personal attachments that have defined her adult life, which spans the years of apartheid. When her husband moves to London, she sells the home where they lived throughout their marriage. A figure for white South Africa under apartheid, this house exists in the novel to be left, or left behind. Vera moves into the annex of a house rented by Zeph Rapulana, a black businessman whom she had represented years before when he was a squatter leader. The end of the novel finds her contemplating the future.

Vera's situation—alone, a tenant in the annex of the house that Zeph rents from the whites who lived there before—asks readers to consider the likely irrelevance, in the coming order, of the personal life that she herself associates with the old regime. But if the end of *None to Accompany Me* illustrates the exhaustion of old plots, it also invites us to envision new ones. In taking Vera Stark past the narrative of sexual desire, even at the cost of emphasizing her isolation, Gordimer might also be looking beyond the old order in which this narrative took shape and in which it is implicated in ways that are not spelled out. If Vera's tenuous position on the margins of a nation in transition raises questions about the location of white women, writers included, in the nations that they inhabit, it also calls for paradigms, not yet manifest, and points to new kinds of relationships—and plots in which they can be narrated—between white women such as Stead, Lessing, and Gordimer and the postcolonial, postimperial nations their novels bring to life.

Works Cited

Abel, Elizabeth. "*The Golden Notebook:* 'Female Writing' and 'The Great Tradition.' " In Sprague and Tiger, *Critical Essays* 101–6.

Abel, Elizabeth, Marianne Hirsch, and Elizabeth Langland, eds. *The Voyage In: Fictions of Female Development.* Hanover N. H.: University Press of New England, 1983.

——. Introduction. In *The Voyage In* 3–19.

Adelman, Janet. *Suffocating Mothers: Fantasies of Maternal Origin in Shakespeare's Plays, "Hamlet" to "The Tempest."* London: Routledge, 1992.

Alcoff, Linda. "The Problem of Speaking for Others." *Cultural Critique* 20 (Winter 1991/92): 5–32.

Allen, Judith. "Breaking into the Public Sphere: The Struggle for Women's Citizenship in New South Wales, 1890–1920." *In Pursuit of Justice: Australian Women and the Law,* ed. Judy MacKinotty and Heather Rodi. Sydney: Hale and Iremonger, 1979. 107–17.

——. "The Invention of the Pathological Family." *Family Violence in Australia,* ed. Carol O'Donnell and Jan Craney. Melbourne: Longman and Cheshire, 1982. 1–27.

Althusser, Louis. "Ideology and Ideological State Apparatuses (Notes towards an Investigation)." *"Lenin and Philosophy" and Other Essays.* Trans. Ben Brewster. New York: Monthly Review Press, 1971. 127–89.

Anderson, Benedict. *Imagined Communities: Reflections on the Origins and Spread of Nationalism.* London: Verso, 1983.

Anderson, Lindsay. "Get Out and Push!" In Maschler, *Declaration* 153–80.

Appiah, Kwame Anthony. "The Postcolonial and the Postmodern." *In My Father's House: Africa in the Philosophy of Culture.* New York: Oxford University Press, 1992. 137–57.

Arac, Jonathan. "The Struggle for the Cultural Heritage: Christina Stead Refunctions Charles Dickens and Mark Twain." *Cultural Critique* 2 (Winter 1985/86): 171–89.

Armstrong, Nancy. *Desire and Domestic Fiction: A Political History of the Novel.* Oxford: Oxford University Press, 1987.

Ashcroft, Bill, Gareth Griffiths, and Helen Tiffin. *The Empire Writes Back: Theory and Practice in Post-Colonial Literatures.* London: Routledge, 1989.

Baker, Houston A., Jr. "Caliban's Triple Play." In Gates, *"Race," Writing, and Difference* 318–95.

Baker, Houston A., Jr., Manthia Diawara, and Ruth H. Lindeborg, eds. *Black British Cultural Studies: A Reader.* Chicago: University of Chicago Press, 1996.

Baker, Rebecca. "Christina Stead: The Nietzsche Connection." *Meridian* 2, no. 2 (1983): 116–20.

Bakhtin, M. M. *The Dialogic Imagination: Four Essays by M. M. Bakhtin.* Ed. Michael Holquist. Trans. Caryl Emerson and Michael Holquist. Austin: University of Texas Press, 1981.

——. "Discourse in the Novel." In *The Dialogic Imagination* 259–422.

——. "Epic and Novel." In *The Dialogic Imagination* 3–40.

——. "Forms of Time and of the Chronotope in the Novel: Notes toward a Historical Poetics." In *The Dialogic Imagination* 84–258.

——. *Problems of Dostoevsky's Poetics.* Ed. and trans. Caryl Emerson. Minneapolis: University of Minnesota Press, 1984.

——. *Rabelais and His World.* Trans. Helene Iswolsky. Bloomington: Indiana University Press, 1984.

Balibar, Etienne, and Immanuel Wallerstein. *Race, Nation, Class: Ambiguous Identities.* London: Verso, 1991. Translation of Balibar by Chris Turner.

Barnard, Rita. *Apartheid, Literature, and the Politics of Place.* Oxford University Press, forthcoming.

Barthes, Roland. *Writing Degree Zero.* Trans. Annette Lavers and Colin Smith. New York: Hill and Wang, 1968.

Bazin, Nancy Topping. "Sex, Politics, and Silent Black Women: Nadine Gordimer's *Occasion for Loving, A Sport of Nature,* and *My Son's Story.*" *Bucknell Review* 37, no. 1 (1993): 30–45.

Bazin, Nancy Topping, and Marilyn Dallman Seymour, eds. *Conversations with Nadine Gordimer.* Jackson: University of Mississippi Press, 1990.

Bhabha, Homi K. "The Commitment to Theory." In *The Location of Culture* 19–39.

——. "DissemiNation: Time, Narrative, and the Margins of the Modern Nation." In *The Location of Culture* 139–70.

——. "Introduction: Locations of Culture." In *The Location of Culture* 1–18.

——. "Introduction: Narrating the Nation." In *Nation and Narration* 1–7.

——. *The Location of Culture.* London: Routledge, 1994.

——. "Of Mimicry and Man: The Ambivalence of Colonial Discourse." In *The Location of Culture* 85–92.

——, ed. *Nation and Narration.* London: Routledge, 1990.

Biddiss, Michael. "Thatcherism: Concept and Interpretations." In Minogue and Biddiss, *Thatcherism* 1–15.

Bloom, James D. *Left Letters: The Culture Wars of Mike Gold and Joseph Freeman.* New York: Columbia University Press, 1992.

Boone, Joseph Allen. *Libidinal Currents: Sexuality and the Shaping of Modernism.* Chicago: University of Chicago Press, 1998.

——. "Of Fathers, Daughters, and Theorists of Narrative Desire: At the Crossroads of Myth and Psychoanalysis in *The Man Who Loved Children.*" *Contemporary Literature* 31 (1990): 512–41.

Boschman, Robert. "Excrement and 'Kitsch' in Doris Lessing's 'The Good Terrorist.' " *ARIEL* 25 (1994): 7–27.

Brenkman, John. "Raymond Williams and Marxism." *Cultural Materialism: On Raymond Williams,* ed. Christopher Prendergast. Minneapolis: University of Minnesota Press, 1995. 237–67.

Brink, Andre. "Mutants of the Picaresque: *Moll Flanders* and *A Sport of Nature.*" *Journal of Literary Studies* 6, no. 4 (December 1990): 261–74.

Broe, Mary Lynn, and Angela Ingram. *Women's Writing in Exile.* Chapel Hill: University of North Carolina Press, 1989.

Brydon, Diana. *Christina Stead.* Totowa, N.J.: Barnes and Noble, 1987.

Burnshaw Collection. Harry Ransom Humanities Center, University of Texas, Austin.

Burton, Stacy. "Exile, Identity, and the Dialogic in Gordimer's *Burger's Daughter* and Lively's *Moon Tiger.*" Paper delivered at International Conference on Narrative Literature, Vancouver, Canada, April 1994.

Busia, Abena P. A. "Silencing Sycorax: On African Colonial Discourse and the Unvoiced Female." *Cultural Critique* 14 (1989/90): 81–104.

Butler, Judith. *Gender Trouble: Feminism and the Subversion of Identity.* London: Routledge, 1991.

Carey, Peter. *Jack Maggs.* New York: Knopf, 1998.

Carter, Paul. *The Road to Botany Bay: An Exploration of Landscape and History.* Chicago: University of Chicago Press, 1988.

Centre for Contemporary Cultural Studies. *The Empire Strikes Back: Race and Racism in 70s Britain.* London: Hutchinson, 1982.

Chevigny, Bell. "Daughters Writing: Toward a Theory of Women's Biography." *Feminist Studies* 9 (1983): 79–102.

Clingman, Stephen. "Literature and History in South Africa." *History from South Africa: Alternative Visions and Practices,* ed. Joshua Brown, Patrick Manning, Karin Shapiro, Jon Wiener, Brenda Bozzoli, and Peter Deling. Philadelphia: Temple University Press, 1991. 105–18.

——. *The Novels of Nadine Gordimer: History from the Inside.* London: Allen and Unwin, 1986.

——. "*A Sport of Nature* and the Boundaries of Fiction." In King, *The Later Fiction of Nadine Gordimer* 173–89.

Conrad, Joseph. *Nostromo.* 1904. Rpt. New York: Penguin, 1986.

Cooke, John. *The Novels of Nadine Gordimer: Private Lives/Public Landscapes.* Baton Rouge: Louisiana State University Press, 1985.

Crewe, Ivor. "Values: The Crusade That Failed." In Kavanaugh and Seldon, *The Thatcher Effect* 239–50.

Curthoys, Ann. "Citizenship and National Identity." *Feminist Review* 44 (Summer 1993): 19–38.

——. "Identity Crisis: Colonialism, Nation, and Gender in Australian History." *Gender and History* 5, no. 2 (Summer 1993): 165–76.

Curtius, Ernst Robert. *European Literature and the Latin Middle Ages.* Trans. Willard R. Trask. New York: Harper, 1953.

David, Deirdre. *Rule Britannia: Women, Empire, and Victorian Writing.* Ithaca: Cornell University Press, 1995.

Davis, Natalie Zemon. *Society and Culture in Early Modern France.* Stanford: Stanford University Press, 1965.

Daymond, M. J. "*Burger's Daughter:* A Novel's Reliance on History." *Momentum: On Recent South African Writing,* ed. M. J. Daymond, J. U. Jacobs, and Margaret Lerita. Pietermaritzburg: University of Natal Press, 1984. 159–70.

Deacon, Desley. *Managing Gender: The State, the New Middle Class, and Women Workers, 1880–1930.* Melbourne: Oxford University Press, 1989.

——. "Politicizing Gender." *Genders* 6 (1989): 1–19.

Deleuze, Gilles, and Felix Guattari. *Kafka: Toward a Minor Literature.* 1975. Trans. Dana Polan. Minneapolis: University of Minnesota Press, 1986.

Derrida, Jacques. "Racism's Last Word." In Gates, *"Race," Writing, and Difference* 329–38.

Docker, John. *Australian Cultural Elites: Intellectual Traditions in Sydney and Melbourne.* Sydney: Angus and Robertson, 1974.

Donaldson, Laura E. *Decolonizing Feminisms: Race, Gender, and Empire-Building.* Chapel Hill: University of North Carolina Press, 1992.

Dostoevsky, Fyodor. *Crime and Punishment.* 1867. Rpt. Trans. Jessie Coulson. Ed. George Gibian. Norton Critical Edition. New York: Norton, 1975.

Drabble, Margaret. "Doris Lessing: Cassandra in a World under Siege." In Sprague and Tiger, *Critical Essays* 183–91.

Draine, Betsy. *Substance under Pressure: Artistic Coherence and Evolving Form in the Novels of Doris Lessing.* Madison: University of Wisconsin Press, 1983.

Duffy, Julia. "The Grain of the Voice in Christina Stead's *The Man Who Loved Children.*" *Antipodes* 4, no. 2 (1990): 48–51.

DuPlessis, Rachel Blau. "Reader, I Married Me: A Polygynous Memoir." In Greene and Kahn, *Changing Subjects* 97–111.

——. *Writing beyond the Ending: Narrative Strategies of Twentieth-Century Women Writers.* Bloomington: Indiana University Press, 1985.

Dyer, Richard. *Brief Encounter.* BFI Classics. London: British Film Institute, 1993.

Edwards, Lee R., and Arlyn Diamond, eds. *The Authority of Experience: Essays in Feminist Criticism.* Amherst: University of Massachusetts Press, 1977.

Eliot, George. *Middlemarch: A Study of Provincial Life.* 1871. Rpt. New York: Penguin, 1965.

Eliot, T. S. "Hamlet and His Problems." *Selected Essays.* New York: Harcourt, 1960. 121–26.

Enloe, Cynthia. *Bananas, Beaches, and Bases: Making Feminist Sense of International Politics.* Berkeley: University of California Press, 1990.

Ettin, Andrew Vogel. *Betrayals of the Body Politic: The Literary Commitments of Nadine Gordimer.* Charlottesville: University Press of Virginia, 1992.

Exell, Arthur. "Morris Motors in the 1940s." *History Workshop Journal* 9 (Spring 1980): 90–114.

Fanon, Frantz. "On National Culture." In *The Wretched of the Earth* 206–48.

———. *The Wretched of the Earth*. 1963. Trans. Constance Farrington. New York: Grove, 1968.

Felski, Rita. *Beyond Feminist Aesthetics: Feminist Literature and Social Change.* Cambridge: Harvard University Press, 1989.

Feminist Review 44 (Summer 1993). Special Issue on Nationalisms and National Identities.

Ferguson, Moira. *Subject to Others: British Women Writers and Colonial Slavery, 1670–1834.* New York: Routledge, 1992.

Fernandez-Retamar, Roberto. "Caliban: Notes Toward a Discussion of Culture in Our America." 1971. *"Caliban" and Other Essays.* Trans. Edward Baker. Minneapolis: University of Minnesota Press, 1989.

Field, Geoffrey. "Perspectives on the Working-Class Family in Wartime Britain, 1939–1945." *International Labor and Working-Class History*, no. 38 (Fall 1990): 3–28.

Finch, Janet, and Penny Summerfield. "Social Reconstruction and the Emergence of Companionate Marriage, 1945–59." *Marriage, Domestic Life, and Social Change*, ed. David Clark. London: Routledge, 1991. 7–32.

Finnegan, William. "The Election Mandela Lost." *New York Review of Books* 20 October 1994: 33–43.

Foucault, Michel. *The History of Sexuality*. Vol. 1, *An Introduction*. New York: Pantheon, 1978.

Frankenberg, Ruth. *White Women, Race Matters: The Social Construction of Whiteness.* Minneapolis: University of Minnesota Press, 1993.

Frederikse, Julie. *The Unbreakable Thread: Non-Racialism in South Africa.* Bloomington: Indiana University Press, 1990.

Freud, Sigmund. "Family Romances." 1908. *The Standard Edition of the Complete Psychological Works of Sigmund Freud.* London: Hogarth, 1959. 9:237–41.

———. "Female Sexuality." 1931. *Collected Papers*, ed. James Strachey. New York: Basic, 1959. 5:252–72.

———. "Femininity." 1931. *New Introductory Lectures on Psychoanalysis.* Trans. and ed. James Strachey. New York: Norton, 1965.

Gamble, Andrew. "Thatcherism and Conservative Politics." In Hall and Jacques, *The Politics of Thatcherism* 109–31.

Gardiner, Judith Kegan. "The Exhilaration of Exile: Rhys, Stead, and Lessing." In Broe and Ingram, *Women's Writing in Exile* 131–50.

———. "Male Narcissism, Capitalism, and the Daughter of *The Man Who Loved Children.*" *Daughters and Fathers*, ed. Lynda Boose and Betty S. Flowers. Baltimore: Johns Hopkins University Press, 1989. 384–99.

———. *Rhys, Stead, Lessing, and the Politics of Empathy.* Bloomington: Indiana University Press, 1989.

Gates, Henry Louis, Jr. "Introduction: Writing 'Race' and the Difference It Makes." In Gates, *"Race," Writing, and Difference* 1–20.

———, ed. *"Race," Writing, and Difference.* Chicago: University of Chicago Press, 1986.

Geering, R. G. Afterword. In Stead, *Ocean of Story* 537–49.

Gellner, Ernest. *Nations and Nationalism.* Ithaca: Cornell University Press, 1983.

Gender and History 5, no. 2 (Summer 1993). Special Issue on Gender, Nationalisms, and National Identities.

Gibson, Gladys. "London." *The Worst of Times,* ed. Nigel Gray. London: Wildwood, 1985.

Gibson, Ross. *South of the West: Postcolonialism and the Narrative Construction of Australia.* Bloomington: Indiana University Press, 1992.

Gikandi, Simon. *Maps of Englishness: Writing Identity in the Culture of Colonialism.* New York: Columbia University Press, 1996.

Gilbert, Sandra M., and Susan Gubar. *The Madwoman in the Attic: The Woman Writer and the Nineteenth-Century Literary Imagination.* New Haven: Yale University Press, 1979.

Gilroy, Paul. *The Black Atlantic: Modernity and Double Consciousness.* Cambridge: Harvard University Press, 1993.

——. "Police and Thieves." In Centre for Contemporary Cultural Studies, *The Empire Strikes Back* 143–82.

——. *"There Ain't No Black in the Union Jack": The Cultural Politics of Race and Nation.* 1987. Chicago: University of Chicago Press, 1991.

Glenn, Ian. "Hodiernal Hillela—Gordimer's Kim." Rev. of *A Sport of Nature,* by Nadine Gordimer. *Contrast* 64 (1988): 75–81.

Goldin, Ian. *Making Race: The Politics and Economics of Coloured Identity in South Africa.* London: Longman, 1987.

——. "The Reconstitution of Coloured Identity in the Western Cape." In Marks and Trapido, *The Politics of Race, Class, and Nationalism* 156–81.

Gordimer, Nadine. "Afterword: The Prison-House of Colonialism." 1980. Rev. of *Olive Schreiner,* by Ruth First and Ann Scott. Rpt. in *An Olive Schreiner Reader: Writings on Women and South Africa,* ed. Carol Barash. London: Pandora, 1987. 221–27.

——. *Burger's Daughter.* 1979. New York: Penguin, 1980.

——. "The Essential Gesture." 1984. In *The Essential Gesture* 285–300.

——. *The Essential Gesture: Writing, Politics, and Places.* Ed. Stephen Clingman. New York: Knopf, 1988.

——. "From the Nobel Lecture." *Poets and Writers Magazine* 20, no. 3 (May/June 1992): 19–24.

——. "The Gap between the Writer and the Reader." *New York Review of Books* 28 September 1989: 59–61. Rpt. in *Bucknell Review* 37, no. 1 (1993): 21–29.

——. Gordimer Collection. Lilly Library, Indiana University, Bloomington.

——. "Interview." With Stephen Gray. In Bazin and Seymour, *Conversations* 176–84.

——. "Letter from Johannesburg, 1976." In *The Essential Gesture* 118–32.

——. "Literature and Politics in South Africa." *Southern Review* 7 (1974): 205–27.

——. "Living in the Interregnum." 1982. In *The Essential Gesture* 261–84.

——. *My Son's Story.* New York: Farrar, Straus, 1990.

——. *None to Accompany Me.* New York: Farrar, Straus, 1994.

——. "Notes of an Expropriator." *Times Literary Supplement* 4 June 1964: 482.

——. "Off the Page." Interview with Jill Fullerton-Smith. In Bazin and Seymour, *Conversations* 299–305.

——. "South Africa's Nadine Gordimer: Novelist with a Conscience." Interview with Diana Loercher. In Bazin and Seymour, *Conversations* 96–100.

——. *A Sport of Nature.* New York: Knopf, 1987.

——. "Where Do Whites Fit In?" 1959. In *The Essential Gesture* 31–37.

——. "Why Did Bram Fischer Choose Jail?" 1966. In *The Essential Gesture* 68–79.

——. *Writing and Being: The Charles Eliot Norton Lectures, 1994.* Cambridge: Harvard University Press, 1995.

Gorra, Michael. *After Empire: Scott, Naipaul, Rushdie.* Chicago: University of Chicago Press, 1997.

Gough, Ian. "Thatcherism and the Welfare State." In Hall and Jacques, *The Politics of Thatcherism* 148–68.

Goulbourne, Harry. *Ethnicity and Nationalism in Post-war Britain.* Cambridge: Cambridge University Press, 1991.

Green, Dorothy. "*The Man Who Loved Children:* Storm in a Teacup." *The Australian Experience: Critical Essays on Australian Novels,* ed. W. S. Ramson. Canberra: Australian National University Press, 1974.

Greene, Gayle. *Changing the Story: Feminist Fiction and the Tradition.* Bloomington: Indiana University Press, 1991.

——. "*The Golden Notebook:* Then and Now." Paper delivered at the annual meeting of the MLA, New York, December 1992.

——. "Looking at History." In Greene and Kahn, *Changing Subjects* 4–27.

Greene, Gayle, and Coppelia Kahn, eds. *Changing Subjects: The Making of Feminist Literary Criticism.* New York: Routledge, 1993.

Greenstein, Susan M. "Miranda's Story: Nadine Gordimer and the Literature of Empire." *Novel* 18 (1984/85): 227–42.

——. "*My Son's Story:* Drenching the Censors—the Dilemma of White Writing." In King, *The Later Fiction of Nadine Gordimer* 191–207.

Haarhof, Dorian. "Two Cheers for Socialism: Nadine Gordimer and E. M. Forster." *English in Africa* 9, no. 1 (May 1982): 55–64.

Hall, Catherine. *White, Male, and Middle Class: Explorations in Feminism and History.* New York: Routledge, 1992.

Hall, Stuart. "The 'First' New Left: Life and Time." In Oxford University Socialist Discussion Group, *Out of Apathy* 11–38.

——. "The Great Moving Right Show." In Hall and Jacques, *The Politics of Thatcherism* 19–39.

——. *The Hard Road to Renewal: Thatcherism and the Crisis of the Left.* London: Verso, 1988.

——. "No Light at the End of the Tunnel." In *The Hard Road to Renewal* 80–92.

Hall, Stuart, and Martin Jacques. Introduction. In *The Politics of Thatcherism* 9–16.

——. "Popular-Democratic vs. Authoritarian Populism: Two Ways of 'Taking Democracy Seriously.' " In *The Hard Road to Renewal* 123–49.

——, eds. *The Politics of Thatcherism.* London: Lawrence and Wishart, 1983.

Hanson, Clare. "Doris Lessing in Pursuit of the English, or, No Small, Personal Voice." *In Pursuit of Doris Lessing: Nine Nations Reading,* ed. Claire Sprague. New York: St. Martin's, 1990. 61–73.

Haraway, Donna. *Primate Visions: Gender, Race, and Nature in the World of Modern Science.* New York: Routledge, 1989.

Harris, Margaret. "Interrogating Ideologies: Christina Stead's American Sequence." Paper delivered at a special session on Stead at the annual meeting of the MLA, San Francisco, December 1991.

Head, Dominic. *Nadine Gordimer.* Cambridge: Cambridge University Press, 1994.

Heilbrun, Carolyn A. "The Character of Hamlet's Mother." *Hamlet's Mother and Other Women.* New York: Columbia University Press, 1990.

Higgins, Susan [Susan Sheridan]. "Christina Stead's *For Love Alone:* A Female Odyssey?" *Southerly* 38 (1978): 428–45.

Higonnet, Margaret R., ed. *Borderwork: Feminist Engagements with Comparative Literature.* Ithaca: Cornell University Press, 1994.

Hill, Christopher. *The World Turned Upside Down: Radical Ideas during the English Revolution.* New York: Viking, 1972.

Hinton, James. "Coventry Communism: A Study of Factory Politics in the Second World War." *History Workshop Journal* 10 (1980): 90–118.

Hirsch, Marianne. "Jane's Family Romances." In Higonnet, *Borderwork* 162–85.

——. *The Mother/Daughter Plot: Narrative, Psychoanalysis, Feminism.* Bloomington: Indiana University Press, 1989.

Hite, Molly. *The Other Side of the Story: Structures and Strategies of Contemporary Feminist Narratives.* Ithaca: Cornell University Press, 1989.

Hobsbawm, E. J. *Nations and Nationalism since 1780: Programme, Myth, Reality.* Cambridge: Cambridge University Press, 1990.

Hobsbawm, E. J., and Terence Ranger, ed. *The Invention of Tradition.* Cambridge: Cambridge University Press, 1983.

Hoggart, Richard. *The Uses of Literacy: Aspects of Working-Class Life with Special Reference to Publications and Entertainments.* 1957. Rpt. New York: Oxford University Press, 1970.

Horkheimer, Max, and Theodor Adorno. "The Culture Industry: Enlightenment as Mass Deception." *Dialectic of Enlightenment.* 1944. Trans. John Cumming. New York: Herder, 1972.

Howe, Irving. *Politics and the Novel.* 1957. Rpt. Freeport, N.Y.: Books for Libraries Press, 1970.

Hughes, Robert. *The Fatal Shore.* 1986. New York: Vintage, 1988.

Hunt, Lynn. *The Family Romance of the French Revolution.* Berkeley: University of California Press, 1992.

Huyssen, Andreas. *After the Great Divide: Modernism, Mass Culture, Postmodernism.* Bloomington: Indiana University Press, 1986.

Irigaray, Luce. "The Power of Discourse and the Subordination of the Feminine." In *This Sex Which Is Not One* 68–85.

——. *This Sex Which Is Not One.* 1977. Trans. Catherine Porter with Carolyn Burke. Ithaca: Cornell University Press, 1985.

Isserlis, Rose. In Johnson, *The Evacuees* 143–48.

Jacobs, Brian D. *Black Politics and Urban Crisis in Britain.* Cambridge: Cambridge University Press, 1986.

Jacques, Martin. "Thatcherism: Breaking out of the Impasse." In Hall and Jacques, *The Politics of Thatcherism* 40–62.

Jameson, Fredric. *The Political Unconscious: Narrative as a Socially Symbolic Act.* Ithaca: Cornell University Press, 1981.

———. *Postmodernism, or, The Cultural Logic of Late Capitalism.* Durham: Duke University Press, 1991.

JanMohamed, Abdul R. "The Economy of Manichean Allegory: The Function of Racial Difference in Colonialist Literature." In Gates, *"Race," Writing, and Difference* 78–106.

Jarrell, Randall. Afterword. *The Man Who Loved Children.* By Stead. 492–503.

Jayawardena, Kumari. *Feminism and Nationalism in the Third World.* London: Zed, 1986.

Jehlen, Myra. "Archimedes and the Paradox of Feminist Criticism." *Signs* 6 (1981): 575–601.

Jenkins, Peter. *Mrs. Thatcher's Revolution: The Ending of the Socialist Era.* London: Cape, 1987.

Johnson, B. S., ed. *The Evacuees.* London: Gollancz, 1968.

Jolly, Rosemary. "Rehearsals of Liberation: Contemporary Postcolonial Discourse and the New South Africa." *PMLA* 110 (January 1995): 16–29.

Jones, Ernest. *Hamlet and Oedipus.* 1919. Rpt. New York: Norton, 1976.

Kafka, Franz. "On Parables." Trans. Willa Muir and Edwin Muir. *Franz Kafka: The Complete Stories,* ed. Nahum N. Glatzer. New York: Schocken, 1976. 457.

Kaplan, Caren. "The Politics of Location as Transnational Feminist Practice." *Scattered Hegemonies: Postmodernity and Transnational Feminist Practices,* ed. Inderpal Grewal and Caren Kaplan. Minneapolis: University of Minnesota Press, 1994. 137–52.

Kaplan, Carey, and Ellen Cronan Rose. "A Genealogy of Readings." *Doris Lessing: The Alchemy of Survival,* ed. Carey Kaplan and Ellen Cronan Rose. Athens: Ohio University Press, 1988. 16–37.

———. "The Power of the Common Reader: The Case of Doris Lessing." *The Canon and the Common Reader,* ed. Carey Kaplan and Ellen Cronan Rose. Knoxville: University of Tennessee Press, 1990. 66–96.

———, eds. *Approaches to Teaching Lessing's "The Golden Notebook."* New York: MLA, 1989.

Kauffman, Linda S. *Special Delivery: Epistolary Modes in Modern Fiction.* Chicago: University of Chicago Press, 1992.

———, ed. *Feminism and Institutions: Dialogues on Feminist Theory.* Cambridge, Mass.: Blackwell, 1989.

Kavanaugh, Dennis, and Anthony Seldon, eds. *The Thatcher Effect.* Oxford: Clarendon, 1989.

King, Bruce. "Introduction: A Changing Face." In King, *The Later Fiction of Nadine Gordimer* 1–17.

———, ed. *The Later Fiction of Nadine Gordimer.* New York: St. Martin's, 1993.

Kingston, Beverly. "The Lady and the Australian Girl: Some Thoughts on Nationalism and Class." *Australian Women: New Feminist Perspectives*, ed. Norma Grieve and Ailsa Burns. Melbourne: Oxford University Press, 1986. 27–41.

Kipling, Rudyard. *Kim*. 1901. Rpt. New York: Penguin, 1987.

Klein, Melanie. "Love, Guilt, and Reparation." In Melanie Klein and Joan Riviere, *Love, Hate, and Reparation*. 1936. Rpt. New York: Norton, 1964. 57–119.

Klug, Francesca. " 'Oh to Be in England': The British Case Study." In Yuval-Davis and Anthias, *Woman-Nation-State* 16–35.

Knapp, Mona. *Doris Lessing*. New York: Ungar, 1984.

Kristeva, Julia. *Powers of Horror: An Essay on Abjection*. Trans. Leon Roudiez. New York: Columbia University Press, 1982.

——. "Stabat Mater." *The Female Body in Western Culture: Contemporary Perspectives*, ed. Susan Rubin Suleiman. Cambridge: Harvard University Press, 1986. 99–118.

Lamming, George. "Caliban Orders History." *The Pleasures of Exile*. 1960. Rpt. Ann Arbor: University of Michigan Press, 1992. 118–50.

Lane, Tony. "The Tories and the Trade Unions: Rhetoric and Reality." In Hall and Jacques, *The Politics of Thatcherism* 169–87.

Langbauer, Laurie. *Women and Romance: The Consolations of Gender in the English Novel*. Ithaca: Cornell University Press, 1990.

Lanser, Susan Sniader. "Compared to What? Global Feminism, Comparatism, and the Master's Tools." In Higonnet, *Borderwork* 280–300.

Lant, Antonia. *Blackout: Reinventing Women for Wartime British Cinema*. Princeton: Princeton University Press, 1991.

Lawrence, Errol. "Just Plain Common Sense." In Centre for Contemporary Cultural Studies, *The Empire Strikes Back* 47–94.

Lawrence, Karen R. *Penelope Voyages: Women and Travel in the British Literary Tradition*. Ithaca: Cornell University Press, 1994.

Layton-Henry, Zig. *The Politics of Race in Britain*. London: Allen and Unwin, 1984.

Lazarus, Neil. "Modernism and Modernity: T. W. Adorno and Contemporary White South African Literature." *Cultural Critique* 5 (1986/87): 131–55.

Leavis, F. R. *The Great Tradition: George Eliot, Henry James, Joseph Conrad*. 1954. Rpt. New York: New York University Press, 1967.

Lessing, Doris. "Doris Lessing at Stony Brook: An Interview with Jonah Raskin." In *A Small Personal Voice* 61–76.

——. *The Fifth Child*. New York: Knopf, 1988.

——. *The Golden Notebook*. New York: Simon and Schuster, 1962.

——. *The Good Terrorist*. 1985. New York: Vintage, 1986.

——. *In Pursuit of the English: A Documentary*. 1960. London: Sphere, 1968.

——. Preface to *The Golden Notebook*. 1971. In *A Small Personal Voice* 23–45.

——. *A Small Personal Voice: Essays, Reviews, Interviews*. Ed. Paul Schlueter. New York: Knopf, 1974.

——. "The Small Personal Voice." In *A Small Personal Voice* 3–22.

——. "A Talk with Doris Lessing." Interview with Florence Howe. In *A Small Personal Voice* 77–82.

——. *Under My Skin: Volume One of My Autobiography, to 1949.* New York: Harper, 1995.

Lidoff, Joan. *Christina Stead.* New York: Ungar, 1982.

Lionnet, Françoise. *Postcolonial Representations: Women, Literature, Identity.* Ithaca: Cornell University Press, 1995.

Liscio, Lorraine. "*Burger's Daughter:* Lighting a Torch in the Heart of Darkness." *Modern Fiction Studies* 33 (1987): 245–61.

Lodge, Tom. *Black Politics in South Africa since 1945.* London: Longman, 1983.

Lodge, Tom, and Bill Nasson, with Steven Mufson, Khehla Shubane, and Nokwanda Sithole. *All, Here, and Now: Black Politics in South Africa in the 1980s.* New York: Ford Foundation / Foreign Policy Association, 1991.

Lurie, Alison. "Bad Housekeeping." Rev. of *The Good Terrorist* and *The Diaries of Jane Somers: "The Diary of a Good Neighbour" and "If the Old Could . . . ,"* both by Doris Lessing. *New York Review of Books* 19 December 1985: 8–10.

Lyotard, Jean-François. *The Postmodern Condition: A Report on Knowledge.* Trans. Geoff Bennington and Brian Massumi. Minneapolis: University of Minnesota Press, 1984.

Mandela, Nelson. *Long Walk to Freedom: The Autobiography of Nelson Mandela.* Boston: Little, Brown, 1994.

Marcus, Jane. *Virginia Woolf and the Languages of Patriarchy.* Bloomington: Indiana University Press, 1987.

Marks, Shula, ed. *Not Either an Experimental Doll: The Separate Worlds of Three South African Women.* Bloomington: Indiana University Press, 1987.

Marks, Shula, and Stanley Trapido. "The Politics of Race, Class, and Nationalism." In Marks and Trapido, *The Politics of Race, Class, and Nationalism* 1–70.

——, eds. *The Politics of Race, Class, and Nationalism in Twentieth-Century South Africa.* London: Longman, 1987.

Martin, Richard G. "Narrative, History, Ideology: A Study of 'Waiting for the Barbarians' and 'Burger's Daughter.' " *ARIEL* 17 (1986): 3–21.

Marx, Karl, and Friedrich Engels. *The German Ideology.* Ed. R. Pascal. New York: International, 1947.

Maschler, Tom, ed. *Declaration.* London: MacGibbon and Kee, 1957.

Mashinini, Emma. *Strikes Have Followed Me All My Life: A South African Autobiography.* 1989. Rpt. New York: Routledge, 1991.

Mattera, Don. *Sophiatown: Coming of Age in South Africa.* Boston: Beacon, 1989.

Matthews, Jill Julius. *Good and Mad Women: The Historical Construction of Femininity in Twentieth-Century Australia.* Sydney: George Allen and Unwin, 1984.

McClintock, Anne. *Imperial Leather: Race, Gender, and Sexuality in the Colonial Contest.* New York: Routledge, 1995.

McClintock, Anne, and Rob Nixon. "No Names Apart: The Separation of Word and History in Derrida's 'Le Dernier Mot du Racisme.' " In Gates, *"Race," Writing, and Difference* 339–53.

Meese, Elizabeth A. "The Political Is the Personal: The Construction of Identity in Nadine Gordimer's *Burger's Daughter.*" In Kauffman, *Feminism and Institutions* 253–75.

Melville, Herman. *Moby Dick.* 1851. Norton Critical Edition, ed. Harrison Hayford and Hershel Parker. New York: Norton, 1967.

Menchú, Rigoberta. *I, Rigoberta Menchú: An Indian Woman in Guatemala.* Ed. Elisabeth Burgos-Debray. Trans. Ann Wright. New York: Verso, 1984.

Meyer, Susan. *Imperialism at Home: Race and Victorian Women's Fiction.* Ithaca: Cornell University Press, 1996.

M. H. "Christina Stead's Fantastic Gallery." Rev. of *The Man Who Loved Children. New York Times Book Review* 20 October 1940: 7.

Miles, Robert, and Annie Phizacklea. *White Man's Country: Racism in British Politics.* London: Pluto, 1984.

Miller, Nancy K. "Decades." In Greene and Kahn, *Changing Subjects* 31–47.

——. "Emphasis Added: Plots and Plausibilities in Women's Fiction." In Showalter, *The New Feminist Criticism* 339–60.

Millin, Sarah Gertrude. *The South Africans.* 1926. New York: Liveright, 1927.

Minogue, Kenneth, and Michael Biddiss. *Thatcherism: Personality and Politics.* London: Macmillan, 1987.

Mitchell, Juliet. "Women: The Longest Revolution." 1966. *Women: The Longest Revolution.* New York: Pantheon, 1984. 17–54.

Modjeska, Drusilla. *Exiles at Home: Australian Women Writers, 1925–1945.* Sydney: Angus and Robertson, 1981.

Mohanty, Chandra Talpade. "Under Western Eyes: Feminist Scholarship and Colonial Discourses." *Third World Women and the Politics of Feminism,* ed. Chandra Talpade Mohanty, Ann Russo, and Lourdes Torres. Bloomington: Indiana University Press, 1991. 51–80.

Moi, Toril. *Sexual/Textual Politics: Feminist Literary Theory.* London: Methuen, 1985.

Monteser, Frederick. *The Picaresque Element in Western Literature.* University: University of Alabama Press, 1975.

Murie, Alan. "Housing and the Environment." In Kavanaugh and Seldon, *The Thatcher Effect* 212–25.

Newman, Judie. *Nadine Gordimer.* London: Routledge, 1988.

Nixon, Rob. "Caribbean and African Appropriations of *The Tempest.*" *Critical Inquiry* 13 (1987): 557–78.

——."Sons and Lovers: Nadine Gordimer Grows Bold Gracefully." Rev. of *My Son's Story,* by Nadine Gordimer. *Voice Literary Supplement* November 1990: 23–24.

Omond, Roger. *The Apartheid Handbook: A Guide to South Africa's Everyday Racial Policies.* New York: Penguin, 1985.

"Opening *The Golden Notebook:* Remembering the Source." *PEN Newsletter,* no. 79 (October 1992): 3–13.

O'Rourke, Rebecca. "Doris Lessing: Exile and Exception." In Taylor, *Notebooks/Memoirs/Archives* 206–26.

Osborne, John. *Look Back in Anger.* 1957. Rpt. New York: Penguin, 1982.

———. "They Call It Cricket." In Maschler, *Declaration* 61–84.

Oxford University Socialist Discussion Group, ed. *Out of Apathy: Voices of the New Left 30 Years On*. London: Verso, 1989.

Paul, Kathleen. *Whitewashing Britain: Race and Citizenship in the Postwar Era*. Ithaca: Cornell University Press, 1997.

Peck, Richard. "What's a Poor White to Do? White South African Options in *A Sport of Nature*." In R. Smith, *Critical Essays* 153–67.

Phillips, Caryl. *Cambridge*. 1991. New York: Vintage, 1993.

Pratt, Mary Louise. *Imperial Eyes: Travel Writing and Transculturation*. New York: Routledge, 1992.

Rabinowitz, Paula. *Labor and Desire: Women's Revolutionary Fiction in Depression America*. Chapel Hill: University of North Carolina Press, 1991.

Radhakrishnan, R. "Negotiating Subject Positions in an Uneven World." In Kauffman, *Feminism and Institutions* 276–90.

Raiskin, Judith L. *Snow on the Cane Fields: Women's Writing and Creole Subjectivity*. Minneapolis: University of Minnesota Press, 1996.

Read, Daphne. "The Politics of Place in *Burger's Daughter*." In King, *The Later Fiction of Nadine Gordimer* 121–39.

Reed, Stanley. In Johnson, *The Evacuees* 217–30.

Reid, Ian. *Fiction and the Great Depression: Australia and New Zealand, 1930–1950*. Melbourne: Arnold, 1979.

Reiger, Kerreen M. *The Disenchantment of the Home: Modernizing the Australian Family, 1880–1940*. Melbourne: Oxford University Press, 1985.

Rhys, Jean. *Wide Sargasso Sea*. 1966. Rpt. New York: Norton, 1982.

Rich, Adrienne. Interview with Elly Bulkin. In Sprague and Tiger, *Critical Essays* 181–82.

Riley, Denise. *"Am I That Name?" Feminism and the Category of "Women" in History*. Minneapolis: University of Minnesota Press, 1988.

———. *War in the Nursery: Theories of the Child and Mother*. London: Virago, 1983.

Roberts, Sheila. "Nadine Gordimer's 'Family of Women.' " In R. Smith, *Critical Essays* 167–79.

Rose, Jacqueline. "Sexuality in the Reading of Shakespeare: *Hamlet* and *Measure for Measure*." *Alternative Shakespeares*, ed. John Drakakis. London: Methuen, 1985. 95–118.

Rothstein, Mervyn. "Doris Lessing and Her 'Fifth Child': Painful Memories of a Difficult Birth." *New York Times* 14 June 1988: C19.

Rowley, Hazel. *Christina Stead: A Biography*. New York: Holt, 1994.

———. "Christina Stead: The Voyage to Cythera." *SPAN*. Newsletter of the South Pacific Association of Commonwealth Literature and Language Studies. April 1988. 33–45.

———. "How Real Is Sam Pollit? 'Dramatic Truth' and 'Procès-Verbal' in *The Man Who Loved Children*." *Contemporary Literature* 31 (1990): 499–511.

Rubenstein, Roberta. *The Novelistic Vision of Doris Lessing*. Urbana: University of Illinois Press, 1979.

Sage, Lorna. *Women in the House of Fiction: Post-war Women Novelists*. New York: Routledge, 1992.

Said, Edward W. *Beginnings: Intention and Method.* New York: Basic, 1975.
——. *Culture and Imperialism.* New York: Knopf, 1993.
——. "Introduction: Secular Criticism." In *The World, the Text, and the Critic* 1–30.
——. *Orientalism.* New York: Pantheon, 1978.
——. "Reflections on American 'Left' Literary Criticism." In *The World, the Text, and the Critic* 158–77.
——. "Reflections on Exile." *Granta* 13 (1984): 159–72.
——. *Representations of the Intellectual.* The 1993 Reith Lectures. 1994. Rpt. New York: Vintage, 1996.
——. *The World, the Text, and the Critic.* Cambridge: Harvard University Press, 1983.
——. "The World, the Text, and the Critic." In *The World, The Text, and the Critic* 31–54.
Scanlan, Margaret. "Language and the Politics of Despair in Doris Lessing's *The Good Terrorist.*" *Novel* 23 (1990):182–98.
Schaffer, Kay. *Women and the Bush: Forces of Desire in the Australian Cultural Tradition.* Melbourne: Cambridge University Press, 1988.
Schor, Hilary. "Homelessness in the Novel: *The Good Terrorist* and Post-Realism." Paper delivered at the annual meeting of the MLA, San Francisco, December 1987.
Schreiner, Olive. *The Story of an African Farm.* 1883. Rpt. New York: Penguin, 1971.
Schweikart, Patrocinio P. "Reading a Wordless Statement: The Structure of Doris Lessing's *The Golden Notebook.*" *Modern Fiction Studies* 31 (Summer 1985): 263–79.
Scott, Joan W. "The Evidence of Experience." *Critical Inquiry* 17 (1991): 773–97.
——. "Gender: A Useful Category of Historical Analysis." *Gender and the Politics of History.* New York: Columbia University Press, 1988. 28–50.
Scott, Virginia. "Doris Lessing's Modern Alice in Wonderland: *The Good Terrorist* as Fantasy." *International Fiction Review* 16, no. 2 (Summer 1989): 123–27.
Sedgwick, Eve Kosofsky. *Between Men: English Literature and Male Homosocial Desire.* New York: Columbia University Press, 1985.
Segal, Lynne. "The Silence of Women in the New Left." In Oxford University Socialist Discussion Group, *Out of Apathy* 114–16.
Shelley, Mary. *Frankenstein; or, The Modern Prometheus.* 1818. New York: Oxford University Press, 1993.
Sheridan, Susan. *Christina Stead.* Bloomington: Indiana University Press, 1988.
Showalter, Elaine. "Feminist Criticism in the Wilderness." In *The New Feminist Criticism* 243–70.
——. "Toward a Feminist Poetics." In *The New Feminist Criticism* 125–43.
——, ed. *The New Feminist Criticism: Essays on Women, Literature, and Theory.* New York: Pantheon, 1985.
Sinfield, Alan. *Literature, Politics, and Culture in Postwar Britain.* Berkeley: University of California Press, 1989.

Sinkler, Rebecca Pepper. "Goblins and Bad Girls." *New York Times Book Review* 3 April 1988: 6.

Smith, Anna Marie. *New Right Discourse on Race and Sexuality: Britain, 1968–1990.* Cambridge: Cambridge University Press, 1994.

Smith, Rowland, ed. *Critical Essays on Nadine Gordimer.* Boston: Hall, 1990.

Solomos, John. *Race and Racism in Contemporary Britain.* London: Macmillan, 1989.

Sommer, Doris. "Textual Conquests: On Readerly Competence." *The Uses of Literary History,* ed. Marshall Brown. Durham: Duke University Press, 1995. 255–69.

Sparks, Allister. *Tomorrow Is Another Country: The Inside Story of South Africa's Road to Change.* New York: Hill and Wang, 1995.

Spivak, Gayatri Chakravorty. "Can the Subaltern Speak?" *Marxism and the Interpretation of Culture,* ed. Cary Nelson and Lawrence Grossberg. Urbana: University of Illinois Press, 1988. 271–313.

——. "Three Women's Texts and a Critique of Imperialism." In Gates, *"Race," Writing, and Difference* 262–80.

Sprague, Claire. "Doris Lessing at the New School, October 14, 1993." *Doris Lessing Newsletter* 16, no. 1 (Winter 1994): 6, 13.

——. "*The Golden Notebook:* In Whose or What Great Tradition?" In Kaplan and Rose, *Approaches to Teaching Lessing's "The Golden Notebook"* 78–83.

——. *Rereading Doris Lessing: Narrative Patterns of Doubling and Repetition.* Chapel Hill: University of North Carolina Press, 1987.

Sprague, Claire, and Virginia Tiger, eds. *Critical Essays on Doris Lessing.* Boston: Hall, 1986.

Sprengnether, Madelon. *The Spectral Mother: Freud, Feminism, and Psychoanalysis.* Ithaca: Cornell University Press, 1990.

Stead, Christina. "Another View of the Homestead." In *Ocean of Story* 513–20.

——. "Christina Stead: An Interview." With Ann Whitehead. *Australian Literary Studies* 6 (1974): 230–48.

——. "Christina Stead in Washington Square." Interview with Jonah Raskin. *London Magazine* ns 9, no. 11 (1970): 70–77.

——. *For Love Alone.* 1944. Rpt. London: Virago, n.d. [1978].

——. "An Interview with Christina Stead." With John B. Beston. *World Literature Written in English* 15 (1976): 87–95.

——. "Interview with Christina Stead." With Rodney Wetherell. *Australian Literary Studies* 9 (1980): 431–48.

——. *The Man Who Loved Children.* 1940. Rpt. New York: Avon, 1966.

——. *Notes on Woolf.* MS4967, box 7, folder 53, Stead Papers. Australian National Library, Canberra.

——. *Ocean of Story: The Uncollected Stories of Christina Stead.* Ringwood, Australia: Penguin, 1985.

——. "On the Women's Movement." *Partisan Review* 46 (1979): 271–74.

——. *Seven Poor Men of Sydney.* 1934. Rpt. Sydney: Angus and Robertson, 1965.

——. "Uses of the Many-Charactered Novel." Draft ms. in the papers of the

League of American Writers. Bancroft Library, University of California, Berkeley.

——. "A Waker and a Dreamer." In *Ocean of Story* 481–93.

——. "A Writer's Friends." In *Ocean of Story* 494–502.

——. "The Writers Take Sides." *Left Review* 1, no. 11 (August 1935): 453–62.

Stewart, Ken. "Heaven and Hell in *The Man Who Loved Children.*" *Meridian* 2, no. 2 (1983): 121–27.

Straus, Nina Pelikan. *Dostoevsky and the Woman Question: Rereadings at the End of a Century.* New York: St. Martin's, 1994.

Summers, Anne. *Damned Whores and God's Police: The Colonization of Woman in Australia.* Melbourne: Allen Lane, 1975.

Taylor, Jenny. "Introduction: Situating Reading." In Taylor, *Notebooks/Memoirs/Archives* 1–41.

——. "Memory and Desire on Going Home: The Deconstruction of a Colonial Radical." In Sprague and Tiger, *Critical Essays on Doris Lessing* 37–44.

——, ed. *Notebooks/Memoirs/Archives: Reading and Rereading Doris Lessing.* London: Routledge, 1982.

Thompson, Leonard. *A History of South Africa.* New Haven: Yale University Press, 1990.

Thorpe, Day. Rev. of *The Man Who Loved Children,* by Christina Stead. *Washington Sunday Star* 7 March 1965.

Tompkins, Jane. "All Alone, Little Lady?" *The Uses of Adversity: Failure and Accommodation in Reader Response,* ed. Ellen Spolsky. London: Associated University Presses, 1990. 190–96.

Turner, Victor. *Dramas, Fields, and Metaphors: Symbolic Action in Human Society.* 1974. Rpt. Ithaca: Cornell University Press, 1994.

Tynan, Kenneth. "Theatre and Living." In Maschler, *Declaration* 107–30.

Wagner, Kathrin. *Rereading Nadine Gordimer.* Bloomington: Indiana University Press, 1994.

Walker, Shirley. "Language, Art, and Ideas in *The Man Who Loved Children.*" *Meridian* 2, no. 1 (1983): 11–20.

Ward, Russel. *A Nation for a Continent: The History of Australia, 1901–1975.* Richmond, Victoria: Heinemann Education, 1977.

Ware, Vron. *Beyond the Pale: White Women, Racism, and History.* London: Verso, 1992.

Waters, Chris. " 'Dark Strangers' in our Midst: Discourses of Race and Nation in Britain, 1947–1963." *Journal of British Studies* 36, no. 2 (1997): 207–38.

Weeks, Jeffrey. *Sex, Politics, and Society: The Regulation of Sexuality since 1800.* 2d ed. London: Longman, 1989.

Weinhouse, Linda. "The Paternal Gift of Narration: Nadine Gordimer's *My Son's Story.*" *Journal of Commonwealth Literature* 29, no. 2 (1993): 66–76.

Wells, Ken. " 'Coloreds' Struggle to Find Their Place in a Free South Africa." *Wall Street Journal* 6 December 1995: A1, 10.

What Happened to "Burger's Daughter"; or How South African Censorship Works. Emmarentius, South Africa: Taurus, 1980.

White, Jonathan. "Politics and the Individual in the Modernist Historical

KING ALFRED'S COLLEGE
LIBRARY

Novel: Gordimer and Rushdie." *Recasting the Word: Writing after Colonialism,* ed. Jonathan White. Baltimore: Johns Hopkins University Press, 1993: 208–40.

White, Richard. *Inventing Australia: Images and Identity, 1688–1980.* Sydney: George Allen and Unwin, 1981.

Williams, Chris. *Christina Stead: A Life of Letters.* Melbourne: McPhee, Dribble, 1989.

Williams, Raymond. *The Country and the City.* New York: Oxford University Press, 1973.

——. *The Long Revolution.* 1961. Rev. ed. New York: Harper Torchbooks, 1966.

——. *Marxism and Literature.* Oxford: Oxford University Press, 1977.

Winnett, Susan. "Making Metaphors/Moving On: *Burger's Daughter* and *A Sport of Nature.*" In King, *The Later Fiction of Nadine Gordimer* 140–53.

Winnicott, D. W. *Playing and Reality.* London: Tavistock/Routledge, 1989.

Woodhull, Winifred. "Exile." *Yale French Studies* 82. 7–24.

Woolf, Virginia. *A Room of One's Own.* 1929. Rpt. New York: Harcourt, 1957.

——. *Three Guineas.* 1938. Rpt. New York: Harcourt, 1963.

Yale French Studies 82/83. "Post/Colonial Conditions: Exiles, Migrations, Nomadisms," ed. Françoise Lionnet and Ronnie Scharfman. New Haven: Yale University Press, 1993.

Yelin, Louise. "Fifty Years of Reading: A Reception Study of *The Man Who Loved Children.*" *Contemporary Literature* 31 (1990): 472–98.

——. "Problems of Gordimer's Poetics." *Feminism, Bakhtin, and the Dialogic,* ed. Dale M. Bauer and Susan Jaret McKinstry. Albany: State University of New York Press, 1991. 219–38.

Yglesias, Jose. "Marx as Muse." Rev. of *The Man Who Loved Children,* by Christina Stead. *Nation* 5 April 1965: 368–70.

Young, Iris Marion. "The Ideal of Community and the Politics of Difference." *Feminism/Postmodernism,* ed. Linda J. Nicholson. New York: Routledge, 1990. 300–323.

Yuval-Davis, Nira, and Floya Anthias, eds. *Woman-Nation-State.* New York: St. Martin's, 1989.

Index

Library of Congress Cataloging-in-Publication Data

Yelin, Louise.
  From the margins of empire : Christina Stead, Doris Lessing,
Nadine Gordimer / Louise Yelin.
    p.   cm. — (Reading women writing)
  Includes bibliographical references (p.   ) and index.
  ISBN 0-8014-3503-X (alk. paper). — ISBN 0-8014-8505-3 (pbk. : alk. paper)
    1. Commonwealth literature (English)—Women authors—History and criticism.
2. Women and literature—English-speaking countries—History—20th century.
3. Lessing, Doris May, 1919–   —Political and social views.   4. Stead, Christina,
1902–1983—Political and social views.   5. National characteristics, British, in
literature.   6. Gordimer, Nadine, 1923–   —Political and social views.
7. Decolonization in   literature.   8. Great Britain—In literature.   9. South Africa
—In literature.   10. Imperialism in literature.   11. Australia—In literature.
I. Title.   II. Series.
PR9080.5.Y45   1998
820.9'9287—dc21

98-7901

Reading Women Writing

A Series Edited by
Shari Benstock and Celeste Schenck

Recasting Autobiography: Women's Counterfictions in Contemporary German Literature and Film
     by Barbara Kosta

Women and Romance: The Consolations of Gender in the English Novel
     by Laurie Langbauer

Nobody's Angels: Middle-Class Women and Domestic Ideology in Victorian Culture
     by Elizabeth Langland

Penelope Voyages: Women and Travel in the British Literary Traditions
     by Karen R. Lawrence

Autobiographical Voices: Race, Gender, Self-Portraiture
     by Françoise Lionnet

Postcolonial Representations: Women, Literature, Identity
     by Françoise Lionnet

Woman and Modernity: The (Life)styles of Lou Andreas-Salomé
     by Biddy Martin

In the Name of Love: Women, Masochism, and the Gothic
     by Michelle A. Massé

Imperialism at Home: Race and Victorian Women's Fiction
     by Susan Meyer

Outside the Pale: Cultural Exclusion, Gender Difference, and the Victorian Woman Writer
     by Elsie B. Michie

Dwelling in Possibility: Women Poets and Critics on Poetry
     edited by Yopie Prins and Maeera Shreiber

Reading Gertrude Stein: Body, Text, Gnosis
     by Lisa Ruddick

Conceived by Liberty: Maternal Figures and Nineteenth-Century American Literature
     by Stephanie A. Smith

Kassandra and the Censors: Greek Poetry since 1967
     by Karen Van Dyck

From the Margins of Empire: Christina Stead, Doris Lessing, Nadine Gordimer
     by Louise Yelin

Beyond Consolation: Death, Sexuality, and the Changing Shapes of Elegy
     by Melissa F. Zeiger

Feminist Conversations: Fuller, Emerson, and the Play of Reading
     by Christina Zwarg